THEOPHRASTUS AND HIS WORLD

This is the first extended study in English of Theophrastus' *Characters*, one of the briefest but also most influential works to survive from classical antiquity. Since the seventeenth century, the *Characters* has served as a model and an inspiration for authors as diverse as La Bruyère, Thackeray, George Eliot and Elias Canetti. This study aims to locate Theophrastus and his *Characters* with respect to the political and philosophical worlds of Athens in the late fourth century, focusing on later imitators in order to provide clues to reading the Theophrastan original. Special attention is paid to the problems and possibilities of the *Characters* as testimony to the culture and society of contemporary Athens, integrating the text into the extensive fragments and testimonia of Theophrastus' other writings. The implications for the historian of the elusive humour of the *Characters*, dependent in large measure on the device of caricature, are explored in detail. What emerges is a picture of the complex etiquette appropriate for upper-class citizens in the home, the streets and other public places in Athens where individuals were on display. Through their resolutely shaming behaviour, the *Characters* illuminate the honour for which citizens should, by implication, be striving. A key theme of the study is Theophrastus' ambivalent position in Athens: a distinguished philosopher and head of the Lyceum, yet still subject to the disabilities of his metic status.

Paul Millett is Senior Lecturer in Ancient History at the University of Cambridge, and a Fellow of Downing College

CAMBRIDGE CLASSICAL JOURNAL
PROCEEDINGS OF THE CAMBRIDGE PHILOLOGICAL SOCIETY
SUPPLEMENTARY VOLUME 33

THEOPHRASTUS AND HIS WORLD

PAUL MILLETT

Published by The Cambridge Philological Society.
www.classics.cam.ac.uk/pcps/pcpshome.html

© The Cambridge Philological Society, 2007

ISBN: 978 0 906014 32 5

This book is available direct from Oxbow Books, Park End Place, Oxford, OX1 1HN.

Printed by Cambridge University Press.
www.cambridge.org/printing

Artemidoro: What book is this?

Ofelia: I was reading Theophrastus' *Characters* just now.
   What an incomparable work!

Artemidoro: For my part, I was reading the Dialogues of the divine Plato,
   which I always have upon me.

La grotta di Trofonio (1785)
Act I, Scene IV
Libretto by Giambattista Casti
Music by Salieri

In Memoriam

Crispin Wendler Brown

1967–1987

CONTENTS

Preface   ix

1 The *kairos* of the *Characters?*   1

2 Theophrastus of Eresus and Theophrastus Such   7

3 Theophrastus the metic   20

4 That's entertainment?   28

5 They do things differently there?   42

6 *Corruption* and the *Characters*   51

7 Honour bright   58

8 Etiquette for an élite: at home   69

9 Etiquette for an élite: away   83

10 Face to face in the Agora   93

11 Conspicuous co-operation?   99

12 Theophrastus Nonesuch   110

Endnotes   118

Appendix 1
Naming the Characters   159

Appendix 2
Characters in *Punch* magazine   165

Appendix 3
Classical allusion in Thackeray's Book of Snobs   167

Bibliography   172

Index of references   183

PREFACE

This piece was first promised some sixteen years ago. Early versions were read to research seminars in Oxford and Cambridge. Although no one probably now remembers, I am grateful for suggestions offered on those occasions. Successive drafts of the present work have been read by Paul Cartledge, Nancy Henry, James Diggle, Robin Lane Fox, Robin Osborne, Ivo Volt, David Sedley, and Michael Pakaluk; all of whom offered valuable advice. The criticism provided by the anonymous reader for the Cambridge Philological Society was thoughtful and constructive. Andrew Goodson has been an acute and informative copy-editor. I have received bibliographical help from Richard Bowring, Rosemary Dean, Karen Lubar, Laura McClure, Marden Nichols, Harriet Moynihan, Stephen Todd, and Anita White. Mark Bradley, Richard Fletcher, John Patterson, David Pratt, Peter Rhodes, Malcolm Schofield, Chris Stray, and Penny Hatfield (Archivist of Eton College) responded willingly to specific enquiries. In the case of Philip Rubery, the contribution was musicological. My greatest obligation is to James Diggle, whose text, translation and commentary surely mark a new era in the study of the *Characters*.

I am grateful indeed to the Cambridge Classical Faculty for making it possible for me to dispense with College administrative duties during the Lent Term, 2006.

I have tried to make my text accessible for non-specialists, with more technical material and detailed argument placed in endnotes which are correspondingly longer. For the same reason, all Greek words and phrases in the text are translated or transliterated. FHS&G identifies numbered passages in the indispensable pair of volumes, *Theophrastus of Eresus: sources for his life, writings, thought and influence*, edited by W. W. Fortenbaugh, P. M. Huby, R. W. Sharples and Dimitri Gutas. Their translations are adopted in the text and notes, with occasional modifications.

It is one of the faults of Theophrastus' 'Tactless Man' that 'When the audience has taken the point, he gets up to explain it all over again'. It frequently happens that a particular part of a Character provides material for two or more separate arguments. Where this is the case, while wary of seeming tactless, I thought it more convenient for the reader on each occasion to quote, paraphrase or summarize the appropriate passage rather then merely cross-reference (though there is still plenty of that). To avoid possible confusion, *Characters* refers to the work by Theophrastus; Characters to the thirty or so individual studies that make up the work. A complete list of the Greek names of the Characters and the English equivalents which I have used can be found in Appendix 1.

I have tended in the text and notes to refer to this monograph as an 'essay'. This reflects not only its length, but also the idea of an attempted exploration of the world of Theophrastus, for which there seemed to be no clear precedent. The reader will find summaries of the structure that emerged and of the overall argument of the essay respectively at the ends of Chapters 1 and 12.

For several years in the 1980s I asked my first-year pupils in Classics to write an essay on what the *Characters* had to offer the sceptical historian. The one from whom I learnt most was Crispin Wendler Brown of Queens' College, to whose memory this essay is dedicated.

PAUL MILLETT   DOWNING COLLEGE, AND
                                                    THE CLASSICAL FACULTY,
                                                            CAMBRIDGE

1

THE *KAIROS* OF THE *CHARACTERS*?

The subject of Cicero's *Brutus* is the history of Roman oratory, presented as a three-way debate between Brutus, Atticus and Cicero himself. Although the setting for their encounter is Cicero's house in Rome, classical Greece is never far away. The three friends sit themselves down on a lawn, close by a statue of Plato (§24). By the time we join the debate, Cicero has provided, as a preliminary, a rapid tour of the development of rhetoric at Athens (§§26–52), including lavish praise of Theophrastus for his elegance and charm as an orator (§§37–8). Theophrastus is about to put in a second, rather different appearance. Approximately half-way through the discussion (§§169–72), Cicero turns aside from Roman orators to list those among 'Allies and Latins'. Brutus interrupts: what are the characteristics of these (as it were) 'foreign orators'? Cicero responds: they are no different from 'City orators', save that their oratory lacks quasi-urban colouring. Brutus asks what Cicero means by this, and is answered with an illustration. Cicero recalls having heard how Titus Tinca of Placentia in northern Italy got involved in a witty exchange with Quintus Granius the Roman auctioneer. Although Tinca was most amusing, he was completely upstaged by Granius through some 'indefinable vernacular flavour'.

Cicero continues: 'So I am not surprised at what is said to have happened to Theophrastus when he pressed a little old lady (*cum percontaretur ex anicula quadam*) about the price for which she would sell a certain item. She answered, and added, "Foreigner (*hospes*), it's not possible [to sell it] for less." It annoyed him that he did not escape the appearance of being a foreigner, although he spent his life in Athens and of all people spoke excellent [Attic Greek]. Similarly, in my opinion, there is among us a certain accent characteristic of the people of the City [of Rome], just as there, of the people of Athens.' The essence of the anecdote is also reported by Quintilian (8.1.2), who adds that Theophrastus was rumbled because, in respect of just one word, he spoke 'too much like a person from Attica.'[1]

It is, of course, highly unlikely that this encounter ever took place; at least, not as recorded by Cicero and Quintilian.[2] Rather, the anecdote embodies themes that are central to this exploration of 'Theophrastus and his world'. First, there is Theophrastus' own ambivalent relationship with the world of Athens (born and brought up at Eresus on Lesbos), exemplified by his cultivation of Attic Greek and apparent desire not to

economy and society, their book seems simultaneously to provide a framework for articulating the world of Theophrastus and also characterizing the *Characters*.[8] Finally, and most immediately relevant to Theophrastus, there is the recent appearance of James Diggle's text of the *Characters* (2004), complete with translation and commentary.[9]

Diggle's synoptic introduction enables discussion of the usual preliminaries to be abbreviated, if not by-passed. The reader is presented with concise, annotated treatments of Theophrastus' life and times, the nature and purpose of the *Characters*, its stylistic merits, date and transmission. Suffice it to say that the work commonly called the *Characters* (more accurately *charakteres ethikoi* or 'Behavioural Types') consists of thirty short caricatures of character-types as they might be met in the imagination in the houses and on the streets of Athens: all male, and all more-or-less negative. It seems likely that Theophrastus was among the first (possibly the first) to cite behaviour, as opposed to speech or physiognomy, as an aspect of *charakter* with the sense of the differentiating feature of a type.[10] A brief, inconsequential preface gives the author's age as ninety-nine and promises good as well as bad characters. Each characterization that follows consists of a one-word title, an abstract definition of the quality concerned, a sequence of concrete examples of appropriate behaviour, and, in certain cases, a moralizing conclusion.

Virtually everything about the text as transmitted is problematic. The Preface has long been recognized as spurious; condemned by both language and content. More recently, the definitions and conclusions have been decisively questioned and identified as Byzantine additions. Moreover, the text as a whole exhibits deep-seated corruption and there are signs of extensive interpolation. The *aponenoemenos* or 'Morally Degraded Man' (6) fairly illustrates of the extent of the problem. Apart from lame definition and epilogue, more than one third of the remainder has been identified as interpolated (§§2, 7), and half a line seems hopelessly corrupt (§3).[11] It is not even clear how many characters are actually represented: almost certainly thirty-one, and probably thirty-two. As transmitted, the text contains parts of two Characters ('Obsequious Man' 5.6–10; 'Offensive Man' 19.7–10) not corresponding to the title or the rest of the Character. In the case of the 'Obsequious Man', the corruption dates back at least as far as a papyrus from Herculaneum.[12] Small wonder the *Characters* has attracted the attention of major figures in classical philology across four centuries and more: Stephanus (1557), Casaubon (1592), Coray (1799), Cobet (1859), Jebb (1870), Wilamowitz (1902), Diels (1909), Pasquali (1919), and Immisch (1923).[13]

If scholarly interest is represented in the range of texts and commentaries, the immediate and enduring appeal of the *Characters* (despite all textual difficulties) is reflected in a host of translations across a variety of languages. Appendix I to this study tabulates a selection of the more recent commentaries and translations, cross-referencing renderings of character-titles. Out of historical interest, the early English and French translations by Healey (1616) and La Bruyère (1687) are also included.[14] These changing perceptions and representations of moral values constitute in themselves a fragment of modern cultural history. While, amongst others, the qualities of the 'Superstitious Man' (16), 'Distrustful Man' (18) and 'Arrogant Man' (24) remain more-or-less constant, assimilation into English of other Characters alters through time. *bdeluria* (11) prompts the sequence: obscene, gross, buffoon, offensive, obnoxious, repulsive; *anaisthesia* (14): blockish, stupid, feckless, obtuse; *authadeia* (15): stubborn, surly, hostile, self-centred; *aedia* (20): tedious, unpleasant, ill-bred, tiresome, bad-taste, disagreeable. Of course, there are also cases where modern variation reflects Greek concepts which, through cultural specificity, defy straightforward translation. *aponoia* (6) presents a perennial problem (reckless, wilful disreputableness, the rough, outcast or demoralized man, shameless man, the man who has lost all sense), while renderings of *philoponeria* (29) tend towards the archaic (patron of rascals, friendship with scoundrels, patronage of scoundrels, friend of villains).[15] Here is our first encounter with an underlying theme of this study: interplay between perceptions of the *Characters* as both strikingly familiar and disconcertingly different.

Several versions of the *Characters* can lay claim to a status approaching historical artefacts. The *editio princeps* by Willibald Pirckheimer (1527) was appropriately dedicated to Albrecht Dürer, delineator of character in another medium. But pride of place goes to Isaac Casaubon, whose text, commentary and Latin translation served to introduce the *Characters* to an educated European public. The first edition appeared in 1592, with further versions in 1599 and 1612. One likely outcome was John Healey's translation of 1616, the earliest rendering of the *Characters* into English; another was the appearance of Joseph Hall's explicitly Theophrastan *Characters of Vertues and Vices*. Hall's imitation appeared in 1608; in 1610 it was translated into French, quite possibly the first literary work in English to receive that distinction, and just possibly a remote inspiration for Jean de La Bruyère, whose massively influential translation and reworking of Theophrastus first appeared in 1688.[16] The relationship of La Bruyère to Theophrastus is explored at length by Octave Navarre (1914), whose own commentary on the *Characters* from 1921 is introduced as a post-War 'tract for the times', defending the claims of French scholarship against 'le prestige de la science germanique' (vi).[17] At the other end of the translation timescale, Vellacott's Penguin Classic of 1967 surely introduced the *Characters* to more English readers than any version before or since.[18] By contrast, Edmonds and Austen describe their innovative commentary from 1904 as 'intended mainly for the Sixth Forms of Public Schools' (v). Hence their 'slight alterations to render the texts more readable'; which is to say, bowd-lerized.[19] But even more revealing of its place and time is Jebb's celebrated edition, first published in 1870 and revised by Sandys in 1909. If Charles Hignett's *Xerxes' invasion of Greece* was described by Momigliano as being (after *Zuleika Dobson*) 'the best book about Oxford', Jebb's *Characters* has plenty to tell about Victorian Cambridge; or, at least, the inhibitions of its upper-middle class.[20]

The ostensible purpose of Jebb's edition, subtitled *An English translation*, was to introduce the 'lighter traits' of the *Characters* to Greekless readers; his commentary relates not to the Greek original, but the text as translated. Even so, as editor, he was at great pains to establish what Theophrastus actually wrote, including a critical appendix of some fifty pages (161–216). Yet there are a dozen or so passages which, through perceived impropriety, Jebb felt 'unwilling to translate', and are omitted in both in English and Greek (viii). These cuts are not signalled in the text, on the ground that this 'would nearly have been equivalent to printing them in capital letters'. Predictable victims of the excision-knife are the 'Repulsive Man' with his deliberate exhibitionism (11.2), likewise (though exposing himself unwittingly) the 'Country Bumpkin' (4.7), the 'Late Learner' visiting a *hetaira* (27.9), and even the 'Obtuse Man' going to the lavatory in the middle of the night and being bitten by the neighbour's dog (14.5). But harder to understand, even making due allowance for high 'Victorian values', are omissions which include belching in the theatre: the 'Repulsive Man' again (11.3); or telling father in all apparent innocence that mother is asleep in the bedroom: the 'Overzealous Man' simply stating the obvious (13.8). Also omitted are having a hairy body, not taking a bath at bedtime, and scratching (or chewing) while sacrificing. Such are a few of the failings of the 'Offensive Man' (19), to whom Jebb takes such exception that he gets cut down to just eight lines of Greek; eighteen lines in Diggle's version for the twenty-first century.[21]

****

In the chapters that follow, attempts are made to isolate the characteristics of the *Characters*, locate the work in suitable contexts, and identify its uses for the historian. Chapter 2 compares Theophrastus' *Characters* against a range of later imitators, focusing on George Eliot's *Impressions of Theophrastus Such* as providing clues to reading the Theophrastan original. Issues emerging from Eliot's reworking include the presence of the author and the implicit ideology shared by Theophrastus and his original intended audience. This leads, in Chapter 3, to a consideration of Theophrastus' headship of the Lyceum while a metic in Athens after Alexander. Chapter 4 tries to supply occasions for the *Characters* that combine its veiled philosophical content with obvious entertainment value. Less formal interludes in Theophrastus' *virtuoso* lectures are offered, alongside symposia, as possible circumstances for performance of the *Characters*. An audience of wealthy, would-be philosophers has implications for presentation of the Characters: themselves conceived as citizens of good standing, but deficient in *paideia*. The elusive humour of the *Characters* is associated with caricature, which introduces the problem of how the text may be read by historians. This theme is further explored in Chapter 5, addressing the issue of 'similarity and difference' between ancient and contemporary character. Also addressed are consequential attempts to relate the content of the *Characters* to events in Athens, and detailed analyses of individual Characters.

Chapters 6 and 7 introduce Horden and Purcell's *The corrupting sea* as a text against which the *Characters* might fruitfully be read, illuminating the connectivity of Athens and its inhabitants within the wider Mediterranean world, and confirming ways in which honour and shame are fundamental concerns for the Characters. Chapters 8 and

9 draw together strands of the Characters' behaviour, constructing systems of etiquette appropriate for the home, the streets, and other public places where individuals were on display. Something of the complex of interpersonal relations in Theophrastus' Athens is exemplified through the Characters' encounters in the Agora, the subject of Chapter 10. In Chapter 11, the attitude of the Characters towards work and leisure is measured against Veblen's *The theory of the leisure class* (1899); the Characters themselves are further compared and contrasted with Aristotle's Great-Hearted Man. In both cases, differences prove ultimately more illuminating than similarities. The final chapter re-presents the broad ideas developed in the essay, invokes Norbert Elias on the sociological significance of etiquette, and closes with speculation over the ongoing appeal of the *Characters*.

2

THEOPHRASTUS OF ERESUS AND THEOPHRASTUS SUCH

'Vertue is not loved enough; because she is not seene: & Vice loseth much detestation; because her uglinesse is secret. ... What need wee more, than to discover these two to the world? This Worke shall save the labour of exhorting and disswasion. I have done it, as I could; following that ancient Master of Morality, who thought this the fittest taske for the ninety and ninth yeare of his age, and the profitablest monument that he could leave for a fare-well to his Grecians.' So wrote Joseph Hall in 'The Proem' to his *Characters of Vertues and Vices* of 1608, taking at face value the preface to Theophrastus' *Characters*. Testimony to the ongoing appeal of the *Characters* is a vigorous and varied afterlife in the hands of imitators, of whom Hall is the earliest and arguably the best. The whole scene of *The Theophrastan 'Character'* is masterfully surveyed by J. W. Smeed (1985), who 'cannot think of a smaller book with greater influence' (5). This is borne out by his identification and elucidation of several hundred relevant texts from antiquity to the later twentieth century. The clustering of English imitations from the seventeenth century is discussed in detail in an older work by Benjamin Boyce (1947). Both books naturally emphasize ways in which imitators develop and diverge from the Theophrastan model. In what follows the process of literary evolution is reversed, with imitators being deployed to demonstrate what is distinctive about the Theophrastan original. The range of character-books I have consulted in detail is necessarily limited: Hall (1608), Overbury (1622), Earle (1628), La Bruyère (1688), Thackeray (1846–7), and Canetti (1979); but still sufficient to throw into relief the technique, range, and content of Theophrastus' original.[22] The uses for the Classicist of George Eliot's *Impressions of Theophrastus Such* (1879) are, however, different in character.

Twentieth-century commentators on the *Characters* are naturally drawn to an observation made by Theophrastus Such himself (16): 'I gather, too, from the undeniable testimony of his [Aristotle's] disciple Theophrastus that there were bores, ill-bred persons and detractors even in Athens, of species remarkably corresponding to the English, and not yet made endurable by being classic...' The passage is invariably cited incomplete, out of context, and without further comment.[23] But the quotation cannot be left to speak for itself; not least, with its riddling semi-self-reference. The context is the second chapter, 'Looking Backward', which, along with the opening chapter 'Looking Inward', seems programmatic, serving to introduce to readers the fictional author: introverted, middle-aged, the bachelor son of a country clergyman with frustrated literary ambitions. He opens chapter 1 with a question: 'It is my habit to give an account to myself of the characters I meet with: can I give a true account of my own?' His acquaintances are as forgetful of his biographical revelations as of a 'dead philosopher', yet they are still aware of things about him of which he himself remains ignorant. These might include singing out of tune, the sound of his foreign accent in the ears of a native speaker, and persevering in behaviour which antagonizes the woman he is pursuing. From this he concludes that others know secrets about him unguessed by himself. By way of illustration, he introduces a miniature case-study (2). As a child he expended much effort in learning the hornpipe, being proud of his supposed superiority as a dancing pupil. Now he can picture the merriment of those watching his solemn face and ridiculous legs. 'What kind of hornpipe am I dancing now?' While laughing at his fellow-men, he knows he must necessarily be among those being laughed at. The chapter concludes how (13): 'in noting the weakness of my acquaintances, I am conscious of my fellowship with them. ... But there is a loving laughter in which the only recognized superiority is that of the ideal self ... holding the mirror and the scourge for our own pettiness as well as our neighbours.'

Much of the detail here, especially the opening page or so, is crypto-Theophrastan, including his bachelor status and the image of the self-betraying, non-native speaker.[24] There is also an autobiographical subtext: the provincial background that Eliot gives to Theophrastus Such echoes both her own extraction and Theophrastus' non-Athenian origins.[25] Of course, not in the least like the original Theophrastus is the narrator's overt reflexivity.

This self-revelatory motif is developed in 'Looking Backward', which paradoxically seems to undercut the work's classicizing title and introductory pages. The author bemoans the fact that although people never wish for different parents, there is a general desire to return to the past, usually that of Pericles or, even better, the 'Aeolic lyrists' (14). But to do so means ignoring what is good in the present, while suppressing ancient unpleasantness. He confesses that he has often wished to be a different person, but not from the conventional classical past. What guarantee is there that, given his modest attainments, he would have fared better there? 'An age in which every department has its awkward squad seems in my mind's eye to suit me better. I might have wandered by the Strymon under Philip and Alexander without throwing any new light on method or organizing the sum of human knowledge; on the other hand, I might have objected to Aristotle as too much of a systematizer, and have preferred the freedom of a little self-contradiction as offering more chances of truth.' (16) Then follows the passage favoured by commentators on the *Characters*, quoted above, after which Theophrastus Such adds how he feels 'better off for possessing Athenian life solely as an inodorous fragment of antiquity.' There are also derogatory remarks about the 'plain men of middle stature and slow conversational powers' of Sappho's Mytilene, whose ranks he would himself have joined. In this way, the author justifies his preoccupation with persons in the present, as represented in the remaining sixteen chapters. A majority concern society types, often minor authors, who reveal their weaknesses through their writings.[26]

Although reminiscences of Theophrastus' technique of characterization do recur, the book is not a collection of characters.[27] 'It is a book about what defines moral character, about how fictional characters are created, and about how the author survives as his or her written text is inherited by successive generations.' The quotation is from the pathbreaking edition of *Theophrastus Such* by Nancy Henry (1994) xii, whose introductory essay illuminates issues of authorship, audience, identity, classical past and modern present, all of them relevant to readers of Theophrastus and his *Characters*.[28] As Henry points out (ix), in the absence of plot and development of characters, Eliot's last work is not a novel along accepted nineteenth-century lines. A sense of unity is generated instead by the voice and vision of the narrator. Critics have struggled (or not even attempted) to assimilate *Theophrastus Such* to the rest of Eliot's work (xiv). For Leslie Stephen, writing in his study of *George Eliot* from 1902, it was (193–5): 'a curious performance ... always apt to become ponderous if not pedantic', and remaining unread, 'except from a sense of duty'. Symptomatic of this indifference is a tendency identified by Henry to misquote the title, 'a practice which ranges from the careless to the comic' (xiv–xv).[29] She argues instead for a reading of the book as both a reflection of Eliot's earlier writings and also an experimental departure from them (ix), 'in what looks like early Modernist experimentation through fragmentation of form. ... In *Impressions* George Eliot goes beyond even her last novel, *Daniel Deronda*, in positing the role of collective memory in the future of national cultures, and the power of literary texts in creating and preserving both.' The same might and will be said of Theophrastus' *Characters*.

One unifying theme is the ambiguity of classical allusion, mediated through Theophrastus Such, who (as we have seen) has mixed feelings about appropriation of the ancient past. Chapter 10, 'Debasing the Moral Currency', is ostensibly concerned with the trivializing of classical texts: 'a burlesque Socrates, with swollen legs, dying in the utterance of cockney puns' (85). The concluding chapter, 'The Modern Hep! Hep! Hep!', refers, without apparent irony, to 'the glorious commonplaces of historic teaching at our public schools and universities, being happily ingrained in the Greek and Latin Classics' (144). The underlying theme is the preservation of national memory as an element and means of national greatness: how the freedom of modern Greece is owed 'to the presence of ancient Greece in the consciousness of European men', and not to the dubious realities of Greek history or the modern Greeks themselves.[30]

The half-hidden allusions to Theophrastus in the opening pages (surely the 'dead philosopher' referred to on the first page) do recur, though with diminished frequency and greater obscurity. Reference to 'an inodorous fragment of antiquity' (see above) may call to mind Theophrastus' own work *De odoribus*. A casual reference to an acquaintance named Glycera (8) may hark back to the alleged mistress of Menander, reputed pupil of Theophrastus. Pummel, the 'sort of valet and factotum' to Theophrastus Such (71–3) may owe his conception to Theophrastus' philosophical slave Pompylus (below, 21). An anecdote concerning the pathological laughter of the Tirynthians is attributed to Athenaeus (86), who, on investigation, actually cites as his source Theophrastus' lost monograph *On comedy* (see n. 126). For those with the wit to uncover it, Eliot exposes her scholarly familiarity with the original Theophrastus.[31] Her friendship with Jebb dated from 1872, shortly after the appearance of his edition, which she may be presumed to have read; but her interest in Casaubon, including his version of the *Characters*, went back thirty years to her time in Geneva, Casaubon's birthplace.[32]

Riddling references to Theophrastus form only a part of the classical story, for which the tone is set before even the title page. On the flyleaf is quoted a six-line extract from Phaedrus: attributed, but unreferenced and untranslated. As correspondence with her publisher shows, Eliot was aware that this ran the risk of alienating Latinless readers by what would be judged by them 'the deepest-dyed pedantry'; but she declined to compromise.[33] The persevering reader would have to grapple not only with the usual Latin tags (*ex pede Herculem, memoria technica, ad libitum, corpus vile*), but also whole sentences ('inventas aut qui vitam excoluere per artes'; 'gratis anhelans, multa agendo nihil agens'). More-or-less familiar names (Homer, Hesiod, Pythagoras, Sophocles, Plato, Tacitus) mingle with the more obscure (Athenaeus, Maro, Flaccus, Pliny [the Elder]). The reader is implicitly challenged to puzzle out (*inter alia*) indirect allusions to the temple of Poseidon at Sounion (22), the Homeric Question (29), Herodotus on the Ionian Revolt (29), the banishment from Sinope of Diogenes the Cynic (81), the Rosetta Stone (113), and Aristotle's *Ethics* (130).[34] If, as Henry suggests (ix), it was Eliot's intention to demonstrate through *Theophrastus Such* the superiority of her own self-learning to that of university-educated men, she certainly succeeded. Contemporary critics complained at the intellectual demands made on the reader: 'No poem is great if only a small coterie admire it.'[35]

Although classical culture predominates, its manipulation has no monopoly in *Theophrastus Such*. Readers are confronted with French, German and Italian languages and literature, mixed in with much historical and scientific material.[36] A case in point is Eliot's preference for apparently classical or classicizing names for her cast of characters. Glycera we have already met; chapter 12 offers in rapid succession: Semper, Ubique, Aliquis, Quispiam, Pilulus, Bovis, Avis, Callista, Meliboeus, Philemon, and Euphemia. In fact, the device of allegorical naming seems to be adapted from La Bruyère, a favourite author of Eliot, to whom she makes explicit acknowledgement.[37] Chapter 10 ('Debasing the Moral Currency') opens with a quotation from his *Caractères de Théophrast*, which the imaginary author declines to translate because of the 'glamour of unfamiliarity conferring a dignity on the foreign names of very common things'. As Nancy Henry points out (xxix–xxx), this introduction adds an extra layer of complexity, as the English Theophrastus opens his chapter on contemporary manners by declining to translate the French Theophrastus, who had prefaced his own work with a translation of the Greek Theophrastus (below, 12).[38]

This blending by Eliot of classical with other cultures, continually testing and tantalizing her readership, also served to demonstrate the richness of contemporary English culture with its complex heritage. Chapter 11 explores this phenomenon while highlighting a further theme: the relationship between Theophrastus Such and Theophrastus of Eresus. Its title, 'The Wasp Credited with the Honeycomb', takes the knowing reader back to Aesop: the animals deduce that a wasp smeared with honey must be responsible for creating honeycomb. Eliot delays her retelling of the fable until the end of the chapter, where it is used as a commentary on the behaviour of one Euphorion, a minor scholar, who (88) 'is disposed to treat the distinction between Thine and Mine in original authorship as egoistic, narrowing, and low'. The scene is set for a discussion of ideas about authorship and originality, culminating with the unattributed borrowing from Aesop, only by convention the author of the work preserved under his name. To quote Henry again (viii), 'The presence of the fable ... raises further questions about the relationship between origination and ownership, and about how the inherited intellectual property of any community binds its members and defines its character.'[39] This helps explain why, having moved so far from the Greek original, the name of Theophrastus remains in Eliot's title. Again from chapter 11 (96): 'We all notice in our neighbours this reference to names as guides in criticism, and all furnish illustrations of it in our own practice; for, check ourselves as we will, the first impression from any sort of work must depend on a previous attitude of mind, and this will constantly be determined by the influences of a name.' So names do matter, and 'first impression' in that passage surely signals to the reader its relevance to *Impressions of Theophrastus Such*.

In fact, the naming of the work is more complicated than at first appears. The original title as conceived by Eliot was *Characters and Characteristics: Impressions of Theophrastus Such*, which, if anything, serves to strengthen the Theophrastan connexion. The shortened form was adopted out of convenience: 'The first two words are truthfully descriptive, but they have been much used, and the book is sure to be called "Theophrastus Such"', wrote Eliot to her publisher (*Letters*, vol. 7, 110–11, from 5 March 1879). She also considered describing herself on the title page as 'editor', reinforcing the reader's notion of Theophrastus Such as the actual author (*Letters*, vol. 7, 111, from 22 March 1879).[40]

As it stands, the title is still significant, with punning associations which have been teased out by Henry (xvi–xix). 'Impressions', in addition to the psychological imprint of characters on the author's mind, implies the process of printing, preservation and transmission. Comparable is the apparent manipulation of the notion of *charakter* by the Greek Theophrastus. There is a further possible ambiguity in that Impressions 'of' Theophrastus Such may mean both 'by' and 'about'. This ties in with Henry's ingenious explanation of the surname 'Such', which she relates to the literal translation of Theophrastus' formulaic phrase *toioutos tis, hoios* ('such a man, who'), used to introduce each Greek character. In the case of Eliot's Theophrastus, the introduction applies to himself (xix): 'The formula introduces – types – Theophrastus, but can only be completed on the completion of the book, and then only in terms of what he does, not in terms of any "first impression" of a name. Theophrastus, "Such a type who writes this book", in writing the book, has made its writing characteristic of him.' To return to the opening chapter (5): 'while I carry in myself the key to other men's experience, it is only by observing others that I can so far correct my self-ignorance as to arrive at the certainty that I am liable to commit myself unawares and to manifest some incompetency which I know no more of than the blind man knows of his image in the glass.' On which Henry adds (xvii), 'Classical Theophrastus does not reveal this kind of self-reflection. In explaining his purpose in writing, modern Theophrastus begins to sound like the familiar novelist George Eliot.'[41]

All this is true enough. On the face of it, Theophrastus as narrator of the *Characters* remains resolutely silent about his purpose in writing, his relationship with his audience and to the world around him. As has been seen, Hellenistic and Byzantine scholars felt the urge to contribute a Preface, pointed definitions, and, in certain cases, sententious conclusions.[42] The sense of 'something missing' (if not amiss) is reflected in the moralizing additions inevitably made by Theophrastus' imitators, both ancient and more modern. The earliest uncontested use of the *Characters* to survive (however precariously) is from the late third century BC by Ariston of Keos, successor at two removes to Theophrastus as head of the Lyceum. Under the heading of 'On Relief from Arrogance', Ariston presents the characters of the 'Hostile Man' (*authades*), the 'Self-Willed Man' (*authekastos*), the 'Know-it-all' (*panteidemon*), and the 'Ironical Man' (*eiron*). Their form, with concrete examples of behaviour, is thoroughly Theophrastan, but here embedded in a ponderous philosophical commentary.[43]

As we have seen, Joseph Hall, some eighteen centuries later, prefaces his *Characters of Vertues and Vices* by describing Theophrastus as 'that ancient Master of Morality'. As befitted a Bishop-to-be, known to contemporaries as the 'Christian Seneca', Hall deployed his twenty-four character-studies in order to demonstrate the practical side of moral philosophy.[44] His collection incorporates observations which are overtly ethical, expressed in abstract as opposed to concrete form. His 'Of the Superstitious' is a case in point. Although owing an obvious debt to Theophrastus in terms of detailed behaviour ('If he heare but a Raven croke from the next roofe, he makes his will'), the Character begins with moralizing antithesis: 'Superstition is godlesse Religion, devout impietie'; and it closes with a paradox: 'Finally, if God would let him be the carver of his owne obedience he could not have a better subject: as it is, he cannot have a worse.' 'The Superstitious' forms a pair with its neighbour 'Of the Profane', which opens: 'The superstitious hath too many gods: The profane man hath none at all'; both correspond with the preceding virtuous Character of 'The Penitent'. What are innovations in Hall – moral abstraction, rhetorical poise and wit, linked Characters, delineation of good as well as bad – become routine in his seventeenth- and eighteenth-century successors.[45]

The perceived moralizing gap in Theophrastus was also conspicuously filled by La Bruyère; according to Smeed (1985) 47, almost certainly independent of Hall's reworking. *Les Caractères ou les moeurs de ce siècle* first appeared in 1688, with an eighth edition in 1694, almost three times the length of the original version. Only a third of La Bruyère's text from 1694 consists of actual characters, the remainder being made up of meditations and maxims. He defends their inclusion on the ground that not only Theophrastus but also Solomon wrote books of or about *Proverbs*. The justification appears in La Bruyère's 'Discours sur Théophraste', an introductory essay to the translation of the *Characters* (3–17). Its content is wide-ranging, introducing Theophrastus to the reader, engaging with the battle of the Ancients and Moderns (someday, we will ourselves be reckoned ancient), and contrasting fourth-century Athens with the French court (n. 94). This develops into exclamatory praise for Athens and its citizens, embracing laws, *politeia*, courage, discipline, perfection in arts and sciences, and culminating in '[la] politesse dans le commerce ordinaire et dans le language!' (13–14). He cites in support (and with embellishments) Theophrastus' exposure as a non-Athenian 'par une simple femme de qui il achetait des herbes au marché', and reports the great man's astonishment that he was unable to acquire through effort what ordinary people possessed through nature. The paragraph closes with La Bruyère reassuring the reader that if Theophrastus stooped to depict ridiculous behaviour, it was to shame the Athenians and cause them to mend their ways. Moralizing is to the fore, explicitly linking back the *Characters* to the *Nicomachean ethics* and *Magna moralia*, and locating La Bruyère's own contribution alongside 'deux ouvrages morales': La Rochefoucauld's *Maximes* (1665) and Pascal's *Pensées* (1670). In drawing up his set of contemporary characters, La Bruyère combines Theophrastus' preference for behavioural detail with his own explicit moralizing.[46]

For further development within the character-genre, there is William Thackeray's *Book of Snobs*. Initially published in weekly issues of *Punch or the London Charivari* between the Februaries of 1846 and 1847, the 'Snob Papers' achieved immediate popularity, being regularly republished in book form.[47] While remaining recognizably Theophrastan in substance, the *Book of Snobs* reaches well beyond Theophrastus, who is never mentioned.[48] Through the fifty-four brief chapters, the author addresses the reader directly, exposing false behaviour at all levels in society, as the self-unaware jostle for recognition of their assumed status. Earlier imitators of Theophrastus had incorporated occasional, implied social comment: La Bruyère's sympathetic though apologetic presentation of peasants: 'en effet ils sont des hommes' (11.128); Overbury's bitterly witty evocation of 'A Prison' as a place where '*Nullum vacuum* (unless in prisoners bellyes) is here truly to be proved' (82–3). But in the hands of Thackeray, barbed criticism emerges as the sustaining theme; specifically, the unjust manipulation of social hierarchy, incorporating clear recommendations for reform. Contexts include 'Military Snobs' and purchase of commissions (ch. 9, 40–3), 'Civilian Snobs' and flogging in the army (ch. 22, 89–92), 'Clerical Snobs' and the privileged confirmation of juvenile aristocrats (ch. 13, 55–7), and 'University Snobs' contrasting treatment of the poorest scholars with aristocratic Fellow Commoners (ch. 14, 58–62). As befitted the then radical pages of *Punch*, Snobbishness is broadly equated with the foibles of 'Society' (ch. 40, 166–9) in the sense of what might nowadays be called the 'Establishment'.[49]

In both reality and pretence, the work grows organically, with its narrator allegedly responding to weekly correspondence, engaging in imagined dialogue with his readers. 'Notes of admiration (!), of interrogation (?), of remonstrance, approval or abuse come pouring into *Mr. Punch's* box.' (ch. 8, 36). The author expresses the hope (approximately fulfilled) that, in time, Court News and the Police Courts in newspapers will be complemented by a 'Snob-department' (ch. 39, 161).[50] In 'Chapter Last' (220–5), he notes how, through these pages, 'The word Snob has taken a place in our honest English vocabulary', claiming that if the snob cannot yet be defined, he or she can now at least be recognized. In fact, Thackeray had created, along the way and by degrees, the modern conception of snobbery; that is, striving to associate with those perceived to be of superior status, while treating disdainfully those regarded as inferiors. From the start, the author makes it clear that he regards himself as a snob, though of the more harmless variety, in that he is a relative (occasional) rather than a positive (perpetual) snob (ch. 1, 7–10). The second chapter (11–14) revolves around his rejection and later forgiveness of a close companion (Mr Marrowfat by name) whom the author catches eating peas with his knife. The formal title of the work was *Snobs of England by one of themselves* and his imagined correspondents address him as 'Mr Snob' (ch. 12, 51; 31, 128; 43, 179). He wonders whether 'it is impossible for *any* Briton, perhaps, not to be a snob in some degree' (ch. 5, 23), and asks himself: 'Art not thou, too, a Snob and a brother?' (ch. 43, 183).[51]

The *Book of Snobs*, with its incorporation into the discourse of an imagined author, has obvious affinities with the supposed self-revelation that is a key feature of *Theophrastus Such*. There may be faint verbal echoes. The 'loving laughter' invoked by Theophrastus Such at the close of chapter 1 (see above) is reminiscent of the laughter and love attributed to Mr Punch in the final sentences of the *Book of Snobs*. The mirror held up by Eliot's Theophrastus to reflect his own pettiness may approximate to the accusation made by a correspondent against Mr Snob that, far from depicting Snobs, 'it is only your own ugly mug which you are copying with a Narcissus-like conceit and fatuity' (ch. 5, 23). The comparison could be extended across to Thackeray's playful manipulation of the Classics. But this also serves to emphasize the distance Eliot has moved on from Thackeray's version, teasing and testing her readers.[52]

For the most part, classical allusion in the *Book of Snobs*, though extensive, is straightforward and intended to reassure rather than challenge its readership. References tend to the commonplace, with context largely explicating allusions. Mr Snob variously compares himself to Curtius ('Prefatory Remarks', 4), Damon or Pythias (ch. 1, 8), Narcissus (ch. 5, 23), Phidias (ch. 8, 37), Brutus (ch. 16, 67) and Cincinnatus ('Chapter Last,' 221). A reference to Orpheus and Eurydice actually directs the reader for further information to 'Lemprière's Dictionary' (ch. 44, 185; cf. 17, 74; below, 169). There is little untranslated Latin: 'Snobbishness is like Death in a quotation from Horace, which I hope you have never heard': a translation of *Odes* 1.4.13–14 follows ('Prefatory Remarks,' 5). Classics are deployed impartially to illustrate snobbery and expose ignorance. The President of St Boniface College, 'a rich specimen of a University Snob', had, by the age of twenty-five, 'invented three new metres and published an edition of an exceedingly improper Greek Comedy, with no less than twenty emendations upon the Greek text of Schnupfenius and Schnapsius...' (ch. 14, 58). The illiterate housekeeper of Castle Carabas points out to visitors how: 'The carvings of the chimlies, representing the buth of Venus, and Ercules, and Eyelash, is by Van Chislum, the most famous sculpture of his hage and country' (ch. 35, 146–7). If anything, Mr Snob is at pains to underplay the extent of his own classical learning. After listing imaginary literary clubs with increasingly implausible classical names (culminating in 'Poluphloisboio Thalasses'). He adds '*I* don't know Greek for one, and I wonder how many other members of these institutions do' (ch. 45, 189).[53]

This device of authorial self-revelation is intensified by Eliot's *Theophrastus Such* so as almost to deconstruct the character-genre. It is difficult to imagine how character-writing could be further refined without annihilating the underlying idea of character.[54] The most distinguished twentieth-century exponent of characters, Elias Canetti, apparently returns in his *Earwitness* to Theophrastan form and simplicity; there is no introduction or moralizing commentary. The closest he comes to comment on the text is *via* his own Character called 'The Earwitness', who (43–4) 'huddles unnoticed in a corner, peers into a book or display, hears whatever is to be heard, and moves away untouched and absent'. Yet Canetti incorporates into the conception and presentation of his characters an element of the fantastic or surreal. Typical titles include 'The King-proclaimer', 'The Tear-warmer', 'The Syllable-pure Woman', and 'The Sultan Addict', who (77):

> installs a harem for herself, locking herself up in it. There she remains forever, never leaving. There she wears transparent clothing as befits the place, and she practices intimate dances, only for him. Then she waits for the sultan, who never comes, and she imagines that he is on his way to her. ... There she throws herself ardently at his feet and begs him for his most abominable desires.

Arguably, character here crosses over the boundary into eccentricity, the Anti-Feminist becomes a fantasist, with individual triumphing over generic. Where characters are not recognizable types, it is difficult or impossible for the reader to rationalize and relate to their actions.[55]

The distance travelled in this selective analysis of the genre (to which we will return) serves to highlight the essential minimalism of the Theophrastan original, where externals alone reveal the inner man. To Theophrastus himself is attributed the saying that honours (*timai*) ought to be the outcome, not of manner and charm (*homilia kai charis*), but of deeds done (*ek ton praxeon*).[56] This stripping down of the *Characters* to cores of descriptive actions has, however, helped to promote two diversionary approaches.

Doubts have regularly been voiced over the integrity of the text. At one extreme, M. L. West has suspected that the *Characters* is in its entirety a Hellenistic compilation of Theophrastan material. This is on the grounds that other Peripatetics (Ariston as above, and Aristotle below) introduce their characters in a theoretical and diverse context.[57] A more common conclusion has been that, although the *Characters* was a contemporary creation by Theophrastus, it was intended more as an appendix than a free-standing composition. Suggested substantive accompanying works include writings on ethics, rhetoric and comedy, either Old or New.[58] Lurking behind this hypothesis are concerns over the perceived poverty of Theophrastus' style in the *Characters*. 'The Greek is sometimes obscure or inelegant, the vocabulary colloquial, the style unvaried and abrupt. Their terseness suggests notes for lectures, and they can hardly have been written for separate publication as a literary work.' So concludes Vellacott (1973) 10, who in part undercuts his own argument by producing an eminently readable translation, independent of his accompanying version of Menander. On a practical level, accusations of stylistic inadequacy have been countered by Diggle (2004), who demonstrates how, through the 'simplicity and economy of his language, Theophrastus can prompt us to think, ask questions, to fill in the details for ourselves and supply the thoughts at which he only hints' (19–25).[59] Theophrastus would probably have agreed. According to Demetrius (*On style* 222 = FHS&G 696), he argued that a speaker ought not to aim at completeness but leave some things for the listener to infer for himself: 'for when he perceives what you have left out, he not only is a listener but also becomes your witness, and in addition more favourably disposed'.

A second defence of the stripped-down *Characters* has led to a more serious misapprehension. Here, the apparently minimalist role of the author in the process of composition is taken as an epistemological virtue, with Theophrastus regularly receiving praise as an 'objective observer', disinterestedly noting down the behaviour of Athenians on display. For Smeed (1985) 5, 'He is a reporter, a deadpan observer of human affairs.' According to Ussher (1966) 65, the *Characters* is 'a series of jottings in the notebook of a keen-eyed and humorous observer'. This chimes in conveniently with Theophrastus' 'day-job' as a philosopher-scientist, so that the *Characters* may also be assimilated to a 'scientific' approach. 'What we have here are the field reports of a scientist botanizing in Athens', writes Anderson (1970) xiv–xv. For Trenkner (1958) 147–8, Theophrastus has written a 'scientific, not a literary work ... in the form of scientific *hypomnemoneumata* [memoranda] without any literary pretensions'.[60] The argument, though seductive, should be discounted. In the first place, it perpetuates the myth of the scientist as, almost by definition, an impartial observer operating in a value-free vacuum. Not so. 'How odd it is that anyone should not see that all observation must be for or against some view if it is to be of any service!' The words are Charles Darwin's, elucidating a fundamental principle of scientific and, by extension, historical enquiry.[61]

Darwin's principle of 'for or against' may be applied specifically to Theophrastus as philosopher and natural scientist. The works on which his scientific reputation has traditionally rested, *Inquiry into plants* and *On the causes of plants*, might superficially seem to consist of material more-or-less randomly collected, analysed and classified.

But even here, Theophrastus deploys his data explicitly to engage with theories of his predecessors. In the *Inquiry* (3.4–6) the views of Anaxagoras, Diogenes, and Kleidemos on the spontaneous generation of wild trees are noted and dismissed as beyond comprehension, in favour of observable phenomena. In *Causes* (1.8.2–4), Democritus' theory of the rate of growth of trees is opposed by actual evidence of different circumstances of planting and the characteristics of named species of trees (cf. 2.9–10). In an extended passage (6.1.1–3.2) the theories of Democritus and Plato on taste are critically examined. Although Aristotle is not mentioned by name in either monograph, his views are silently corrected.[62]

All this conforms with ongoing revaluation of Theophrastus' status as a thinker. As Steinmetz points out in his thoughtful overview of the *Characters* (1970) 91, scholars of the later twentieth century (and now beyond) have concentrated on isolating Theophrastus' independent contribution as a philosopher, distinct from Aristotle. These are major concerns of contributors to 'Project Theophrastus', who have singled out logic, metaphysics, ethics in politics, rhetoric and poetics, ecology and psychology (especially animal psychology); all areas where Theophrastus' contributions were significant and 'in many cases represented advances far beyond their Aristotelian antecedents' (FHS&G vol. 1, 1–2). Specifically, Richard Sorabji, having posed the question 'Is Theophrastus a significant philosopher?', enthusiastically answers 'yes', with regard to his writings on god, motion, place, and the killing of animals for food.[63]

As pointed out by Jørgen Mejer (1998) 19, traditional datings make Theophrastus one of Aristotle's earliest associates with an age difference of less than fifteen years. They may therefore better be approached as colleagues rather than teacher and student. It is likely that Theophrastus began publishing while Aristotle was still alive. Balme (1962) has made out a detailed case for locating Theophrastus' views on spontaneous generation in his *Metaphysics* as poised between those in Aristotle in *Metaphysics* and in *De generatione animalium* and *Historia animalium*. Lynch (1972) 77 suggests possible Theophrastan influence on Aristotle across their twenty-year association, with the former's *Metaphysics* rejecting Aristotelian ideas.[64]

Finally, the notion of Theophrastus of the *Characters* as disinterested observer may be countered by one of the lessons learnt from *Theophrastus Such*, where Eliot has provided what is virtually a commentary on the process of character-writing. Specifically, she suggests that the author is inevitably present in his or her text, even if that presence is neither intended nor explicit ('What kind of hornpipe am I dancing now?'). The focus of observation necessarily reveals something about the observer. On a basic level, selectivity is unavoidable, with consequential suppression or omission. Theophrastus Such himself in 'Looking Inward' (5–6) makes a comparison with Rousseau's *Confessions*; in spite of Rousseau's efforts at self-revelation, half of the reader's impression of his character comes from what he leaves unsaid. In the *Characters*, that consideration may be applied to both choice of characters and their range of actions. An obvious case is the absence from Theophrastus of female and 'lower-class' characters, who are such a feature of his imitators; likewise his exclusion of non-Athenians. By contrast, from the eighty-three Overburian characters, ten are women, twenty-three are from the 'poorer classes', and four are not English.[65]

The implications of choice are thrown into still sharper relief by reference to so-called 'Estates Literature', dating from the twelfth to the sixteenth century, and seeking to locate and describe all manner of significant men and women within the frame of contemporary English society. Typically, Estates Satire aimed at confirming divine sanction for the various estates, stressing their interdependence, lamenting their various shortcomings, and recommending remedies. Jill Mann in her *Chaucer and medieval Estates satire* (1973) has staked out a strong claim for the General Prologue to the *Canterbury Tales* as an outstanding specimen of Estates Literature with its 'satiric representation of all classes of society' (1). She suggests (5) how the Estates framework provides an ordering of experience without which detailed observation would have little sociological significance. As will be seen, the *Characters* has its own ordering (52). She further identifies Chaucer's distinctive contribution in the detail of the occupations of his pilgrims (10–16): 'The *Prologue* proves to be a poem about work' (202). Daily occupation, including anti-social practices, determines and constitutes character. But this is accompanied by what she terms 'omission of their victims' (86–105, 190–1), whereby the harmful effects of dubious practices are left unstated. It is in this and other ways, according to Mann (197–8), that Chaucer consistently removes from the reader the possibility of moral judgement. The contrast with the world of the *Characters* is evident, indicative of different choices and directions not taken. Theophrastus no less than Chaucer was an artful observer.[66]

There have been sporadic attempts to credit Theophrastus with an imaginary thirty-first Character: typically that of the 'Philologist', as if those writing on Theophrastus cannot bear to be left out of the action. A more appropriate additional Character, could we supply it, would be that of Theophrastus himself.[67] Of course, direct knowledge of the character of Theophrastus, in the sense of 'personality', is an impossibility. What we are told by Diogenes Laertius and others verges on the banal: how Theophrastus was 'most intelligent and industrious', 'ever ready to do a kindness and a lover of words' (Diog. Laert. 5.36–7 = FHS&G 1.10–12), and how, according to Diogenes the Cynic, he possessed *barutes* or 'gravity' (*Suda* no. 1141 = FHS&G 55). 'Anecdotes about Theophrastus are deplorably few,' writes Mejer (1998) 9, concluding that that 'the few preserved anecdotes do give us a fairly consistent impression of Theophrastus' (28). Those hinting at reputed character are sparse and generally consistent with a reputation for hard-working asceticism: how Theophrastus would be the last person in Athens to dress indulgently, wearing linen (Diog. Laert. 6.90 = FHS&G 23); how he would constantly say that time was a 'costly expenditure' (Diog. Laert. 5.40 = FHS&G 1.44–5); his view that intellect and a good mind are gained not by prayer but by study (*Gnom. Vat.* 323 = FHS&G 471). For further consistency, see below (25). The difficulty lies in discerning what this uniformity reflects: perceived reality or invented persona? For those hoping for the former, analogies with anecdotes about ancient authors and on Roman emperors are not encouraging.[68]

An alternative approach seeks to highlight the Theophrastus behind the *Characters* by locating him within a range of contexts. Two have already been briefly considered: that of Theophrastus' other writings, and the relationship of the *Characters* to its imitators; both serving to confirm the individuality of his own perspective. A third may be prompted by *Theophrastus Such* with its questioning of attribution, its emphasis on the presence in the text of the author/narrator, and the heightened idea of an imagined audience or readership; that is, a group which has its identity defined and solidarity strengthened by informed engagement with the text. As we have seen, in Eliot's hands, Classics plays a key role in this process; similarly, though less subtly, in Thackeray's *Book of Snobs*. This approach offers at least the possibility of reconstructing something of the ideology necessarily shared by the author and those for whom the work was intended. Absence of moralizing guidance for the reader in the original *Characters* may be explained in terms of an understanding common to Theophrastus and his intended audience.[69] Smeed notes with reference to eighteenth-century England (74) how characters thrive on consensus of opinion. What follows is an attempt to identify and articulate that consensus with regard to the *Characters* in later fourth-century Athens, beginning with the setting of the Lyceum.

3

THEOPHRASTUS THE METIC

'Bury me wherever seems to be especially suitable in the garden, doing nothing excessive concerning the burial nor concerning the monument. In order that the maintenance of the shrine and the monument and the garden and the walk (*peripatos*) may be continued after me, Pompylus, too, is to have joint charge of these things, living nearby and giving attention to the other matters as [he did] even formerly. And those who hold these things are to be attentive to his welfare.' The quotation is from Theophrastus' will, preserved by Diogenes Laertius (5.53–4 = FHS&G 1.324–30); garden, shrine and walk refer to locations in the Lykeion.[70] The instructions indicate Theophrastus' close identification with the Lyceum (though unobtrusive in death), hint at its physical form, and demonstrate something of the set of relationships there encompassed. It is illuminating to compare Aristotle's will, also preserved by Diogenes (5.11–16), which is almost entirely concerned with private affairs. We catch a glimpse there of Theophrastus himself, appointed one of five executors ('if he should be willing and it should be possible for him'), and being placed in line to look after Aristotle's son and daughter, with the possibility (not fulfilled) of marriage to the latter (5.12–13 = FHS&G 19). By contrast, Theophrastus' own will makes provision for maintenance of the Mouseion or sanctuary of the Muses in the Lykeion, completion of statues of the goddesses, placing of a statue of Aristotle in the shrine, replacement there of existing votive offerings, rebuilding a small portico next to the Mouseion, setting tablets with maps of the earth in the lower portico, repairing of the altar, and completion of a life-size statue of Nicomachus, father of Aristotle. Then, after the quotation with which this chapter began, there follows a detailed record of domestic arrangements and bequests, ending with a list of executors and elaborate instructions for safekeeping of the will.[71]

This is easily the most detailed of the four Peripatetic wills preserved by Diogenes. Readily apparent is Theophrastus' extensive wealth, with property in Stageira (presumably inherited from Aristotle), family property in Eresus, unspecified financial agreements in Chalcis, and household possessions in Athens. There are sizable monetary bequests (reckoned in talents and thousands of drachmas) and instructions regarding ten household slaves: three to be freed immediately, two conditionally freed, four given away, and one sold on. But what stands out is Theophrastus' concern with securing personal bonds between his followers, designed to safeguard the future well-being of the philosophical school. As a broad indication, the will mentions forty indi-viduals by name: several in different sets of circumstances; approximately twice as many as Aristotle. Paramount are arrangements for the philosophers to continue to commune together (5.52–3 = FHS&G 1.311–20):

> The garden and the walk and all the dwellings next to the garden I give to those of [my] friends listed below who wish at any time to study and to philosophize together in them – since it is not possible for all men always to be in residence – [on condition that] they neither alienate [them] nor anyone appropriate [them] for his own private use, but rather that they possess [them] in common (*koinei kektemenois*) as if a shrine, and that in addition they should treat one another in a familiar and friendly manner (*kai pros allelois oikeios kai philikos chromenois*), as is fitting and just. Let the common partners (*hoi koinonountes*) be Hipparchus, Neleus, Strato, Callinus, Demotimus, Demaratus, Callisthenes, Melantes, Pancreon, and Nicippus.

The terminology is rich in its implications. The members of the school effectively constitute a *koinonia* and are to treat another as befits *oikeioi* and *philoi*.[72]

Several services are specified in the will itself (5.54–6 = FHS&G 1.320–56). The senior residents are encouraged to take care of Aristotle's grandson, supporting his philosophical endeavours. As we have seen, the *philoi* are further requested to make sure that the freedman Pompylus should have necessary support in acting as caretaker of the Lyceum. The will goes on to apportion furniture for his use and secure a gift of 2000 drachmas and two slaves for Pompylus and the freedwoman Threpte, who may plausibly be identified as his wife. The insistent detail – how the money along with any previous gifts and their own earnings is to be 'safely theirs, as I have often discussed with Melantes and Pancreon themselves, and they have agreed with me in everything' – may reflect the vulnerability of bequests to former slaves. Two thousand drachmas was a substantial sum: the level of wealth needed to qualify for the restricted franchise under Antipater (below, 35). Theophrastus also gives detailed explanation of arrangements made for Hipparchus, acting as sole-executor. He tells how he would have appointed as co-executors Melantes and Pancreon, had not Hipparchus helped them (and Theophrastus himself) in the past, and were his own affairs not now 'ship-wrecked'. As under these circumstances it would be awkward for Melantes and Pancreon to act alongside Hipparchus, they are to receive compensation from the estate of one talent each.[73]

The sense of community may be reinforced by the location and configuration of the Lyceum itself. Until recently, the preferred placing for the Sanctuary of Apollo Lykeios (based on admittedly fragile evidence of inscriptions) was an area to the east of the city, immediately outside the Themistoclean wall, in the vicinity of what is now Syntagma Square. However, relatively recent excavations to the east of Rigillis Street, close by the bed of the Ilissus, have uncovered a large, rectangular building-complex, surrounded on three sides by stoas. The structure, plausibly identified as a palaestra, seems to date from the last quarter of the fourth century BC, being rebuilt at least twice before being abandoned in the later fourth century AD. On the basis of size, location and repeated reconstruction, the excavators have concluded that this is indeed the Gymnasium of the Lykeion, originally the work of Lycurgus (pseudo-Plutarch, *Ten Orators* 841C-D).[74] What are the implications of this relocation? The Lyceum now appears as rather more remote from the city: approximately two kilometers from the Agora as the crow flies, and slightly further out than the Academy. Not far, perhaps, in absolute terms, but even small distances may acquire symbolic significance; what might be termed the 'Girton College effect'. The chorus of farmers in Aristophanes' *Peace* complains that (353–7): 'For quite long enough we've been killing ourselves and we've worn ourselves out, wandering to the Lykeion and back, spear-shield-and-all.'

Although nothing much should be read into the simple physical separation of the Lyceum from the city, shared, as it was, by all three philosophical schools centred on gymnasia, the sense of ideological distance may be more significant. In part, the appeal of the gymnasium for philosophers was practical: a pleasant ambience with shade and running water. Existing buildings could be utilized: the Mouseion, stoas, shrine and walk mentioned in Theophrastus' will. The Mouseion itself may have served as a storeroom-cum-library. Wycherley suggests that the peripatos of the gymnasium in the Lykeion might have supplied the place needed for large-scale lectures; a reminder that, with its variety of public spaces, philosophers had no monopoly in their non-athletic use of gymnasia. The process whereby gymnasia evolved into places for education seems clear enough: locations where young men (and others) with time and money to spare might conveniently train mind as well as body.[75]

The Agora might appear to provide an urban equivalent, the obvious gathering-place within the city for instruction-through-conversation. But what served to mark off Agora from gymnasia was its different blending of people and activities. I have tried elsewhere to demonstrate Plato's and Aristotle's deep-seated dislike for the Athenian Agora, combining necessary civic functions (politics, religion, justice) with activities they deemed unworthy (chiefly buying and selling), attracting too many of the 'wrong' type of people. The little old woman who allegedly discountenanced Theophrastus is a possible case in point. The 'Morally Degraded Man' (6.9) downgrades himself still further by taking in hand *polloi agoraioi*. It is in this spirit of exclusivity that Theophrastus' 'Oligarchic Man' (26.3) advises his like-minded crony: 'We must meet and discuss this on our own and be rid of the mob (*tou ochlou*) and the Agora.' For their part, Plato (in the *Laws*) and Aristotle (in the *Politics*) offer an identical, ideal solution: avoiding lower-class contamination by separation of agora-activities into discreet and segregated areas. In the case of their own philosophizing, they were able to put the principle into practice. Although teaching in gymnasia could hardly be private, at least the right kind of people turned up to heckle: in the case of Plato, a Sicilian doctor (Athenaeus 2.59d-f).[76]

That said, the setting of Plato's *Protagoras* does offer a more insulated, urban alternative to the Agora as a place for intellectual debate: the house of Callias, which, with its courtyard and colonnades, is apparently big enough for a gathering of some forty visitors. A doorkeeper keeps at bay the wider, unwanted world. Wycherley identifies the arrangement of the gymnasium, with its palaestra and stoas, as effectively reproducing Callias' house writ large: 'It has been said quite rightly that a Greek philosophical school was essentially a specialized extension of a Hellenic household.' Such an extension forms part of the house of the 'Conspicuous Consumer' (5.10), with a designated area which he rents out to sophists who need an audience.[77]

The older idea that the philosophical schools, in particular the Lyceum, resembled nothing so much as Oxbridge colleges, complete with Master, Fellows and Scholars, has happily fallen from favour. John Lynch in his important study *Aristotle's school* (1972) has clarified the status of the Lyceum as a secular educational institution, not, as used to be thought, having the legal basis of a religious foundation (1–8, 106–34).[78] But calling for further thought is the peculiar overlapping of public and private that seems characteristic of the Lyceum. Implicit in the story so far has been a division between the state-owned land and buildings that were the gymnasium of the Lykeion, and the privately-owned property of Theophrastus. In his will, a distinction has been detected between those instructions prefaced by *boulomai* ('I wish') referring to public property, and *didomi* ('I bequeath') dealing with private possessions.[79] The distinction is helpful, but should not be pressed too far. After all, some instructions necessarily refer to things to be done rather than 'given'. A specific problem arises out of Theophrastus' wishes relating to the public property of the Mouseion, stoas, shrine and altar, which include rebuilding, renovation, adornment, and additions to the fabric. It does seem remarkable that a private individual (not even a citizen) could propose in a personal document such extensive interference with public property. There comes to mind the so-called 'Spring House Decree', whereby the *demos* unambiguously rejected an offer by Pericles and his sons to bear the cost of rebuilding a public fountain house. Of course, by the time of Theophrastus' death, Athens was no longer that self-conscious kind of democracy.[80]

Theophrastus' encroachment on the public sphere may be tied in with another anomalous feature of the will: his apparent ability, though not a citizen, to bequeath to ten further non-citizens the use of garden, walk and dwellings, as if his private property. This is apparently explained by a sentence from Diogenes (5.39 = FHS&G 1.38–40): 'It is said that he even came into possession of his own garden (*idion kepon schein*) after the death of Aristotle, since Demetrius of Phalerum, who was also his friend (*gnorimos*), helped him [to obtain it] (*touto sumpraxantos*).' The presumption is that Demetrius, former pupil at the Lyceum and Macedonian regent (*epimeletes* or *epistates*) of Athens, used his influence in the Assembly to secure a decree of *enktesis* for Theophrastus, giving him the right to own real property; and that may well be right. It is on this ground that Theophrastus has been hailed as formal founder of the Peripatetic school.[81] But other possibilities at least deserve consideration. The nature of the relationship between Theophrastus and Demetrius of Phalerum remains problematic. From the vantage-point of the fourth-century AD, the philosopher Themistius could harangue a sophist (real or imagined) for not rejecting the financial favours of the archons, 'as Theophrastus did those from the Phalerean' (Orations 21 252B = FHS&G 29).[82]

It was the norm for non-citizens to rent property in Athens, through the agency of a citizen *prostates* or patron. This included Aristotle all his time in Athens, and Theophrastus at least until the intervention of Demetrius; unless, that is, they were lent accommodation by some citizen-friend. We can only speculate over the identity of Aristotle's and Theophrastus' *prostatai*, which might change over time, with, in addition to the individual required by law, the possibility of informal and non-Athenian patrons and protectors. As overall executor of his will, Aristotle nominated the all-powerful Antipater (5.11). Lane Fox (1996) 134 intriguingly suggests that Theophrastus, 'in order to secure his bequests to his school and friends', hedged his political bets by having one copy of his will deposited with Adeimantus (identified as 'a top Macedonian courtier'), and another with Olympiodorus ('democracy's top general').

In the case of Theophrastus' help from Demetrius, what needs to be noted is the legal neutrality of Diogenes' wording, as rightly in Sollenberger's careful version given above: *schein* means 'come to possess' not 'own'; *idion* as 'private' in the sense of 'his own' not 'private property'; *sumprattein*: 'assist', not 'assist in obtaining'. A straightforward grant of *enktesis* to Theophrastus would not have enabled him to bequeath the property to non-citizens. We should reckon with the possibility of a more personal, extra-legal involvement on the part of Demetrius, who conceivably bought the garden on behalf of his friend, with title (though that is not the right word) devolving informally over time on Theophrastus and his followers. By the same token, across the years a similar blurring of public and private may have occurred over formal responsibility for, and possession of the Mouseion and other buildings on the site.[83]

Theophrastus, then, the metic. As in the case of Aristotle, we can only guess at the tensions generated by an inferior civic status for an otherwise obvious member of the élite.[84] On the one hand, alongside Theophrastus' personal wealth went further marks of distinction. According to Diogenes (5.37 = FHS&G 1.13–14), in addition to his friendship with Demetrius, as intellectual heir to Aristotle he was 'welcomed' by Cassander, and his presence was sought (unsuccessfully) by Ptolemy. Set against these connexions was the institutional inferiority imposed by metic status. Apart from the need to nominate a citizen-*prostates*, there was the obligation to pay the monthly metic tax: both on pain of enslavement. Theophrastus himself in his *Laws* explained the proverbial phrase 'more mute than a bowl' as a reference to metics carrying bowls in public processions. 'Whenever they [the Athenians] wanted to point out a metic, they said "bowl" or "bowl carrier". Because he had no freedom of speech (*aparresiaston*), they could threaten to make him more mute than a bowl.'[85]

Although, as we have seen, certain disabilities might be evaded through powerful connexions, these brought their own risks, as demonstrated by the earlier experiences of Aristotle.[86] As a result of the violent overthrow in 307 of the régime ruled over by Demetrius, democracy was temporarily restored and steps taken against perceived supporters of the Macedonians. A committee of *nomothetai,* appointed to revise the law-code operating under Demetrius, approved a proposal from one Sophocles that all heads of philosophical schools had first to secure approval of the *boule* and *demos.* In protest, all philosophers, including Theophrastus, withdrew from Athens. Lara O'Sullivan in 'The Law of Sophocles' (2002) plausibly associates the impulse behind Sophocles' legislation with the known Macedonian connexions of the Peripatetics, and specifically the favouritism shown to Theophrastus by Demetrius.[87] Within a year, however, the philosophers were back in Athens. Philon, a citizen and a Peripatetic, challenged Sophocles in court with having introduced an illegal measure; the defence mounted by Demochares, nephew of Demosthenes and insistent advocate of Athenian independence, proved unsuccessful.[88]

The bare bones of the story are told by Diogenes (5.38 = FHS&G 1.22–9), who explains that the Athenians' motive for convicting Sophocles (whom they allegedly fined a massive five talents) was specifically to ensure the return of Theophrastus. But that is best taken as part of Diogenes' theme of the ongoing popularity of Theophrastus with the Athenians. He describes how he was earlier brought to trial for impiety by Hagnonides, an established opponent of Macedonian domination, who ended up almost being fined, because 'his [Theophrastus'] acceptance among the Athenians was so great'.[89] This alleged Athenian love-affair with Theophrastus culminates in a mass funeral procession, escorting his body to the Lyceum (5.41 = FHS&G 1.60–2). But Diogenes (or his source) surely over-compensates. Theophrastus' post-Sophoclean influence in Athens was apparently insufficient to engineer the return from self-protecting exile of the politician Dinarchus. Although originally from Corinth, Dinarchus spent most of his active political life in Athens, where he is said to have been a pupil of Theophrastus and Demetrius ([Plut.], *Ten Orators* 850C). Friendship with Antipater and Cassander, then the ending of Demetrius' régime, prompted his removal from Athens. According to Dionysius of Halicarnassus (*Dinarchus* 2 = FHS&G 30), Theophrastus was one of a number of friends in Athens on whom for fifteen years Dinarchus pinned his hopes. Only in 292, shortly before his death, was Theophrastus able to prevail on Demetrius Poliorcetes to authorize Dinarchus' return ([Plut], *Ten Orators* 850D).[90]

The anecdotal evidence may be read both ways: collaboration, political persecution, voluntary exile, and a trial for impiety at which, as a metic, Theophrastus would necessarily be disadvantaged.[91] We may create our own, alternative anecdotal motif: the 'divine speaker' baffled and bested by native Athenians. According to Aelian (8.12 = FGH&S 32A), Theophrastus broke down while addressing the court of the Areopagus. The occasion was presumably his trial for impiety. Theophrastus' excuse, that he was overcome by the majesty (*to axioma*) of the council, was countered by Demochares' riposte 'in a very stinging and quick-witted manner (*pikrotata ... kai*

hetoimotata)', that 'those doing the judging were Athenians, not the twelve gods'.[92]
Compare a story retold by Cicero in *On the nature of the gods* (1.93 = FHS&G 61A):

> Was it by relying on these [Epicurean] dreams that not only Epicurus and
> Metrodorus and Hermarchus spoke against Pythagoras, Plato and Empedocles,
> but also the prostitute (*meretricula*) Leontion dared to write against
> Theophrastus? She did indeed say witty things, and in Attic dialect, but really! –
> Such great licence did the garden of Epicurus have.

The notion of a woman of low status exercising her wit in Attic Greek at Theophrastus'
expense has obvious affinities with the anecdote, again from Cicero, with which this
essay began.[93] Also significant here is Pliny the Elder's oblique reference to the
Leontion story (*Natural histories* 1 Preface 29 = FHS&G 61B): 'Just as if I don't know
that even a woman wrote critically of Theophrastus, a man so great in eloquence that
he acquired a divine name from it, and that from this [criticism] arose the proverb of
choosing a tree for hanging oneself.' The saying presumably refers to provoking
criticism through an inept choice of name: a hostage to fortune. The clustering of ideas
is at least consistent, emblematic of Theophrastus' less-than-complete integration into
the Athenian scene. Hence, perhaps, Theophrastus' insistence, as recorded by Vitruvius
(6 Intr. 2 = FHS&G 491) that, 'Of all men the educated man alone is neither a stranger
in foreign places nor lacking in friends, when the members of his household and
relatives are lost. Rather, he is a citizen in every state...'[94]

The established tradition attributes to Aristotle the process of renaming
Theophrastus (Diog. Laert. 5.38 = FHS&G 1.30–1): 'He was called Tyrtamus, but
Aristotle changed his name to Theophrastus on account of the divine character of his
speech.' The reliability of the anecdote is assessed by Sollenberger (1992) 3833–6, who
notes that other philosophers (including Plato, formerly Aristocles) are credited with
name-changes. He also contrasts 'Divine Speaker' with the apparently colourless
'Tyrtamus', a form of the word 'Fourth' (as in 'fourth-born'), which may well have
been specific to Asia Minor. By contrast, 'Theophrastus' was a relatively common
name for Athenians from the fifth to third centuries BC. This raises at least the
possibility that Tyrtamus was seeking a replacement-name both agreeable to his
reputation and also not obviously 'foreign'.[95]

The formulation of the attack on Theophrastus ascribed to Leontion may reflect a
broader perspective on the Lyceum, with reference to the other major philosophical
schools. The supposed 'metic' character of the Lyceum has often been noted. All five
so-called 'scholarchs' from Aristotle down to Ariston of Ceos were non-Athenian, as
was perhaps a majority of their followers. Theophrastus' will, it should be recalled,
referred to 'dwellings' next to the garden, available for occupation for those wishing
to philosophize together, 'since it is not possible for all men always to be in residence'.
The resultant 'insecurity' of the Lyceum's membership has been put forward by Lynch
(1972) 152–4 as a significant factor in its early relative decline. Admittedly, this may

overstate the case. Other schools had their own high-profile non-Athenians (including scholarchs), and a consolidated list of Theophrastus' pupils includes several Athenian citizens (FHS&G 18).[96] But the strands of evidence drawn out in this chapter lead off in the same direction; how, from its foundation, the heads of the Lyceum and its membership could be seen as somehow 'less Athenian' in orientation, disassociated from the civic mainstream. This supports the idea of a heightened sense of community, reinforced by its location outside the city. Although it would be an obvious exaggeration to envisage the public place of the Lykeion as a philosophical outpost, the burial there of Theophrastus might almost seem reminiscent of an oikist.

Aristotle's emphasis on his followers as a community of *philoi* is well attested in Book 9 of the *Nicomachean ethics* (1164b3, 1171b29–72a9). Although philosophers elsewhere (certainly the Academy and the Epicureans) conceived of themselves as *philoi*, Lynch has demonstrated (1972) 85–7 how Aristotle diverged from the traditional terminology of philosophical association, dropping *suneinai* ('being together') in favour of *koinonein* ('combining together'). The effect was to highlight the co-operative aspect of the Lyceum, marking off its distinctive brand of philosophy: the cumulative effect of shared tasks, as opposed to the dialectical process of the Academy. 'For while no single person can find a significant measure of the truth, it is possible for everyone to contribute to its discovery, so that by the combined work of many something considerable will be achieved.' Continuation of the co-operative ideal under Theophrastus is evident from the phrasing of his will, reflecting the strengthening of communal institutions. Let us see how these features might provide a context for the *Characters*.[97]

4

THAT'S ENTERTAINMENT?

Close to the beginning of his pedants' banquet, Athenaeus has one of the learned diners cite Hermippus of Smyrna (1.21b = FHS&G 12), a biographer from the third century BC, who describes how: 'Theophrastus would arrive at the *peripatos* punctually, smart and well dressed, then sit down and deliver his lecture, in the course of which he would use all kinds of movements and gestures. Once, when he was imitating a gourmet (*opsophagon*), he stuck out his tongue and licked his lips.' Apart from providing a glimpse of Theophrastus' routine as teacher, the vignette supplies a possible context for the *Characters* in terms of 'performance culture'. Theophrastus puts on a distinctive display (*epideixis*), cultivating his individual appearance (*schema*) before the gaze (*theoria*) of a committed and critical audience. The occasion is competitive; a contest (*agon*) not merely to win over those present, but ideally to gain an advantage over philosophical rivals. The idea of competition is made explicit in a metaphor attributed by Plutarch to Zeno (*Moralia* 545F = FHS&G 15), who, 'seeing that Theophrastus was admired for having many pupils, said, "His chorus is larger, but mine is more harmonious".'[98]

One difficulty in locating the *Characters* lies in reconciling its obvious comedy with the predominantly serious business of philosophy. The view has already been encountered, and discounted, that the work was intended as an appendix to a more substantial composition on ethics, rhetoric, or comedy. Although that is based on a misapprehension, some kind of philosophical connexion seems undeniable, implicit in the work's full title (above, 3). In terms of method, the *Characters* resembles the remainder of Theophrastus' surviving works only in the most general sense of a preoccupation with the principle of classification.[99] Concerning content, however, there are acknowledged affinities with passages in a range of Aristotle's works: *Rhetoric*, *Nicomachean* and *Eudemian ethics*, *Magna moralia* and possibly (but probably not) the pseudo-Aristotelian *Physiognomica*. Physiognomy, in the sense of relating facial features to inner character, has its formal origins in the *Physiognomica* attributed to Aristotle, written either by Peripatetics, or persons under their influence. But physiognomics play virtually no part in delineation of individuals in the *Characters*, who are only occasionally described in terms of facial appearance.[100]

Relevant passages from Aristotle are marshalled by Diggle (2004) in his compact discussion of 'Antecedents and Relations' (5–8). In the *Rhetoric* (1389a3–1391a29), Aristotle describes in more-or-less detail a range of characters (*ethe*) including young men, old men, the middle-aged, those who are well-born, rich, and powerful. In the *Nicomachean ethics* (1115a4–1128b33) he personalizes various characteristics, including the Coward (*deilos*) and the Courageous Man (*andreios*). But as Diggle notes (7), in contrast to Theophrastus, 'his persons exist, for the most part, out of time and space, moral paradigms, not flesh and blood'. A case in point is the Coward. According to Aristotle, the Courageous Man will best demonstrate his bravery either at sea or in an infantry battle. These are the precise locations for Theophrastus' 'Coward' (25), but here embedded in lively scenes of action. In fact, the divergence may be followed further. Whereas Aristotle observes that the dangers of warfare are superior to those at sea as offering opportunities for enhanced nobility, Theophrastus' 'Coward' exploits battle in terms of its enlarged scope for deviousness: seeing men falling, he abandons the phalanx to retrieve his sword which he then hides, finally claiming false credit for rescuing a wounded comrade.[101]

Where overlap with Aristotle does occur is in the structural presentation of virtues and vices. In the *Nicomachean ethics* (1106b16–1108b6), moral qualities are deployed by Aristotle to establish virtue as a mean between corresponding vices of deficiency or excess. Thus *aletheia* (truth) is poised midway between *eironeia* (irony) and *alazoneia* (boasting). Both are Theophrastan (1, 23), as are a further seven of the twenty-six paired vices listed by Aristotle. Theophrastus in a substantial fragment from his own writings on ethics preserved by Stobaeus similarly frames his thoughts in terms of co-ordinates, comparing those present at meetings who chatter, are taciturn, and 'say only what is necessary and so lay hold upon due measure (*ton kairon*)' (*Anthology* 2.7.20 = FHS&G 449A). Stobaeus here quotes from a summary account of Peripatetic ethics thought to be by Arius Didymus from the first century BC. The passage goes on to paraphrase 'several sets of co-ordinates in conformity with his [Theophrastus'] teacher'. Precise overlap of the seven triads with faults of the *Characters* occurs in *sophrosune, akolasia, anaisthesia; andreia, thrasutes, deilia; eleutheriotes, asotia, aneleutheria*.[102]

The formulation of virtues as means may help to explain why collections of 'good' characters consistently fail to engage the reader, in that nothing about their behaviour can be provocative or piquant. A case in point is Aristotle's *megalopsuchos* or Great-Hearted Man (1123a34–25a16), regularly seen as anticipating the *Characters* in form, but lacking their direct appeal. As will be seen (ch. 11), the relationship between the Great-Hearted Man and the notional ideal from which the Characters deviate is complex and potentially revealing. 'Must the "Characters" of Ideal Types be Dull?', asks Smeed (1985) 190–8), to which his own answer is, not necessarily, but in the pleasure-giving stakes bad characters do enjoy a head-start. It has been pointed out how Theophrastus' Characters may exasperate, annoy, and even disgust, but none is truly evil; very few of their actions would lead to being prosecuted and locked up, even under Athenian law. Whatever the banality of evil, behaving badly would seem to be endlessly diverting.[103]

There is surely an unvoiced expectation that the bad behaviour of the Characters will bring its own retribution; characteristically, foregoing the benefits of the mutuality that they exploit or shun. The exception to the rule is the *aponenoemenos* or 'Morally Degraded Man' (6.7), who through theft spends more time in gaol than in his own house. Appropriately so, in that his character encompasses insensitivity to the shame that is obvious to all around him, which is its own punishment. By contrast, the 'Talker' (7.9) seems fully aware of his weakness, confessing to a 'well-oiled tongue', causing him to 'twitter like a swallow'; all the more reprehensible that he carries on regardless: 'It's hard for me to keep quiet'. How does the severity of the failings of the other Characters match up with those attributed by Theophrastus' imitators? Joseph Hall termed the faults of his characters 'vices' (Hypocrisy, Profanity, Envy); suitably serious in that the moral boundaries being transgressed were sanctioned by religion: Jebb (1909) 25. His successors, as will be seen (35), regularly insert characters destined by their occupations to evil-doing (Overbury's Pirate, Usurer, Canting Rogue, Roaring Boy, and the like). As a broad counter-indicator, the anti-social behaviour of Theophrastus' Characters rarely, if ever, inflicts *hubris*.[104]

A series of sayings, more-or-less remotely attributed to Theophrastus, may hint at how the behaviour of his Characters is to be registered on the scale of wrongdoing. That they are not envisaged as *kakoi* may be inferred from a saying of Theophrastus preserved by Stobaeus (*Anthology* 3.38.30 = FHS&G 444): how wicked men are not so pleased with their own good things as with the evils afflicting others (*epi tois allotriois kakois*). A possible implication is that any pleasure felt at the behaviour of Characters cannot be the result of their connexion with evil. Compare (more tenuously) the sentiment attributed to Theophrastus by Seneca (*On anger* 1.12.3 = FHS&G 446): 'It cannot happen … that a good man is not angered by evil (*malis*)'; presuming for the *Characters* an audience of amused rather than angered 'good men'. More tenuously still, preserved in Arabic by Mubassir (FHS&G 454) as one of the *Choicest maxims and best sayings*, 'Theophrastus said: "The educated person is he who talks about the good qualities of people and conceals the evil".'[105]

Not philosophy then, but the work of a philosopher, and arguably meant for the appreciation of other philosophers. Consensus seems to have developed over an informal status for the *Characters* so as to allow adequate scope for entertainment. The approach may be traced back to Jebb (1909), who rightly identified the difficulty in attributing a serious purpose to the *Characters* as being (13): 'not that the descriptions are amusing, but they are written as if their principal aim was to amuse.' He therefore envisaged Theophrastus writing short character-sketches for his own and his friends' amusement. These passed haphazardly from hand to hand, a process that continued after his death. In this way, Jebb sought to account for the perceived peculiarities of the text as transmitted; more or fewer, longer or shorter Characters, and their apparently random ordering. Diggle (2004) 14–16, disagreeing with Jebb's diagnosis of the state of the text, revives a theory of Pasquali: how the sketches were intended as lighthearted diversions in more formal lectures on ethics. In support, Diggle invokes Hermippus' striking sketch of Theophrastus-as-lecturer cited above, speculatively extending via the *Characters* the likely range of actions and gestures. How would the audience have responded to Theophrastus' presentation of the 'Tactless Man' as teacher (12.9), getting up to explain all over again the point his pupils have already grasped?[106]

The broad idea is attractive and the performance element may be reinforced by Theophrastus' apparent concern, expressed elsewhere, over the importance of *hupokrisis* in the sense of rhetorical delivery. According to the late grammarian Athanasius (*Rhetores Graeci* 14 177.3–8 = FHS&G 712), Theophrastus said that *hupokrisis* was of the greatest help in persuasion, including movement of the body and pitch of the voice. Cicero in *De oratore* (3.221 = FHS&G 713) emphasizes the importance of changing facial expression: 'Theophrastus indeed says that a certain Tauriscus used to say that one who in delivery makes his speech while gazing fixedly upon something is "an actor with his back turned".'[107]

Crucial to the context of performance is the encompassing ideology; in this case, the humorous effect of the *Characters* as an expression of knowledge and values shared by Theophrastus and the community of scholars, confirming and reinforcing their sense of solidarity. Shared experience and expectations provided an implicit moral commentary on the *Characters*, which later generations have found it necessary to supply for themselves. Effectiveness of the process depended on a common sense of separateness and superiority. This might be manifested through the recognition of philosophical allusion: veiled reference to Arisotle's *Ethics* as equivalent to modern, unattributed quotation of Virgil, Horace and Phaedrus (above, 10).[108] The resulting psychological reaction is potentially complex. Informed members of the audience might combine a sense of pleasure in philosophical recognition, denied to outsiders, with a feeling of moral superiority over the Characters themselves: 'At least I don't behave like that, but then I've read and understood my Aristotle.' According to the *Gnomologium Vaticanum*, a late collection of sayings (no. 325 = FHS&G 522), Theophrastus was emphatic that to praise and blame should not be open to everyone, but was the prerogative of those who had distinguished the good and bad with regard to man. But additional layers of response would be created by the realization of personal deficiencies, possibly resulting in a mental note to avoid certain actions for the future. Again, according to the *Gnomologium Vaticanum* (no. 329 = FHS&G 473), Theophrastus 'said to one who was irritated with himself on account of his own errant actions and was feeling regret, "if before doing bad things (*ta phaula*) you were just as irritated with yourself as [you are] after having done them, you would not have erred".'[109]

In his valuable study 'The uses of laughter in Greek culture', Stephen Halliwell (1991) has explored what he describes as (280) the 'strong tendency for [Greek] views and judgements of laughter to gravitate towards the poles of a fundamental contrast'. The one pole he labels by association with Greek terminology (*paizein, paidia*) as 'play'; that is laughter which is largely free from practical consequences and repercussions. Other considerations include (283): 'lightness of tone; autonomous enjoyment; psychological relaxation; and a shared acceptance of the self-sufficient presuppositions or conventions of such laughter by all who participate in it'. The opposing pole of 'consequential laughter' is implicated in some practical and (para-doxically) serious process: 'causing embarrassment or shame, signalling hostility, damaging a reputation, contributing to the defeat of an opponent, delivering public chastisement; the feelings aroused may not be shared by all concerned'. Pressed too far, the abuse of consequential laughter spills over into *hubris* (287), 'challenging an individual's identity and injuring his status'. 'Educated *hubris*' is how Aristotle in the *Rhetoric* defines *eutrapeleia* or 'wit' (1398b10–12). Theophrastus himself apparently knew where to draw the line. According to Plutarch, *Quaestiones cconvivales* (633B = FHS&G 31): 'men laugh when they are teased about a hooked or snub nose, as the friend of Cassander was not offended when Theophrastus said to him, "I am amazed at your eyes, for they do not sing, though your nose gives them the pitch".' The nose presumably resembled a pipe. The natural location for the witticism would be a dinner or a symposium. Halliwell identifies a range of occasions, 'paradigmatically those of conviviality and festivity', on which laughter was expected to fulfill a prominent function, allowing for shared perceptions of 'playful' laughter (290).[110]

The circumstances already envisaged for performance of the *Characters* combine essentially playful laughter, ostensibly directed at imagined characters outside the group, with an element of consequential laughter, implicitly informing members of the group able to recognize among the Characters their own failings. This is reminiscent of Theophrastus Such's 'loving laughter in which the only recognized superiority is that of the ideal self ... holding the mirror and the scourge for our own pettiness as well as our neighbours' (above, 8). Plutarch in his *Quaestiones convivales* (631D-E = FHS&G 711) attempts to explain the working of 'jests' (*skommata*); how 'the enjoyment afforded by cleverness causes pain to persons mocked and pleases those present. For by taking pleasure in what is said, they seem to believe the speaker and to participate in the ridicule. For according to Theophrastus, jest is a concealed rebuke for error. Consequently the listener supplies mentally on his own what is missing, just as if he knows and believes it.' With the Characters, the implied rebuke is impersonal, internalized by those who need it, and consequently concealed from others present.[111]

Implicit in the performative approach to the *Characters* is the notion that people (specifically the young) can be guided towards better behaviour. Elsewhere, Theophrastus expresses their openness to change (Stobaeus, *Anthology* 4.11.16 = FHS&G 539); how it is difficult to prophesy about young people: 'for [the character of] youth is hard to guess at and marked by many changes, being carried on different occasions in different directions.' Yet it is possible to provide appropriate guidance. Plutarch (*Agis and Cleomenes* 2.1–3 = FHS&G 467) describes how in the young, the virtues 'are still growing and sprouting'; virtues which, according to Theophrastus, 'are established through praises of things done rightly and thereafter developed by being stirred with pride'. Presumably the same applies to implied criticism of wrongdoing. Theophrastus is said to have reassured a blushing youth with the words 'Cheer up! For virtue has just such a colour!' (Antonius Melissa, *Loci communes* 2.71 = FHS&G 470); but the story is also attributed to other thinkers (see n. 68).

The exclusivity of this conniving relationship between teacher and audience presumes relatively small groups of students; certainly not the 2000 that Diogenes tells us came to Theophrastus' school (5.37 = FHS&G 1.16), which may best be read as part of his ongoing theme of Theophrastus' popularity with the Athenians. If taken at face value, 2000 may refer to the total number of pupils taught in the course of his career (averaging out at sixty or so per year), or to the *exoterikoi peripatoi* (almost 'extra-mural lectures') traditionally offered by the Lyceum, which took place in the afternoons or evenings.[112]

Informal composition and presentation of the *Characters* has the additional advantage of explaining, if not resolving, the long-standing problem of its 'date', whether that be dramatic date, date of composition, or of publication. The difficulty arises out of conflict between events referred to by individual Characters, chiefly the 'Rumour-Monger' (8), which indicate an oligarchic Athens after Alexander, and repeated references to democratic institutions; notably Assembly, popular courts and liturgies, as made by the 'Oligarchic Man' (26).[113] Later democratic niches into which the *Characters* have been slotted (none of them entirely convincing), are surveyed by Diggle (2004) 27–37, who favours an extended period of composition, theoretically through Theophrastus' career as a teacher. Lane Fox (1996) 134–8 argues for a collection of Characters beginning in Alexander's lifetime (he dates the bragging of the 'Boastful Man' before 323) and extending down to c.309, which is where he locates the incidental detail of the 'Rumour-Monger'. We are therefore to imagine ongoing changes and additions to the text.[114] A fragment of Theophrastus' correspondence quoted by Diogenes (5.37 = FHS&G 1.16–21), suggests that he was a regular reviser at least of his lectures. 'In the letter to Phanias the Peripatetic he discussed, among other things, matters concerning the lecture-hall (*peri deikteriou*) as follows: "Not only is it not easy to get a public assembly (*panegurin*), but not even a small number of listeners (*sunedrion*) as one would like. Public readings lead to revisions. The present generation (*hai helikiai*) no longer tolerates the deferring of everything and lack of care".'[115]

Apart from lectures and other formal teaching, we may visualize a range of occasions in the Lyceum on which solidarity might be expressed and enhanced; not least, opportunities for wining and dining which (as we shall see) are such a feature of the *Characters*. Indeed, these gatherings might provide suitable settings for recitation of party-pieces, including the *Characters*. The 'Self-Centred Man' (15.10) is censured for refusing to recite at what is presumably a dinner-party or symposium.[116] We remain ignorant of the Lyceum's domestic arrangements, save in one predictable respect. Athenaeus names Aristotle as framing *sumpotikoi nomoi* or 'rules for the symposium' (5.186b). This may tentatively be tied in with Diogenes' throwaway comment that Aristotle 'made it his custom in his school to appoint someone *archon* (president) every ten days' (5.4). Although this *archon* was presumably responsible for day-to-day running of the school, the office has also been identified with that of symposiarch or leader of the symposium.[117] Theophrastus is reported to have left money to support communal dining (Athen. 5.186a = FHS&G 36), and the will of his successor, Strato, specifically mentions 'all the furnishings of the dining-room (*sussition*), the cushions and the drinking-cups' (Diog. Laert. 5.62). The role of symposia in generating and maintaining a sense of élite solidarity is well established. 'The symposium's ritualized space and costume provided a space for the performance of song, but also, and more importantly, for the displays of erotic courtship and other aspects of male bonding from political pressure groups to philosophical circles' (Goldhill (1999) 24). Altogether an appropriate environment for aspiring philosophers with more intense interaction than in lectures. According to Diogenes (5.40 = FHS&G 1.40–2), Theophrastus advised a man who remained silent throughout a symposium, though not necessarily one held at the Lyceum: 'If you are uneducated, you are behaving sensibly, but if you are educated, foolishly.'

But exclusivity came with a price, both literal and metaphorical. Teles the Cynic, from the later third century BC, tells how one Metrocles, a pupil of Theophrastus, was embarrassed by the extravagant way of life of the student circle (*Sermones* 4A, Hense 40–1; cf. Diog. Laert. 6.94–5): 'For the common table (*sundeipnon*) he had to see that the breads were good, the dainties (*opson*) above the ordinary, the wine sweet, the entertainment appropriate... For among them such a life is considered to be liberal (*eleutherios*).' Metrocles eventually found his way to the less costly school of the Cynics (below, n. 84).[118] Lycon, Strato's successor as scholarch, is said by Antigonus of Carystus, an admittedly hostile source, to have held banquets so luxurious as to have inconvenienced existing members and to have discouraged others from joining the community (Athen. 12.547d-48b). Indicative of the unsurprisingly high level of wealth of students at the Lyceum are the few exceptions singled out in the sources. Alleged nonconformists (apart from the slave Pompylus) include Bion of Borysthenes, reputed to be an ex-slave (Diog. Laert. 4.46–7), and Cleanthes from Assos, said to have arrived in Athens with only four drachmas and to have supported himself by watering gardens and crushing grain at night (Diog. Laert. 7.168–9).

The overall wealth of the intended audience has consequences for the detailed presentation of the *Characters*. For gratification to be an acceptable response to moral failure, the Characters as individuals need to be provided with every means of behaving well. We scorn Theophrastus' well-to-do 'Penny-Pincher' (10.6), turning the house upside-down to ferret out the *trichalkon* coin dropped by his wife, but sympathize with the poor woman of Luke's gospel (15.8–10), who searches diligently for her lost drachma.[119] Aristotle's Great-Hearted Man does not deign to despise the lowly (*hoi tapeinoi*), or even people of the middling sort (*mesoi*); that would be equivalent to extending one's strength against the weak (1124b19–24). Accordingly, the *Characters* are all constructed as mature, male citizens of good standing. Lane Fox (1996) 132 also points out how Theophrastus does not poke fun at youth. That is presumably because young persons were perceived as a 'soft target', not having benefited from the appropriate *paideia*. All this seems supported by a key passage from Theophrastus in praise of education, preserved by Stobaeus (*Anthology* 2.31.124 = FHS&G 465): 'For *paideia* seems, and all agree on this, to tame the souls [of men]. It removes brutality and senselessness and further results in dispositions becoming more affable and compliant. Perhaps someone might not rebuke the many (*tois pollois*), because they do not have resources (*dia to me echein exousian*), but it is just to bring accusation against all those who, having enjoyed a liberal upbringing (*traphentes eleutherios*) and having sufficient means to enter upon any sort of life whatsoever, fail to ask what life is best.' Theophrastus goes on to bemoan the fact that whereas men take care in planning and seeking guidance for a journey, the crucial choice concerning the best life (*bios aristos*) is left to chance, without critical reflection. The passage as preserved closes with a proverb: 'What is said repeatedly seems to be true, that all men deliberate least concerning themselves.'

Although the Characters are much involved with educating their children, concern seems to stop short with elementary schooling (below, 79). This is not for want of resources, as demonstrated by cumulative references to liturgies, public contributions, ownership of real property, horses, and conspicuous consumption in general. A slave or slaves appear incidentally in half the Characters, almost always attending and waiting upon them. A scholion on the *Nicomachean ethics* (1145a10–11 = FHS&G 461) reports Theophrastus as relating practical wisdom to theoretical wisdom, 'in a way similar to the way in which slaves acting as stewards of their masters are related to their masters. For they do everything which must be done within the house, in order that their masters may have leisure for the pursuits appropriate to free men.'[120] In a judicious analysis, Lane Fox (1996) 130–3 concludes that although not every one of the Characters qualifies as a potential liturgist, they all fall well within the 'upper nine-thousand' citizens worth 2000 drachmas or more, retaining the franchise under the restrictive régime of Antipater in 322 (Diodorus 18.18.4–5). Even the *agroikos* or 'Country Bumpkin' (4.3) is conceived as a man of some substance: 'He distrusts friends and family, preferring to discuss important business with his slaves, and he reports the proceedings of the assembly to the hired labourers working on his farm.' If the *aponenoemenos* or 'Morally Degraded Man' (6.5) tries his hand at 'keeping an inn or brothel or being a tax collector, and is ready to work as an auctioneer, hired cook or gambler', that is to be understood as his own choice, a regrettable manifestation of his amorality. The fact that his association with Agora-people is considered a cause of shame (6.9) implies a degree of social distance.[121]

This marks a significant divergence between Theophrastus and his imitators. Joseph Hall added one character, 'The Good Magistrate', defined primarily by position in society rather than any particular quality. The departure into character-by-occupation was developed systematically by Hall's English successors, extending the range downwards through society. Perhaps a majority of the Overburian characters are conceived as being no better than they ought to be: 'A Servingman', 'An Ostler', 'A Sayler', 'A Souldier', 'My Taylor', 'A Whore', 'A Very Whore', and many more. This signals an explosion of categories of character; Overbury's ten women and four foreigners (including 'A Drunken Dutchman Resident in England') have already been noted. All Earle's characters are English and only two are female, but twenty are 'lower-class', and the sequence, which starts with 'A Child', includes 'A Tavern', 'A Bowling Alley', 'Paul's Walk', and 'A Prison'. Characters created by later authors include animals, a Law-Term, and a Newspaper. Why this profusion in contrast to Theophrastus? According to Smeed (1985) 38, 'Theophrastus had been confronted with a fairly unified society'. Rather, what is unified about the *Characters* are the constraints, described above, under which author and audience operated. Variety in English characters reflects the complex relationship between the hierarchy implicit in civic society (as represented in earlier Estates Satire), and the absence of any closely shared community on the part of authors and readers. Between them, Hall, Overbury and Earle had experience of the overlapping worlds of court, church and university. All three spheres are represented by their characters.[122]

What unifies disparate characters from seventeenth-century collections is the expression of wit, communicated by the author to knowing readers. The first impression of Overbury from 1614 promised on the title page 'Many Witty Characters'. The increasing dependence on wit may be traced through subsequent, expanded editions of *The Overburian Characters*. The ninth impression of 1616 includes as its final item, 'What a Character is', concluding (92): 'To square out a Character by our English levell, it is a picture (reall or personall) quaintlie drawne in various colours, all of them heightened by one shadowing. It is a quicke and softe touch of many strings, all shutting up in one musicall close. It is wits descant on any plaine song.' Forty years later (1665), Ralph Johnson could offer in his *Scholar's guide* a section on *A Character ... Rules for making it*. '1. Chuse a Subject, *viz.* such a sort of men as will admit a variety of observation... 2. Express their natures ... by witty Allegories, or Allusions ... still striving for wit and pleasantness, together with tart nipping jerks about their vices or miscarriages. 3. Conclude with some witty and neat passage, leaving them to the effect of their follies or studies.'[123]

Part of the exercise of wit for the reader consisted in identifying elaboration on the work of predecessors in the genre. When the slave of Theophrastus' 'Penny-Pincher' (10.5) 'breaks a pot or a dish, he deducts the cost from his rations'. Hall gives the story a twist by having the servant of 'The Covetous' break a dish 'through want of light' (83); yet further elaborated by Overbury's 'A Covetous Man' (81), who 'never spends candle but at Christmas (when he has them for new-yeeres gifts) in hope that his servants will break glasses for want of light which they doublie pay for in their wages'. Theophrastus' 'Country Bumpkin' (4.5) ignores everything in the city-streets save for passing goats or donkeys, Earle's 'Plain Country Fellow' (22) goes one better, standing 'dumb and astonished' at the sight of a 'good fat cow', and, 'though his haste be never so great, will fix here half an hour's contemplation'. By contrast, the Overburian 'Country Gentleman' (15–16) when in London is so taken with the city-sights that he 'becomes the prey of every cut-purse'. Alternatively, readers are invited to unpick a combining of two or more Theophrastan Characters. Overbury's 'Ignorant glory-hunter' (9) mixes up Theophrastus' 'Boastful Man' with the 'Man of Petty Ambition'.[124]

Elsewhere, 'wit's descant' resides largely in riddling references. A case in point, chosen almost at random, is Overbury's 'A Water-Man' (68). After opening sentences depending on punning references to the terminology of Thames boatmen: 'Little trust is to be given to him, for he thinks that day he does best when he fetches most men over. His daily labour teaches him the Art of dissembling; for like a fellow that rides to the Pillory, hee goes not the way he lookes... When he is upon the water, he is Fare-company... And to conclude, nothing but a *great Presse*, makes him flye from the River; nor anything, but a *great Frost*, can teach him any good manners.' Much of the remainder is, to the modern reader, witty to the point of incomprehensibility. It is hard here to disagree with Gordon writing of 'Theophrastus and his imitators' (1912) 60: strip many English characters of the author's wit and little remains. That means hard work for the historian. The tendency is prominent in the treatment of 'lower-class' characters, presumably reflecting élite ignorance of their actual way of life. This burlesquing of poorer people winds its way through character-collections until the mid-nineteenth century and Henry Mayhew's *London labour and the London poor* (1851). With this pioneering sociological study of submerged sections of society, told largely through their own words, character-writing is replaced by reportage.[125]

The hard-hitting description at the heart of Mayhew's *London labour* is reminiscent of the concrete detail already isolated as the distinguishing feature of the *Characters*. Otherwise, the grim smile of Henry Mayhew's world could hardly be more remote from the comedy created by Theophrastus. What constitutes the underlying humour of the *Characters*? It would be agreeable if an answer could be given through Theophrastus' own writings, but from his *On comedy* (*Peri komoidias*) and *On the laughable* (*Peri geloiou*) only the merest fragments have survived.[126] We are therefore left to fend for ourselves. Broad considerations include terseness and avoidance of over-complexity, though these are at best ancillary. Writing on Joseph Hall's *Vertues and Vices*, Müller-Schwefe (1972) 245 identifies two features shared by the vices: 'a *disproportion* between *appearance and reality*, which leads to "making evil good, or good evil"; and a harmful *lack of self-knowledge* throughout'. True enough of Theophrastus, but neither feature necessarily generates humour. A possible way forward involves the relatively modern idea of caricature, as has been sporadically applied to the *Characters*. Those opposing stress the essential realism of the character-genre, which must render, according to Bennet and Hammond (1902) xxxix–xl, 'an accurate report of nature and not a caricature'; for Zimmern (1961) 216–7, the *Characters* are 'drawn from life, with hardly a trace of exaggeration or caricature'. He takes at approximately face value their pettiness and quarrelling, as does Ferguson (1911a) 92–3, for whom they represent glimpses of 'the whole farrago of human life'. Those arguing for naturalism in the *Characters* are prepared to press their case as far as the representation of individuals. Ussher (1993) 5 feels that Theophrastus is often 'dealing with flesh-and-blood Athenians ... contemporaries well known in the city and recognizable by any reader'.[127]

Opposition to the 'Characters as real people' might almost seem a matter of instinct: peopling Athens with a bunch of unlikely eccentrics. But Fortenbaugh (2005) has acutely observed how Theophrastus provides no consistent motive for individual actions within each character (88–90, 139–40). He illustrates the phenomenon with respect to the 'Friend of Villains' (29), who on different occasions acts in order to increase his personal power (§2), illicitly to bolster democracy (§5), and to bear down indiscriminately on opposing litigants, who are unlikely both to be in the wrong (§6). We have already met the 'Coward's' split personality (29): in storms at sea, embarrassingly afraid; in battle, creatively devious. Yet the 'Coward' is singled out by Edmonds and Austen (1904) xx as 'bearing the stamp of first-hand information'. A clue (if needed) is supplied by Thackeray in his *Book of Snobs* (ch. 8, 37): 'As Phidias took the pick of a score of beauties before he completed a Venus, we have to examine, perhaps, a thousand Snobs, before one is expressed upon paper.' More practically, Smeed (1985) 265 wonders whether it is possible to write a typical character 'without in some way drawing on living specimens'. In this way, successful character-writing represents a compromise between individual and generic. Fortenbaugh compares the underlying discrepancies within a single Character with the inconsistency of minor characters in New Comedy; in both cases overridden, it might be added, by the willing suspension of disbelief.[128]

The essence of caricature resides in blending realism with elements of distortion, so as to introduce the potential for humour: affectionate, savage or somewhere in between. Although most familiar in the drawn sense (Thackeray and his contemporaries referred to our cartoons as caricatures), it may be helpful to recall the original sense of the Italian *caricare* as 'to load', 'charge', and so 'exaggerate'. In their classic study *Caricature* (1940) 3–10, Gombrich and Kris draw a formal distinction between the depiction of comic types and the mock-portraiture of individuals, which they consider as true caricature. Hence, in their assessment, its relatively late appearance, at the hands of Annibale Carracci (1560–1609), who invented not only the particular art-form but also the word 'caricature'.[129] Caricature fails if recognition is not more-or-less immediate; arguably, part of the viewer's pleasure lies in almost simultaneous puzzlement and apprehension. Gombrich and Kris (12) refer to the 'shock of surprise to which we respond with laughter'. Even so, our own experience of drawn caricatures suggests how far a skilful artist may load the balance towards distortion.

Historians engaging with the *Characters* need to locate the shifting boundary between naturalism and exaggeration across and even within individual Characters. In the absence of any hard-and-fast rule, there may still be rules of the game. Take as point of departure a Character's individual actions: the externals from which the inner man emerges. At its simplest, a Character might consist of an accumulation of discrete actions, disconnected save that they indicate an identical disposition. The 'Chatterbox' (3) consists of deliberately disjointed observations directed at a stranger: family, dreams, dining, changing standards of behaviour, prices, foreigners, the date, weather, plans for the future, life-experience, other people's extravagance, civic architecture, personal health, public holidays. Arguably, each element taken in isolation is unexceptionable, forming, under appropriate circumstances, an acceptable topic of conversation. In reality, no one mentions all these things together to an unknown person. Diogenes Laertius (5.40 = FHS&G 1.41–2) records how Theophrastus advised that an unbridled horse was more to be trusted than disorganized speech (*logos asuntaktikos*).[130] Identically obsessive is the unrelenting umbrage of the 'Self-Centred Man' (15.10) over innocent questions, stubbed toes, missed appointments, and invitations to sing, recite or dance. Anyone can have an off-day, but not every day.

The implication is that these actions, when disaggregated, represent unremarkable behaviour for Athenian citizens. Such is Bolkestein's technique with the 'Superstitious Man' (1929), reading his behaviour as a catalogue of actions that ordinarily pious Athenians might perform on a piecemeal basis. But as Lane Fox demonstrates in detail (1996) 152–4, correspondence with reality is not so straightforward; even individual actions of the 'Superstitious Man' may contain built-in exaggeration. His over-reaction to a dream (16.11), visiting not only dream-analysts, but also seers and bird-watchers, contrasts with the 'Chatterbox' (3.2) and 'Coward' (25.2) merely telling chance acquaintances of their dreams.[131] The 'Shabby Profiteer' (30.11), in the simple act of measuring out grain-rations for the household, contrives to be triply avaricious: using an older, smaller measuring-tin (a Pheidonian pint in place of an Attic litre), denting in its bottom, and brushing the top flat. It was arguably not his job in the first place (below, 78). The 'Distrustful Man' (18) elevates suspicion to an art-form. His insistence on witnesses being present when debtors make monthly interest payments may seem pointless if not perverse, but he characteristically looks ahead lest they later try to dodge repayment of the principal.[132] Elsewhere, distrust distorts his way of life: wasteful of his slaves' time (sending one to check up on another), wasting his own time (sitting down in the street *kata stadion* to re-count his money), going without sleep (to check the house is locked up), shunning the best cloak-repairer (in favour of the best-insured), alienating friends and relatives (by lending only reluctantly), and insulting fellow-citizens (by refusing to lend at all).

Heightening the potential for exaggeration are connexions between individual actions. 'Every action is shaded by another action, just before it or behind it', observes Gordon (1912) 60. True enough, and there are occasions when sets of actions cohere, concentrating evidence of bad character into a single scenario. In exceptional cases, every action combines to tell a story; most obviously about the 'Coward' (25), afloat and ashore. The 'Chatterbox' (3) appears on a single stage, focusing his random comments onto a solitary stranger. More commonly, sets of snippets within a Character combine to form short vignettes: the 'Morally Degraded Man' (6.9) lording it over the stall-holders in the Agora, the 'Man of Petty Ambition' (21.11) making a metaphorical meal out of a public sacrifice, the 'Boastful Man' (23.3–4) holding forth to someone he meets on the road about his extensive personal contacts. As a final refinement, several Characters seem to 'sign off' with a clinching detail, often in direct speech, heightening the sense of the ridiculous. The 'Talker' wears down everyone he meets, but his children know how to handle him: ' "Talk away to us, daddy", they say, "and send us to sleep" ' (7.10).[133]

Attempts to identify aspects of realism in the *Characters*, in the sense of recurring or representative behaviour, are bound to bring to bear expectations based on pre-existing knowledge of the culture and society of classical Athens, and beyond. Witness the mass of material enshrined in all the best commentaries: from Barbara Pym's Lady Nollard on the excellence of bone-broth to Professor Hug on the history of hugging.[134] Smeed (1985) 132–3 offers common-sense arguments against the use of character-collections as the sole source for reconstructing contemporary society: authors did not aim at supplying posterity with systematic accounts of the world around them. Even John Earle's *Microcosmography* is more modestly subtitled *A piece of the world discovered*. Smeed has a point. A reconstruction of Theophrastus' Athens based solely on the *Characters* would be without Acropolis and Areopagus, let alone the philosophical schools and pederasty. On the other hand, absence of any intention on the part of authors to write as if for posterity ensures that their testimony, at least in that respect, is unwitting. Of course, information flows in both directions. Apart from testimonia unique to the *Characters* (Spartan walking-sticks were somehow twisted; Athenian cavalrymen wore spurs, the names of children's games), Lane-Fox (1996) notes concentrations of evidence in the *Characters* relating to coinage, dining, children, tombstone-inscriptions and sacrifice (143, 147–50), which serve to confirm and focus scattered testimony found elsewhere. Possible contributions made by individual Characters are discussed below (48).[135]

Historians and others 'mining' the Characters for information relevant to their specific concerns unavoidably introduce their own ideological expectations. A case in point is the treatment of the *bdeluros* or 'Repulsive Man' (11.2), 'the kind who lifts up his clothes and exposes himself in front of freeborn women'. Here is how this fragment of behaviour is negotiated in H. D. F. Kitto's deservedly popular account of *The Greeks* from 1951: still in print at time of writing, it offers a cogent and humane, though necessarily dated, account of Greek civilization. Kitto takes obvious pleasure in introducing to the reader (213) 'the very acute and amusing *Characters* of Theophrastus, of which no one interested in humanity ought to remain in ignorance for ten minutes longer than he can help'.

One section of *The Greeks* to raise post-feminist eyebrows is Kitto's treatment of Athenian women, beginning (218): 'Most men are interested in women, and most women in themselves.' What follows (218–35) is remarkable for its ingenious attempts, not all of them misplaced, to argue away the then prevailing view that women suffered 'oriental seclusion' and were 'regarded with indifference, even contempt'. In representing this conventional opinion, Kitto cites amongst other negative legal and literary testimony Theophrastus' 'Mean Man' (as he translates *aneleutheros*) carrying home his own shopping while the wife stays at home (22.7). Eventually, Kitto's own humanity breaks in (222): 'The Athenian had his faults, but pre-eminent among his better qualities were lively intelligence, sociability, humanity and curiosity. To say that he treated one-half of his own race with indifference, even contempt, does not to my mind make sense.' There follows a range of arguments in support of empathetic relations between husbands and wives. 'But she was not allowed out unless she had someone to keep an eye on her? The lively Theophrastus helps us here.' Kitto harks back to the 'Mean Man' doing the shopping himself, and also, although his wife brought him a dowry of £5000, declining to provide her with a permanent slave attendant (*therapaina*). Instead, when she needs to go out, he hires one for her from the women's agora. He glosses *aneleutheria* as 'conduct unbecoming a gentleman', observing that 'for a lady to be attended when she went abroad was only her due'. Kitto clinches the argument ('with a conventional apology for its coarseness') with the exhibitionist behaviour of the 'Coarse Buffoon', as he renders *bdeluros*. 'There were all sorts on the streets of Athens. There were perhaps very good reasons for not allowing girls to go about unguarded.'[136]

Thus the voice of the self-confessed 'late Victorian'. Earlier in his account (224), Kitto puts suitable words about reverencing women into the mouth of Gladstone.[137] But forty years later, Robert Garland in his *Greek way of life* (1990) also infers from the *bdeluria* passage Theophrastus' opinion that deliberate displaying of genitals to freeborn women was a sufficiently widespread nuisance to form part of a stereotypical portrait of the *bdeluros*, for whom he tentatively suggests the translation 'Dirty Old Man' (270–1). Although there is nothing in the character to suggest old age, Garland introduces this snippet into a discussion of the psychology of ageing Athenian males. By contrast, the 'Late Learner' (27.2) is explicitly said to be sixty. As Garland suggests, in the youth-oriented culture of Athens, this Character pursues learning not for its own sake, but in order to demonstrate how he remains intellectually and physically unimpaired by the ageing process. In light of his ludicrous failures, Garland concludes that he is 'instantly recognizable and truly pathetic – surely the most pathetic among the thirty characters who populate Theophrastus' gallery of stock Athenians' (206–7). That is a matter of opinion.[138] Kitto introduces his own vignette of the 'Late Learner', whom he incorrectly identifies as 'seventy or more', as a possible *nouveau riche*, for which there is no supporting evidence. He adds (238–9): 'Theophrastus is hard to leave, and I will not leave him without at least introducing the Officious man and the Slow and Stupid man, irrelevant though they may be…' Details follow, down to a manifest piece of *praeteritio*: 'But we must return to our argument, even though that means passing over the Tactless man, who…'

What seems to be missing from both Kitto and Garland is some overall strategy for reading the *Characters* as history, underpinning more personal responses. In what follows, we will explore possible 'Rules of Evidence' relevant to the *Characters*, building on the contexts set out in the chapters above.[139]

5

THEY DO THINGS DIFFERENTLY THERE?

'I sent off Theophrastus three days ago. You will be amused I think by the Eresian if you have not expected too much of him. His real interest is this. Other writers, whose name is legion, prove to us that the great, the organic, lines of human nature are the same to-day, yesterday, and for ever. Theophrastus is one of the few who survive to remind us that the lighter traits also of character are permanent and universal. The bore of the Fourth Century B.C. is essentially the bore of the Nineteenth Century A.D.' So wrote Jebb (1907) 103 in a letter of 1870 to an unknown friend, staking out a familiar claim for the *Characters*. His initial modesty on behalf of Theophrastus is echoed by other supposed enthusiasts. '[A]t least a valuable footnote in the history of civilization', advise Edmonds and Austen (1904) xiii, having first queried its status as literature. '[A] pleasant little book for the casual reader', is how Rusten opens the preface to his edition (2002). Editorial caution has implications for readers' expectations.[140]

More problematic, however, is Jebb's conviction that 'people don't change'; a preoccupation of translators and commentators that can be traced back at least as far as La Bruyère. In the preface to his translation of the *Characters* (12–13), after contrasting the simplistic purity of Theophrastus' Athens with the richness of contemporary life at court, La Bruyère marvels how, across so much space and time, it is still possible to recognize ourselves, our friends, our enemies, those with whom we live. 'En effet, les hommes n'ont point changé selon le coeur et selon les passions; ils sont encore tels qu'ils étaient alors et qu'ils sont marqués dans Théophraste.' Three centuries later, Smeed (1985) cites the comparative timelessness of Theophrastus' 'Bore' and 'Superstitious Man' as demonstrating concern with perennial human types, which he associates with the *Characters*' enduring popularity (5); later adding that 'none of his thirty types has disappeared from the social scene' (288). Expressions of discontinuity are typically directed at specific actions: the 'Conspicuous Consumer' at fault for keeping his teeth white (5.6); the 'Tactless Man' taking as a dancing-partner someone who is still sober (12.14); the 'Arrogant Man's' haughtiness in refusing to receive visitors while in the bath (24.12).[141]

Although recognition of modern among the ancient characters is probably a universal and even pleasurable experience, much hinges for historians on whether this remains the dominant response: how the reader handles the interplay between the unexceptionable and the unfamiliar. Over-emphasis on familiarity may hinder appreciation of what is arguably different and distinctive. So Ussher (1993) declines to comment on, 'every-day activities which centuries and distance do not alter: house-keeping, marketing, sending to the laundry, borrowing and lending among neighbours' (25 n. 107). At least three of those activities might result in monographs detailing distance between ancient and modern practices. Perhaps they have.[142]

Lane Fox (1996) strikes an effective balance, briefly asserting essential continuity in character (128, 156–7), while highlighting significant cultural differences. He identifies the need for additional characters to reflect our own changing circumstances: the Cruel Man, the City Man, the Politically Correct Man. By the same token (though he would not agree), several of Theophrastus' original Characters might now seem redundant. This is reflected in the often-remarked clustering of Characters with broadly similar traits. Four describe species of greed (9, 10, 22, 30), four verbosity (3, 7, 8, 28), four grossness (6, 11, 15, 19), three self-regard (21, 23, 24), two flattery (2, 5), and two tactlessness (12, 13).[143] These similarities are interpreted by Jebb (1909) as evidence for the provisional state of the text, providing his warrant for regrouping associated Characters (9, 19–21). In fact, all cognate characters are divided by more-or-less subtle and sustained distinctions; in line with Theophrastus' concern in his scientific writings with establishing *diaphorai* or 'differences' (see n. 99). Rusten (2002) 149–50 introduces Aristotle's division between deficient giving and excessive taking (*Nicomachean ethics* 1121b12–22a3) to separate out features of the four 'greedy' Characters. Appropriate, as we shall see, to the reciprocity-bound world of Athens, but less so for us. Similarly, the varieties of loquaciousness (idle chatter, compulsive talking, rumour-mongering, slandering) might seem comprehensively to challenge the security of the spoken word in a predominantly oral culture: 'the city of words' in Goldhill's evocative phrase.[144]

Also weakening the idea of unchanging character-traits is instability in the meaning of particular qualities. Jebb begins his introduction (1909) by noting the chief value of the *Characters*, not as offering pictures of men and manners, but in explaining and illustrating the precise meaning of thirty key words (1–2): 'We have, in fact, in this book, a fragment of the social language of Athens interpreted by a very full and explicit commentary.' But the exercise runs into trouble with the opening Character of the *eiron* or 'Dissembler'. Repeated and failed attempts to assimilate his 'irony' to other Greek uses of the term are catalogued by Diggle (2004) 166–7. *deisidaimonia* ('fear of the divine') had the earlier sense not of superstition but conventional piety (349); *philotimos* might seem, according to circumstance, either selfish-minded or public-spirited (405); *alazon* might mean 'liar' as opposed to 'boaster' (431).[145] Here and elsewhere, the problem seems to lie in the assumption of some enduring, core meaning: 'the invariable presence of certain common properties' is how the principle was classically formulated by Stanley Jevons; cited and then challenged by Rodney Needham in his own influential expression of 'Polythetic classification' (1975). According to his alternative reading, characteristics are to be considered as collections of overlapping attributes (Witgenstein's 'family resemblances'), with no single attribute necessarily common to every usage.[146] The ongoing problems of translation, apparent from the range of titles in Appendix I to this essay, are a further argument against the straight-forward universality of all thirty-one character-traits.

Contrasting (but not necessarily opposed to) the timeless reading of the *Characters* is the time-specific approach, tied to the narrative of political events. Although this might seem unpromising, given the *Characters'* indeterminate date of composition, no text touching on classical Athens can entirely escape attention.[147] Giglioni's detailed study (1980) contains a helpful analysis of the notional status of the Characters, but is compromised by the conviction that its content must somehow interlock with what is known of contemporary events in Athens. This on the ground that Theophrastus as a demonstrably acute observer would not be able to ignore the marked changes around him (102). Accordingly, Giglioni (79–83) identifies conspicuous consumption of foreign goods by individual Characters as behaviour appropriate to the *nouveau riche* in the changed circumstances of Macedonian domination: the wealth of Alexander's conquests, as exemplified by the treasure disbursed by Harpalus. The 'Chatterbox's' comment that (3.3) 'Wheat is on sale in the Agora at a bargain price' is used to introduce the notion of a return to settled agriculture (87–90). Regarding the reactionary régime of Demetrius, Theophrastus is presumed to have steered a middle course, as represented by the deliberately opposed Characters of the 'Oligarchic Man' (26) and the 'Friend of Villains' (29) (91–5). The Character of the 'Country Bumpkin' (4) is deployed to demonstrate the increased separation of city and countryside (97–8). It will be appreciated how, in each of these cases, alternative readings are possible. What seems striking about the *Characters* is the absence of evidence for structural political change, with an analogy in the apparently non-politicized drama of Menander.[148]

Alternatively, omission of high politics from the Characters' agenda has itself been read as a sign of changed times. 'Denied the exhilarating study of national questions, they fell back on the narrower study of their neighbours', suggests Gordon (1912) 52. Anticipatory shades here of the unlamented theory of a generalized 'fourth-century crisis'.[149] The Characters have occasionally been held up as representatives of Victor Ehrenberg's post-Socratic, 'apolitical bourgeoisie, enjoying the great art and mild excitement of New Comedy' (1973) 384. A leading exponent was Michael Rostovtzeff (1941), deploying the 'charming, humorous picture of Athenian society in the *Characters'* alongside Menander in support of his theory of the increasing *embour-geoisement* of Athens in the late fourth century (1.163–4, 3.1352 n. 7). Ironically, Alfred Zimmern (1961), hardly a denigrator of things Athenian, had already singled out the *Characters* as evidence for the 'old Greek atmosphere of poverty and discomfort' (216–17). Claude Mossé (1973) closely follows Rostovtzeff, arguing that the absence of any precise political context for the Characters (save for friendly relations with Antipater, or the defence of oligarchy), is 'no chance phenomenon, but reflects the Athenian bourgeoisie's growing detachment from political affairs, which were increasingly left to professional politicians, who tended to become administrators in a society where the *polis* lost the power to make important decisions' (117).[150]

The Rostovtzeff-Mossé reading may be opposed twice over. Even if 'bourgeois' were an appropriate term of reference for Athenian citizens (which it surely is not), a majority of the Characters would be too wealthy to qualify (above, 35). Nor are the Characters apolitical at the level of everyday participation in the political process, involving Assembly, administration and courts. The 'Talker' (7.7) is asked in the street for the latest news from the Assembly; the 'Arrogant Man' (24.4), having been voted into office, declines on the ground that he is too busy. In fact, as has been noted, the detail of civic activity is at odds with the dating of events which are themselves broadly political, relating to Athenian involvement with Macedon. What is missing from the *Characters* (and Menander) is individual, élite participation in ways familiar from historians and the Attic Orators, but not lending itself to the character-genre. A part-exception is the 'Talker' (7.7), who includes in his conversational repertoire not only an account of a famous Assembly-debate from Athens' past ('in the time of the orator Aristophon'), but also 'the public speeches for which he himself received acclaim in the past'. Not that he is meant to be seen as a successful politician. We may imagine his Assembly-speeches as being compromised by the gratuitous abuse for the masses he introduces into his street-narratives, alienating the audience (80).[151]

The tradition that Theophrastus was the teacher of Menander, recorded by Diogenes Laertius (5.36 = FHS&G 11–12), seems plausible enough given the intellectual linkages of later-fourth-century Athens. Several of those described as Theophrastus' pupils were not in fact members of the Peripatetic school (FHS&G 18). But Lane Fox (1996) 139–40 is surely right to argue for an 'affinity of outlook' between Theophrastus and Menander, rather than any direct connexion. The relationship between the *Characters* and the plays now calls for reassessment in light of Susan Lape's forceful arguments in favour of a political function for Menander's comedy. She demonstrates in *Reproducing Athens* (2004) how the dismantling of democratic institutions by Antipater in 322 did little to disturb the underlying Athenian commitment to the values and beliefs associated with the developed democratic régime. She remarks (3 n. 6) on 'the tenacity of democratic identity ... the fact that individual Athenian men continued to see themselves first and foremost as democratic citizens'. As a symbol, Lape cites the decree from 270/69 honouring the Athenian mercenary Kallias of Sphettos, who, in assisting his native polis in its revolt of 286 against Demetrius Poliorcetes, 'did not act against the laws or against the democracy of all the Athenians'. As its editor Shear notes (1978) 11–12, the decree as a whole is 'redolent with the rhetoric of democracy'. And not empty rhetoric, as reflected in repeated Athenian attempts down to 260 to restore a thoroughgoing democratic constitution.[152]

Lape detects ongoing enthusiasm for democracy in the innovations of New Comedy, which as a genre coincides almost exactly with the decades of upheaval in Athens, from 323 down to the capture of the city by Antigonus Gonatas in 261 and the final extinction of realistic democratic aspirations (9). She interprets the Athenians' initial exposure to Macedonian authoritarianism under Demetrius of Phalerum as teaching them how best to negotiate and to compromise. Although the Macedonians targeted obvious democratic institutions (Assembly, law-courts, the idea of the citizen-soldier), they apparently left alone deep-seated cultural practices, including marriage (42). Lape argues that far from representing apolitical escapism, Menander's plots with their focus on marriage and citizen-succession are 'deeply and emphatically political' (68): an attempt to assert polis-values against Macedonian monarchy (12). This challenging hypothesis is supported by a close reading of the plays themselves. She explains how the 'Braggart Soldier' parodies and satirizes the idea of the Hellenistic military ruler (62–5); how plots driven by questions of citizen-status presume traditional birth-based norms and ignore criteria of wealth, twice over imposed by the Macedonians (68). Lape presses further in reading the plays as not merely mirroring current political and cultural phenomena, but as having their own part to play in forming them (11): 'comedy's role as a producer rather than a product of ideology'. 'Comedy ... made things happen in the world by offering narratives that enabled civic audiences to make sense of the manifold changes taking place in the early Hellenistic period within a traditional polis-based conceptual framework, and at the same time crucially reinforced democratic matrimonial and gender practices' (18). She invokes the speech-act theory of J. L. Austin (1962), likening the comic narrative to a 'performative speech act, an utterance that does what it says. ... Thus the performative efficacy of a comedy is not identical with the play itself, but rather arises from the narratives it offers audience members to think about and identify with.' Performance culture as here presented comes close to the context envisaged for the *Characters* (28).[153]

The overall argument of *Reproducing Athens* does not in any way depend on Theophrastus. This is understandable, in light of the different perspectives on Athens and its democratic ideology necessarily held by Theophrastus, Menander, and their respective audiences. Notable is the inclusion by Theophrastus of some hints of what was 'arguably among the most tumultuous and eventful periods in Athenian history' (17), with Characters mentioning by name Alexander, Antipater, Polyperchon and Cassander. But Lape's underlying thesis has clear implications for contextualizing the *Characters*. What she describes as (60), 'The remarkable stability of Athens's democratic ethos' helps on a basic level to explain the inclusion in the *Characters* of democratic institutions as essential parts of Theophrastus' frame of reference. Crucially, her insistence on the survival of democratic ideology reinforces the idea of Theophrastus as concerned with exploring appropriate behaviour in a polis that was still essentially egalitarian in outlook. That is a theme to which we will return.[154]

'Finally, there is a scattering of material throwing light on the contemporary social history of Athens in the *Characters*', writes Podlecki in his survey of 'Theophrastus on History and Politics' (1985) 241. No details are forthcoming. This somewhat dismissive comment in an otherwise helpful piece on Theophrastus' political publications demonstrates the diminished status of the *Characters* among those for whom it represents the 'wrong kind' of history; that is, 'with the politics left out'.[155] This has all too frequently been the fate of the *Characters*: as footnote-fodder for studies of 'everyday life' in Athens, supplying more-or-less colourful snippets of information.

'The residual view of social history' is how Eric Hobsbawm labels this perspective on the past, in his influential essay 'From social history to the history of society' (1971) 72. As a genre, it is essentially descriptive, capable of varying degrees of detail, but with little analytical depth; in Hobsbawm's words, 'rather superficial and journalistic'.

The best illustration of the possibilities and limitations of the genre is amongst the earliest: Wilhelm Becker's *Charicles*; first published in Germany in 1840, and translated into English five years later. This remarkable production conceives the story of Charicles, a young visitor to Athens, as a peg on which to hang a detailed account of *Privatleben*. Twelve loosely connected 'Scenes' ('The Friends of Youth', 'The Ancestral Abode', 'The Banquet', 'The Wedding') are matched by appropriate and lengthy Excursuses ('Education', 'The Grecian House', 'The Meals', 'The Women'). The actual story is densely annotated (occasionally just two or three lines of text per page), and accompanied by some distinctly racy line-drawings (104, 150, 207, 339, 345, 460). In all this, the *Characters* looms relatively large, providing detailed testimony: slaves carrying money for masters (57), pilfering fruit in the Agora (62), pigeon-fancying (77), spitting to avoid the evil eye (132), the popularity of jugglers (187), use of the abacus (232), public festivals resulting in school holidays (234). Similar lists could be compiled for later, less obsessive expressions of Athenian 'daily life'.[156] However antiquarian in approach, all such treatments remain subject to the perspective of the author: what material to include and how individual citations are to be read. With regard to this type of history, authorial intentions are rarely made explicit, beyond a vague inclination either to mourn the 'world we have lost' in ancient Athens, or highlight the Athenians' essential modernity. The testimony of the *Characters* may be deployed, albeit selectively, in support of either reading.[157]

The importance of perspective is apparent in a historically more rewarding variant on the everyday-life approach: the systematic manipulation and development of material within individual Characters. The process here is akin to the creation of a 'thick description'; that is, expanding outwards from material in each Character rather than zoning in on isolated elements (as in the 'mining operations' detailed above).[158] A case in point, already met, is Bolkestein's treatment of the 'Superstitious Man', whereby the Character forms the basis of a wider-ranging examination of the phenomenon of superstition. More recently, Spina (1981) has argued for a new, later-fourth-century style of oligarchy, based on a close reading of the 'Oligarchical Man'.[159] In work on usury, patronage, and exchange, individual Characters have provided key concentrations of material: respectively, the 'Morally Degraded Man' (6), the 'Toady' (2), and 'Shabby Profiteer' (30).[160] To the list might now be added the behaviour in battle of the 'Coward' (25.3–8). On a tactical level, the actions of the 'Coward' offer support for the new orthodoxy of the 'open' phalanx. From his vantage point, presumably well towards the rear, the 'Coward' is able to see those in the front ranks falling, and decides to quit his place in the rear ranks. His retreat would not be feasible if the whole phalanx were involved in a close-packed shoving-match; nor could the wounded man he so realistically tends ('flicking the flies off his wound') possibly be carried out of the fight.

More generally, selecting a conventional hoplite battle as the context for a display of cowardice reinforces Hanson's insistence on the exemplary character of hoplite warfare.[161] Here and elsewhere the role of subjectivity seems clear: the *Characters* promoting different readings (in some cases radically different) of Athenian religion, politics, economy and society, and warfare.

There is nothing new about the character-specific approach. Building on material within individual Characters was something of a speciality with Otto Ribbeck who, in the later nineteenth century, produced detailed 'ethological studies' (his phrase) of the *eiron* (1876), *alazon* (1882), *kolax* (1884) and *agroikos* (1888). His technique is two-sided, using the full range of material both to elucidate and extend the content of each Character: 'theils zu erlautern, theils zu ergänzen' (1882) 3. Accordingly, his study of *agroikia*, based loosely around Theophrastus' 'Country Bumpkin', combines cognate material from Homer to Cicero and beyond. But how is all this to be read as history rather than ethology? Already noted is Giglioni's theory, dependent on Theophrastus, of increased separation between city and countryside. Likewise, Austin and Vidal-Naquet (1977) 372–5, under the heading 'From the peasant-citizen to the boor', contrast the idealized peasant-citizen-soldier, hailed by the chorus of Aristophanes' *Peace* (1159–90), with Theophrastus' *agroikos*: 'a worthless citizen, who is closer to his slaves than his fellow-citizens from the town, and an object of ridicule for them'.

In a recent, important book on rural Athens by Nicholas Jones (2004), the *agroikos* puts in a double appearance, providing a convenient case-study. On the first occasion (43–4), he is offered as a key piece of literary evidence in support of rural residence in farmsteads, as opposed to villages. Theophrastus' *agroikos* is conceived as a comfortably-off citizen, who travels from his farm to the city, having a dog which he presents to visitors as simultaneously guarding both farm and house (*to chorion kai ten oikian*). The second, more substantial, treatment with full translation (211–14) is interpreted along with other Characters to show up the separate identities of city and countryside. This is at the heart of Jones's analysis, attempting to demonstrate (14) 'not unity or cooperation but rather a consistent state of estrangement, alienation, even hostility'. It should be noted that Jones argues for structural dissociation of city and countryside; not as with Giglioni, and Austin and Vidal-Naquet, separation as a later-fourth-century phenomenon.

Jones's initial point need cause no difficulty. In addition to the *agroikos*, he provides a range of arguments for giving greater emphasis to isolated, rural dwellings (17–49). The problem, as Jones disarmingly confesses, lies in the detail of this Character's behaviour, turning up to the Assembly, visiting the town for festivals, haircuts and marketing (to which add patronizing the public baths), which seems to undercut his overall conception of the typical rural Athenian as a 'farmstead-residing isolationist with at best perfunctory association with his country deme, much less with a remote town' (212). He argues instead that the circumstantial detail is suggestive of the city-visit as a special event. The *agroikos* has lost touch with prices, needs a haircut, does not know the date, and buys salt-fish to keep until the next visit. As for attending the

Assembly, the fact that 'everything' happening there is told to his hired hands hints at an isolated appearance. In any case, argues Jones, comic interaction between countryman and the town could not take place without fictive movement between the two spheres. He concludes that, although such visits did occasionally occur, they were relatively rare and comparable with present-day visits to Pittsburgh zoo by local Amish or Mennonite communities (214). Jones writes as Professor of Classics at the University of Pittsburgh.

Let us examine the force of these counter-arguments. Overall, Jones emphasizes the reality of the portrait of the *agroikos*, with its 'quasi-sociological realistic orientation' (43), arguing that its comic effect would be lost if not easily recognized as stereotypical. But where does stereotyping end and comedy begin? Indeed, in connexion with the *agroikos*' earlier appearance, Jones identifies as part of his stereotypical behaviour 'paying regular visits to the *asty* [city]' (44). His detailed argument is ingenious but suffers from over-interpretation. It does not seem profitable to speculate on the frequency of haircutting (or taking a bath), or how easily one might forget the date (as does Theophrastus' *adolesches* (3.3)), or how even those living in the city might buy salt-fish. As for the Assembly (twice mentioned in connexion with the *agroikos*), the comic effect seems to depend on telling absolutely everything to those who should know nothing. Here is one of the keys to this Character: insensitive to crucial status-differences, he answers the door himself, actively distrusts his family and friends, sharing private business with his slaves, and tries it on with the slave-girl, before helping her grind flour for the household.

Two issues remain in dispute. First is the question of the universality of Theophrastus' *agroikos*. Jones envisages the likely readership of the *Characters* as wealthy, city-dwelling citizens, who find 'ruralites' inherently laughable (213). But as argued above, the pupils at the Lyceum might provide an audience with a different, if overlapping focus: basing its humorous response primarily on the *agroikos*' ignorance through his lack of *paideia* rather than straightforward residence in the country. Like Strepsiades in the *Clouds*, he is wealthy enough to have done better. Jones points out that the *agroikos* is placed by Theophrastus alongside wholeheartedly disagreeable Characters, confirming a negative meaning for *agroikia*. He concludes that, by this time, *agroikos* had ceased to have the neutral sense of 'rustic' in favour of 'boor'. But the home environment of the remaining twenty-nine (or thirty) Characters is the city, implying that, in the minds of Theophrastus and his audience, country-people had no monopoly of inappropriate behaviour. Moreover, Ioannis Konstantakos (2005) draws on the evidence of New Comedy to demonstrate the ongoing, positive presentation of *agroikoi*.[162] The second unresolved matter concerns the likely frequency of visits to the city by country people. This is not the place fully to engage with this major issue, but Jones, in line with his view of the essential self-sufficiency of Attic farmers (21), down-plays their economic integration into the life of the city. Yet our own *agroikos* hires labourers, wants to know the price of hides and salt-fish, buys his fish, pays for a haircut, and rejects a suspect silver coin.[163]

Jones explains Theophrastus' rural types as the product of 'an active urbane curiosity and imagination', resembling the 'Pennsylvania Dutch of the media' (compare his analogy of city-visits by local Amish and Mennonite rural families). I would prefer to point to the disjunction between the caricaturing of country people in London in the pages of later-nineteenth-century *Punch* with the relatively high level of mobility then prevailing between city and countryside. The phenomenon was demonstrated for an earlier, pre-railway period by Wrigley in his classic paper giving 'A simple model of London's importance in changing English society and economy 1650–1750' (1967) esp. 44–9. Aside from temporary dwellers, pre-industrial cities are typically net consumers of people, maintaining and increasing their population through immigration: all those corpses reported to the 'Obtuse Man' as being ferried through the Erian Gates (14.13).[164]

6

CORRUPTION AND THE CHARACTERS

In 1949 two schoolteachers, Claude Taylor and David Macindoe, lightened post-War austerity for some by publishing *Cricket dialogue*, a handbook of the basic principles of cricket, presented in the form of a Platonic dialogue. At the end of the chapter on 'Equipment' (33–4), Macindoe proposes: 'Just to finish off, let us ram home the points which we have made about appearance by drawing a picture of the Impossible Cricketer.'

T. Good idea. Well, he arrives late.
M. Without a shirt to wear.
T. His pads are dirty.
M. His boots are muddy.
T. And several spikes are missing in them.
M. His batting gloves are riddled with holes.
T. As are his trousers, because he omitted to put them in moth-balls last winter.
M. He wears a wrist-watch while playing.
T. His loose change jangles in his pocket.
M. His uncut hair flops in his eyes, because he doesn't wear a cap.
T. His socks are dark blue.
M. He wears a leather belt to keep his trousers up.
T. He is horrible.
M. Loathsome.
T. An eyesore.
M. A disgrace to the game.
T. I hope he reads this chapter.
M. And buys this book, instead of borrowing it.

It seems more than likely that the authors deliberately imitate the *Characters*. Both read Greats at Oxford and taught Classics at Eton College.[165] Whether by accident or design, the 'Impossible Cricketer' demonstrates a central aspect of the *Characters*; namely, reinforcing ('ramming home') general principles of conduct by stating instances of the opposite. Implicit in the presentation of the 'Impossible Cricketer' is the Perfect

Cricketer; at least, as conceived by the authors and their cricketing audience of the 1940s. By the same token, it is possible to read character-collections as sequences of transgressed norms, from which the norms themselves may be reconstructed.[166] In the case of the *Characters* that means, as has been argued, standards of behaviour aspired to by Theophrastus and his philosophically inclined audience. As we have also seen, transgression might be indicated in a variety of ways: by an exaggerated accumulation of actions which, taken individually, are approximately normal; or, less frequently, by actions which are abnormal in themselves. Moreover, transgression occurs with respect to a range of occasions and institutions relevant to living in Athens as an upper-class member of the citizen-élite. Seen from this angle, the *Characters* begins to look like a relative rarity from classical Athens; an implied code of behaviour written (unlike oratory and drama) for an élite audience, engaging with the practicalities of their lives within the polis. The implied end-product of this process of norm-reversal might resemble the Peripatetic ideal of a citizen, tempered to suit the circumstances of a demo-cratically-minded polis. We could label him 'Theophrastus' Man'.[167] Here is a frame for analysing material in the *Characters* so as to identify and exploit the peculiar possi-bilities it offers the historian; the equivalent of Jill Mann's 'ordering of experience' with regard to the *Canterbury Tales* (above, 18), without which the naturalistic detail would have 'only the barest sociological significance'.

For analysis to proceed an appropriate focus is needed: Darwin's conviction that 'all observation must be for or against some view if it is to be of any service'. In what follows, the intersecting worlds of Theophrastus and his *Characters* are explored alongside the broad hypotheses of Horden and Purcell's *The corrupting sea* (2000). The choice might seem perverse. The authors are, after all, emphatic from the start that their concern is with the history *of* the Mediterranean world, rather than history taking place within it (2). Also, given their fundamental concern with Mediterranean micro-ecology, in so far as Theophrastus enters into their seven-hundred-page exposition, it is as botanist rather than as the author of the *Characters* (202, 224, 248, 285). Nevertheless, as they explain in a subsequent paper (2005) 357–8, *The corrupting sea* was conceived as a 'backdrop against which [those] other kinds of history could be written'. Two broad considerations are here assessed in conjunction with Theophrastus: the fragmentation of the Mediterranean world into connected microecologies; and, at greater length, the ubiquity of honour and shame as underlying and distinctive Mediterranean values. What follows might constitute a modest test-case for these key aspects of *The corrupting sea*.[168]

For Horden and Purcell, the essential unit for analysing human settlement in the Mediterranean is the microregion. 'The Mediterranean world at all periods must be understood as a vast conglomeration of tiny sub-regions and larger groups of sub-regions: more fragmented, we have urged, than most of its neighbours. The individual identity of these small areas is human, topographical and environmental' (343). Fragmentation generates connectivity through mobility of resources – material, human and intellectual – both within and between each microregion, 'resulting in aggregates that may range in size from small clusters to something approaching the entire Mediterranean' (123). The two phenomena are complementary (175): 'We have identified extreme topographical fragmentation as one of the two key environmental ingredients – along with the connectivity provided by the sea itself – in a distinctly Mediterranean history.' Two metaphors recur: 'the kaleidescopic mosaic of the Mediterranean is distinguished by "structures" which overcome the fragmentation, and above all by maritime communications' (79; cf. 122); 'and ... "Brownian motion" [*cabotage*]: on the Mediterranean's perimeter that does most to fill the conceptual gap between potentially all-round communications ... and the restricted shipping lanes connecting major harbours' (142). It is the apparent density of inter-regional connectivity, along with the aim of Horden and Purcell to dethrone the city as a category central to their analysis, that proves most challenging for Greek historians working within polis-based orthodoxy. As they put it (100), 'Our "microecological model" encourages us to see towns less as separate entities and more as loci of contact or overlap between different ecologies.' Let us see how these matters might relate to Theophrastus and the world of the *Characters*.

Theophrastus in his earlier career could be seen as a paradigm for personal mobility. Although our knowledge is far from full, we can trace something of his movements around the Aegean world. After being born and brought up at Eresus on Lesbos, he travelled as a young man to Athens, where he was possibly a pupil of Plato, certainly of Aristotle. It is thought that around the time of Plato's death (348), Theophrastus travelled with Aristotle to join a philosophical enclave at Assos in the Troad. He was possibly involved in arranging Aristotle's next move to Mytilene on Lesbos (345/4). It is presumed that Theophrastus accompanied Aristotle to the court of Philip II of Macedon (343/2). For what it is worth, Aelian tells that Philip 'honoured' Theophrastus, along with Plato and Aristotle (4.19 = FHS&G 28). Eight years later (335), Aristotle returned to Athens, with Theophrastus as his associate, to found the Peripatos. These travels are to be regarded as a minimum.[169] During his thirty-six years as head of the School, it is hard to imagine Theophrastus remaining permanently in Athens, given the mobility characteristic of philosophers. Travel could be involuntary: the career of Aristotle, uncertain at the close over his place of burial (Diog. Laert. 5.16), shows how internal politics could inflict even on philosophers a variety of 'Brownian motion' (see n. 86). There was Theophrastus' own withdrawal from Athens in 307, in response to the threat of prosecution (above, 25). But intellectuals broadly benefited from the relative tolerance of the Greeks for outsiders wishing to visit or remain among them. In the *De nuptiis* attributed to Theophrastus by Jerome (*Against Jovian* 1.47–8 = FHS&G 486.20–2), the author warns against marriage on the ground that, 'If there is a very learned teacher in some one of the cities, we can neither leave our wives nor make the trip with [such] a burden.'[170]

Additional overseas journeys for Theophrastus, to Egypt and Cyrene, have been inferred from the detailed presentation of material in his scientific writings, which by themselves bear witness to the connectivity of knowledge. The Theophrastan monograph 'Concerning Weather Signs' offers practical advice for travellers, advising that note must be taken of the local conditions where one is placed (§3).[171] The botanical writings bridge, however precariously, the limits of the known world; indeed, playing some part in making them 'known'. 'In the "outer sea" near the Pillars of Hercules grows the "sea-leek", as has been said [4.6.4]; also the well known plants which turn to stone, as *thyma*, the plants like bay and others. And in the sea called the Red Sea, a little above Coptos in Arabia, there grows on land no tree except that called the "thirsty" acacia, and even this is scarce by reason of heat and lack of water.' (*Inquiry into plants* 4.7.1).

The geographical scope of Theophrastus' writings on plants with respect to the Middle East and the western Mediterranean is brilliantly evoked by P. M. Fraser (1995). Reports from the East in Books 4 and 5 are plausibly and on occasion explicitly connected with the campaigns of Alexander. An extended report, including mangroves (4.7.3–4), originates from 'an expedition of those returning from India sent out by Alexander' According to Fraser (187), the *Inquiry into plants*, with its wealth of information about flora from the east, 'provides an objective picture of the immense change wrought in the world by Alexander'. He contrasts (182–7) Theophrastus' well-founded knowledge of plants in the East with his relative ignorance of the flora of the western Mediterranean.[172] There are also clusters of information closer to a variety of homes: Chalcidice and Chalcis, Philippi, Pontus, Lesbos and the Troad, Crete and Arcadia.[173] Detail occasionally surfaces about informants: woodcutters in Arcadia pass on to one Satyrus (possibly a pupil) specimens of cedar (3.12.4); information about the myrrh-tree derives from adventures ashore during a coasting voyage (*paraplous*) in the Arabian Gulf (9.4.3–6). At the other extreme of connectivity, the microecological environment narrows down to Attica: 'At Athens the partridges on this side of Corydallus, towards the city, cackle, but those beyond it twitter' (Athen. 9.43 = FHS&G 355B); and even the Lyceum itself: 'The plane-tree by the watercourse in the Lykeion when it was still young sent out roots a distance of thirty-three cubits, having both room and nourishment' (1.7.1).[174]

The *Characters* is the only work to survive by Theophrastus with an obviously Athenian focus. To date, comment has centred on its urban setting, with praise reserved for its sharp observation of life within the city of Athens. Not that this need be entirely positive. According to Gordon (1912) 60, 'Nothing could be more parochial than the life which Theophrastus describes.'[175] And yet, the undeniable Athenocentricity of the *Characters* is shot through with varieties of connectivity. Take the case of the 'Chatterbox' (3). Apart from personal concerns (inappropriately singing his wife's praises to a stranger), he is certainly parochial, commenting on the large torch one Damippus set up at the Mysteries, asking how many pillars there are in the Odeion, and remarking on the timing of specifically Athenian festivals (Mysteries, Apatouria and Rural Dionysia). But he also expresses an interest with the world of Athens outside the confines of the city (more rain would be good for the crops; what land he will cultivate next year); the wider world as it impinges on Athens (how many *xenoi* live in the city); and Athens' connexions with the Mediterranean world beyond (how the festival of

Dionysus marks the beginning of the sailing season). This serves to establish a pattern for connectivity in the *Characters*: interplay of city and country within the Athenian polis, intrusion of the wider world into the city of Athens, and outreach of Athenian interests and involvement.

The issue of contact between inhabitants of city and countryside has already arisen over the detailed behaviour of Theophrastus' *agroikos*; further exemplified by the oxen, donkeys and goats at which he gawps on the streets of Athens (4.5). The impression of connectivity given there is reinforced by more-or-less incidental hints in the remainder of the Characters. Whereas with the *agroikos* the countryman came to the city, elsewhere the reverse seems the case. Though broadly conceived in terms of the city, several of the Characters resemble the 'Chatterbox' in owning farmland. The 'Toady' (2.12), having praised the flatteree's beautifully built house, comments on the fine planting of his farm. The 'Penny-Pincher' (10.8–9) won't let anyone pick figs from his garden, or walk over his land, or pick up a fallen olive or date. He inspects his boundary-stones on a daily basis: all the more pointed if it involves a trek into the country. When the 'Obtuse Man' (14.3, 11) should be defending a court case in the city, he pays a visit to his farm; and it is on the farm that he boils up his soup, adding double the salt. Other contacts with the countryside are more casual. It is surely on a journey through the country that the 'Overzealous Man' (13.7) leads people on a short-cut and gets everyone lost. The 'Late Learner' (27.10) rides out into the country on a borrowed horse, attempts fancy horsemanship, and falls off. The 'Shabby Profiteer' (30.19) leaves town in order to avoid buying a wedding-present for a friend or a friend's daughter who is getting married. Along with the city-visiting *agroikos* all this might seem to confirm at a micro-level Horden and Purcell's 'constant "ebb and flow between country and town" [that] is part of the overall mobility which characterizes the Mediterranean countryside'.[176]

According to the testimony of the *Characters*, the wider Mediterranean world impinged on Athenian city-dwellers on several levels, open to varying degrees of moral manipulation. As a reminder of the routine presence at least within wealthier citizens' households of slaves from overseas, there is the behaviour of the 'Shameless Man' (9.4), who takes bread and meat from his host's table, hands it to his slave and says for everyone to hear, 'Enjoy your meal, Tibeios'. The name, common among slaves from Paphlagonia, derived originally from Tibeion in Phrygia. Whether a particular slave so named actually hailed from Paphlagonia is an open question; but there could be no doubt about the exotic (and expensive) origins of the Ethiopian slave whom the 'Man of Petty Ambition' (21.4) procures to attend on him in public. Non-Greek origins preoccupy the 'Slanderer' (28.2), who adroitly manoeuvres around the implications of naming and shaming. 'When asked "Who is so-and-so?" (?he responds?) in the style of the genealogists, "I shall begin with his antecedents. His father was originally called Sosias; but in the army he became Sosistratos, and when he was enrolled in a deme, Sosidemos. His mother, however, is a Thracian of good family. At all events she is called (…?), and in their own country women like her are reputed to come from a good family. He himself, with parents like this, is naturally a criminal with a tattoo.' 'Sosias' seems deliberately ambiguous, referring in Athens to slave or free, but more frequently the former; Sosistratos and Sosidemos are always the latter. The Thracian mother's garbled name presumably refers to the tattoos that were reputedly in Thrace the mark of high birth, which ties in with the alleged tattooing of her son, reserved in Athens for runaway or otherwise delinquent slaves.[177]

Alongside barbarian slaves were visitors to Athens, medium and short term: the *xenoi* so conspicuous in the eyes of the 'Chatterbox'. As Whitehead points out (1977) 40–1, Theophrastus the metic never uses the word *metoikos*. The two species of *xenoi* involved with the Characters are either foreigners, broadly equated with metics as inferiors, or 'guest-friends', as notional equals. Into the former category fall the *xenoi* assured by the 'Obsequious Man' (5.4) that they speak more justly than his fellow-citizens; also the *xenoi* to whom the 'Boastful Man' (23.2) feels secure in spinning yarns in the Piraeus. From the perspective of guest-friends, the 'Shameless Man' (9.5) lets his *xenoi* treat him to a seat in the theatre, and the next day adds insult to injury by having them fork out for his sons and their slave attendant. The 'Shabby Profiteer' (30.3) stoops to borrowing money from a *xenos* staying overnight as a guest in his house. The 'Conspicuous Consumer' (5.8–9) makes sure the whole polis knows how he buys up and sends to his *xenoi* all manner of luxury goods available in the Athenian entrepôt: Spartan dogs to Cyzicus, honey from Hymettus to Rhodes, an unknown commodity to Byzantium. In effect, with his personal possessions, he is a one-man study in a specific type of Mediterranean connectivity: a pet monkey, oriental pheasants, pigeons from Sicily, knucklebones made from gazelle horn, spherical oil-flasks from Thurioi, twisted walking-sticks from Sparta, and a tapestry embroidered with Persians. Presumably, his own, far-flung *xenoi* provide a reciprocal service.

All this finds a faint echo in the 'Man of Petty Ambition' (21.9), who has (or had) a dog from Malta, which fact he inscribes on its tombstone as if commemorating a metic.[178] Reliance on travellers as bringers of news into the community is a feature of the technique of the 'Rumour-Monger' (8.4, 8), who claims to have received information about Polyperchon's victory and the capture of Cassander from 'a man just back from the actual battle – a soldier, or a slave of the piper Asteios, or the contractor Lycon'. As supporting evidence, he claims to know how the men of affairs have hidden someone away, 'who arrived from Macedonia four days ago and knows the whole story'.[179]

The tendency of the Characters themselves to travel may be exemplified by the 'Boastful Man' (23.3), who is initially located in the Piraeus, holding forth to strangers about his money in overseas trade and the scale of his money-lending. He fantasizes to the person walking with him about seeing service with Alexander, with whom he was on familiar terms, romancing about the number of jewelled cups he brought back home, maintaining that the craftsmen of Asia are better than those of Europe. He fabricates personal links with Antipater, who has sent 'no fewer than three letters telling him to come to Macedonia, and how he has been offered the right to export timber duty-free', which he has naturally declined, so as to avoid any false accusation of trading with the enemy. All this, despite the fact that 'he has never been outside the polis'.[180] Other

Characters do better than voyage in their imagination. The sufferings of the 'Coward' at sea (25.2), though self-inflicted, are real enough to him. His reactions give something of the flavour of travel by sea with its dangers and possible counter-measures. Sailing close to shore he mistakes promontories for pirate ships. When a swell gets up, he asks if anyone aboard is not initiated into the mysteries: those practised at Samothrace, offering a degree of protection to seafarers. He pesters the steersman, who presumably needs all his wits about him, with questions about the duration of the voyage and how the heavens are looking. Literally, he asks him about 'the affairs of the god [Zeus]', which moves him to share with his neighbour a dream that has frightened him. He therefore undresses so as to be better able to swim for it, encumbers his slave with his clothing, and pleads to be put ashore. It is to be presumed that his service as a hoplite also takes him outside Attica (§§3–8); likewise the suitably-named Sosistratos (27.2), and the 'Overzealous Man' (13.7), who takes it upon himself to question the commander as to when he intends to take the field and his orders for the day after tomorrow.

Other Characters travel on public business, as befits their status. The 'Illiberal Man' (22.5) serves as trierarch and commandeers his steersman's bedding so as to save his own from wear and tear. When travelling on an embassy, the 'Shabby Profiteer' (30.7) leaves his public allowance at home and borrows from his fellow-ambassadors. No doubt he anticipates that their loans will turn into gifts (§20). When abroad with people he already knows, he makes use of their slave attendants, hires out his own slave, and pockets the proceeds (§17). Introducing religious ceremonial as a motive for travel is the action of the 'Man of Petty Ambition' (21.3), unnecessarily taking his son to Delphi for his coming-of-age haircut. There were, after all, plenty of shrines in Attica, to say nothing of barbershops.

Even the restricted testimony of the *Characters*, when aggregated, demonstrates from the perspective of Athens' élite patterns of movements in commodities, individuals and information, within the polis and around the wider Mediterranean world. 'The city's role as a central place in the definition of networks of connectivity is the one that matters to the Mediterranean historian', write Horden and Purcell with respect to religious landscapes (438), but with an obviously wider significance. With regard to the mobility of goods and people (386), they comment how all this travel 'reinforces, extends, diversifies the network of reciprocity and the structures of self-definition, and furthers the cultural, intellectual and social homogeneities which have been so prominent a part of the history of the Mediterranean'. Apart from furthering a sense of civic identity, connectivity in the *Characters* has a strong ethical dimension with its scope for conspicuous display and implied etiquette of travel. Already apparent are proper motives for travelling, supportive relationships between fellow-travellers, the demeanour of the traveller himself, and legitimate expectations on the part of *xenoi*. Refinements are added by the 'Tactless Man' (12.7), inviting those returning from a long journey to go for a walk; by the 'Disagreeable Man' (20.3), who, far from speeding the parting guest, detains people who are about to set sail; and by the 'Arrogant Man' (24.10) who, when travelling, sends someone ahead to announce that his arrival is imminent.

7

HONOUR BRIGHT

One of Theophrastus' less engaging Characters (to us) is the 'Slanderer' (28). We have already seen how he seeks to undermine his victim's claim to citizen-status by more-than-hinting at his father's servile birth and the barbarian origins of his mother. The 'Slanderer' is particularly concerned with the womenfolk of the households he wishes to denigrate, going on to tell how (§3): 'These women grab passers-by off the street', and 'This is a house with its legs in the air. In fact, what's being said isn't idle talk: they couple in the streets like dogs', and 'The only word for them is she-devils', and how 'They answer their own front doors'. He is a consummate gossip, being careful never to seem to initiate a character assassination, but only reinforce views already expressed (§4). 'You can be sure that when he hears others talking slanderously he will join in with "There is nobody I detest more than that man. He's got a repulsive face. And his depravity has no equal. I tell you: his wife brought him a dowry of a talent, but since she presented him with a child he has given her only three coppers a day for food, and he makes her wash in cold water in the month of Posideon."'[181] He is also active in the public sphere (§5). In the Assembly, when someone stands up to speak, he talks to those sitting around him, abusing the speaker and his close relatives (*hoi oikeioi*). Finally (§6): 'He will particularly speak ill of his own friends and relations and of the dead, claiming that slander is only another word for free speech and democracy and liberty (*parresian kai demokratian kai eleutherian*), and he is never happier than when he is engaged in it.'

This Character anticipates several of the themes that come together in this chapter. Overall is a concern with the regulation of honour and shame; manifested here by protecting and even raising one's own status by systematically lowering the reputation of others. The technique employed is that of gossip; here dignified as 'free speech' and presented as an essential component of democracy. There are also the topics the 'Slanderer' chooses to manipulate, both public and (nominally) private. In the context of the polis, sensitive to civic standing, citizen-status offered an obvious target. For those actively involved in politics, public appearances were fair game. The attack the 'Slanderer' makes on the relatives of the Assembly-speaker demonstrates the significance of kinship solidarity, at least within immediate family. Here, however, the 'Slanderer' reveals his distorted character; so obsessed with ill-speaking that he does down even his own friends and relations, on whose support he ought to depend. Moreover, in pointlessly speaking ill of the dead, he theoretically brings himself within the reach of Athenian law. The law in question, attributed to Solon (Plutarch, *Solon* 21.1), was apparently still in force in the later fourth century (Demosthenes 20.104; 40.49).

Of particular interest are the attacks made by the 'Slanderer' on the two households. In the one, the husband is presented as an oppressive *kurios*, exploiting his wife who is in no position to resist. Having produced a son, in the event of her death (made more likely through under-nourishment and hypothermia), her dowry would remain with the husband. In the other household, the imagined *kurios* is alleged to be ineffectual in curbing his womenfolk, who therefore run out of sexual control. All this resonates with the ongoing debate on 'honour and shame', which has been such a feature of Mediterranean anthropology since the 1950s, and is the subject of the final part of *The corrupting sea* (485–523).

The authors wish to establish whether, along with their conception of a history of the Mediterranean, there goes a distinct Mediterranean anthropology; that is, whether as a region it constitutes in anthropological terms a 'discrete and coherent subject of study' (485). From the topics available for assessing the extent of unity and distinction – gender relations, the evil eye, class conflict, patronage – they choose 'honour and shame'; suitable as a test-case on the grounds that these are the concepts for which Mediterranean-wide applicability has been most sharply questioned. Honour and shame are here conceived as complementary poles of evaluation within society. In Peristiany's formulation (1965a) 9, they are 'the reflection of the social personality in the mirror of social ideals'. For Pitt-Rivers (1965) 21–2, honour is 'the value of a man in his own eyes but also in the eyes of his society', providing a nexus between the ideals of a society and their reproduction in the individual through his aspiration to personify them.[182]

Anthropological attention has tended to focus on the honour side of the equation. Enhancing our understanding of the revelation of shame is Bernard Williams' reassessment of *Shame and necessity* (1993). Williams' broad aim is to demonstrate unacknowledged similarities between Greek conceptions and our own (2); how, by coming to understand more acutely the ethical concepts of the Greeks, we may recognize them in our own society and so free ourselves from misunderstandings (10–11). At the heart of his analysis are the different responses of guilt and shame and the part they play in the individual's conception of personal identity. The essential experience of shame is 'being seen, inappropriately, by the wrong people, in the wrong condition'. Williams goes on to establish a straightforward connection with nakedness; he notes how *aidoia*, cognate with *aidos*, is a standard Greek word for genitals; 'The reaction is to cover oneself or hide' (78). The behaviour of the 'Repulsive Man' (11.2) is the exact opposite, deliberately showing off *to aidoion* to freeborn women. The proper reaction to a shameful act is *nemesis*, which might mean, according to the context, shock, contempt, malice, indignation or righteous anger (80). But, contrary to a common view, reactions of shame do not depend on being 'found out'. In fact, the 'imagined gaze of an imagined other' will do just as well (81–2). On the positive side, shame gives to individuals through their emotions a sense of identity. 'It mediates between act, character and consequences, and also between ethical demands and the rest of life.' There is the need for an 'internalised other', embodying perceptions of social reality. In this way individuals are able to assess how their behaviour will affect their lives in the community (102).[183]

Williams concludes that what the Greeks termed *aidos* does correspond quite closely to what we call 'shame' (88). While accepting that many and perhaps all cultures – 'from Iceland to Japan' – function with regard to some system of honour and shame, Horden and Purcell believe that 'some societies use these forms of evaluation with greater frequency and articulacy than do others' (488). The possibility that this was (and is) the case with respect to the Mediterranean world is initially investigated through a series of discrete anthropological studies (489–515). They provisionally conclude that (507): 'honour and shame reveal just the sort of loose unity that we might have hoped to find. ... Most of the individual local vocabularies and dramas of evaluation recognizably belong to one single family.' That guarded assessment is supported by their own, admittedly brief historical investigation of honour, from Dark-Age Greece to eighteenth-century Andalusia (515–23), concluding that: 'a case – inevitably patchy and incomplete – can be made for there having been a non-aristocratic honour ... that characterizes the Mediterranean microecology' (522). Specifically 'non-aristocratic' as demonstrating the reach of honour-based values down through society; a phenomenon that has been disputed, in contrast to the codes of honour uncontroversially characteristic of aristocracies: Homeric heroes, Roman patricians, medieval knights, renaissance courtiers and the like (488). From the ancient Greek world, Horden and Purcell glance at Hesiod in the *Works and days*, with his countryman's sense of shame and excellence (*arete*), which they tentatively extend across to the 'less well-off citizen of a Greek city-state in the age of Aristotle' (519). The *Characters* complement this picture, offering a glimpse of the value-system appropriate to a better-off, though not narrowly aristocratic group of imagined citizens.[184]

Post-War anthropological studies from the Mediterranean have typically been concerned with the opposite of aristocracies: small-scale, rural communities peopled by the relatively poor. Such is the point of departure chosen by Horden and Purcell for their own analysis of honour and shame in the Mediterranean: J. K. Campbell's classic study *Honour, family and patronage* (1964). In what follows, themes from this deservedly influential book are selectively re-presented so as to be measured against the community of the *Characters*.[185]

Honour, family and patronage was the outcome of fieldwork in the mid 1950s among a community of some 4000 Sarakatsani: Greek transhumant shepherds, who spent summer with their flocks in the central Zagori mountains, part of the Pindus range in Epirus. A major part of Campbell's study is concerned with the ramifications of kinship. The Sarakatsani recognize as kindred all cognatic relatives on both the father's and mother's sides, as far as second cousins, encompassing perhaps 250 souls (36–8). Kinsmen play a crucial role in offering information, advice, and moral and practical support (38–42). But it is the immediate or elementary family that forms the fundamental and enduring social unit, where the individual shepherd finds unqualified support, affection, and a sense of moral obligation (38). This is the group to which the individual owes almost exclusively his or her time, energy and loyalties. The sense of solidarity is highly developed; in principle, all its members are held to be responsible for the action of any other member (185–203). The family is not simply a matter of blood relationships; it is crucially an economic unit, owning in common all significant property, and also a religious community in miniature with its own sacred objects (37; cf. 53). Family solidarity is expressed and enhanced through ongoing rivalry between non-related families. As Campbell puts it (262): 'Hostility directed outwards is, of course, the counterpart of the immensely strong jural and affective solidarity of the family.' This rivalry is predicated on the idea of the 'limited good': fixed and barely adequate material resources encourage the belief that one family's success must be at the expense of some other or others (204). Such opposition has the ultimate, theoretical aim of annihilating adversaries (211).[186]

Thus far, fit with the world of the *Characters* might seem poor; indeed, fitting only where it touches. Although there is broad correlation between the Sarakatsan family unit and the Athenian *oikos*, with corresponding composition and sense of group solidarity, similar equivalences may be found in any number of non-Mediterranean rural communities.[187] There are obvious major discrepancies in terms of physical scale: Athens with a population of perhaps 250,000 across c.1000 square miles, as opposed to the 4000 or so Sarakatsani spread over c.380 square miles. Also, the Athenian urban dimension, with its differentiated, hierarchical social structure, contrasts sharply with the broad homogeneity of the Sarakatsan pastoral community. Equally marked are differences in terms of overlapping, organizational groupings. As already noted, from the perspective of each Sarakatsan shepherd, the community is effectively polarized between kinsmen and non-kinsmen: 'own people' and 'strangers' (148). As Campbell records (8–9), the shepherd normally has no membership in other social groupings which might conflict with his exclusive duties to the family. The community lacks any structure of overall authority or effective organization; nor are there any institutions of local government. The Sarakatsani are typically linked to wider Greek society through informal links of patronage (213–62). By contrast, an Athenian citizen, sharing in the *koinonia* of the polis, would have to reconcile family concerns with membership of deme, phratry and tribe. Again, in contradistinction to the insecurity of each polis within the wider Greek world, Campbell points to the rarity of occasions on which the whole Sarakatsan community might be threatened, causing unrelated families to combine together (263–5).[188]

However, these different worlds show clear signs of convergence with regard to honour and shame: both directly, and modified to suit the urban context of the polis, with its rival socio-political groupings and strong central authority. Campbell sets it out programmatically (19): 'Sarakatsani are deeply concerned about three things: sheep, children (particularly sons), and honour.' As subsequently formulated (263–9), honour is the central element in the 'prestige' (*goetro*) or 'name' which concern the Sarakatsani in all their public actions: 'Better to lose your eye than your name', runs a common proverb. 'This intense competition of families to maintain their prestige against the permanent threat of denigration, and the continual evaluation of other people's conduct, which is fed by an insatiate and hostile curiosity, result in a certain hierarchical ordering of Sarakatsan family groups' (265). Men care passionately about their own prestige, that of their families, and of their kinsmen: three sets of reputations which form a single, shared complex (39). Prestige is in part compounded of material elements: numbers of sons and brothers within the immediate family, wealth in terms of flocks, lineage, and marriage connexions; also the ability successfully to display pride (297–306). But fundamental to all else is the preservation of honour or *time*, which is conferred in recognition of an individual's perceived excellence. Honour reflects the integrity and social worth of a family as judged by the community. As Campbell explains (268–9), possession of sufficient honour renders a family more-or-less 'untouched' if not invulnerable in the face of physical injury and verbal insult. However, if some violation should occur, then 'the outraged family must answer at once, and with violence, if its reputation is to survive' (cf. 273–4).

Without at this stage going into detail, preoccupation with honour and shame is a major theme with the *Characters*, at once apparent through several broad Character-types. The 'Slanderer' would have felt at home among the Sarakatsani, at least with his relentless attacks on the reputations of other households, and the implied importance of family solidarity, which in his own case he perversely subverts. In general terms, the Characters drive home lessons about honour by shaming themselves. The 'Toady' (2) demeans himself by deliberately and systematically placing himself in a position of inferiority. The 'Morally Degraded Man' (6.5–6) could not care less about his own relentlessly shameful behaviour, spending more time in gaol than at home. Dishonour is explicit in the title of the *anaischuntos* or 'Shameless Man' (9), who repeatedly compromises his reputation in return for minor material gain. He finds a close associate in the 'Shabby Profiteer' (30), literally a 'shameful-gainer' (*aischrokerdes*), who will exploit anyone, including his friends, for a trifling profit. Finally, the *mikrophilotimos* or 'Man of Petty Ambition' (21) certainly aims at increasing his *time*, but does so in paltry ways that expose him to ridicule.[189] The detail of their actions and reactions, and of other self-shaming Characters, does on the face of it diverge markedly from the behaviour of the Sarakatsani. The paradigmatic situations in which their honour might be threatened are dramatic: homicide, drawing of blood, verbal insult, seduction, rape, and broken betrothal (268–9). Responses are in theory equally drastic: 'The most direct blow to the strength of another family is simply to kill one of its men' (193). Accordingly, for Sarakatsan males, an intrinsic principle of honour is 'manliness' (*andrismos*), manifested in courage and fearlessness, accompanied by physical and spiritual strength, and justified self-confidence (269–70). On a direct reading,

Campbell's detailed characterization of 'The Honourable Man' (274–97) might seem to have little in common with his upper-class Athenian equivalent, implicit in the *Characters*.

In fact, the theme of physical courage is not entirely absent from the *Characters*. Whereas Sarakatsan shepherds need to call on resources of bravery and strength in the everyday business of their lives (29), with Theophrastus' 'Coward' (25.3–8), courage is transferred to the civic context of military service. Appropriately, the people from whom he falsely seeks honour for having 'saved one of our men' are not family, but his fellow-demesmen, clansmen and tribesmen.[190] A different register of violence (closer in spirit to the everyday experiences of the Sarakatsani) is the lot of the 'Late-Learner' (27.9). Having fallen for a *hetaira*, he lays siege to her door, and gets beaten up by a rival lover, whom he then takes to court. Humour here seems to lie in the muddling of two distinct systems of retribution. Young men involved with *hetairai* must expect to take and return blows as a matter of course, whereas seeking formal redress in the courts was for more weighty disputes. According to Campbell (193), honour among the Sarakatsani is not so much concerned with justice as 'strength or prepotency'. There were circumstances in which having recourse to the law in place of self-help might be read as a sign of weakness. The action of the 'Overzealous Man' (13.5), interfering in a fight between people he does not know, might imply that normal practice on the streets of Athens was to let people get on with it.[191]

'How violent was Athenian society?' asks Gabriel Herman; 'among the less violent societies of pre-industrial Europe' is his conclusion (117). He highlights the discrepancy between the 'theory and practice' of revenge in classical Athens, with no apparent evidence for vendetta or blood feud (108–13). Instead, the place was notable for 'the internalization of a set of suprapersonal powers which transcended the realm of private, familial and tribal interests' (116). Broad respect for decisions reached in the courts, sanctioned by a 'power élite', concentrated the competition for honour and shame at lower levels of engagement.

By the same token, the overall level of violence among the Sarakatsani is lower than might be expected from the extreme principles governing their quest for honour, falling far short of wholesale annihilation of adversaries. From the decade 1945–55, Campbell could confirm only two cases of successful revenge killing (194). Practical reasons include the constant and far-flung demands of shepherding, which limit the circumstances placing one man at the physical disadvantage of another (211). The activities of the police, combined with prison and voluntary exile, tend to remove potential victims from the community (194–5). But there are also institutional checks. 'There is a limit to the amount of openly expressed hostility that this community is able to tolerate. Shepherds and their sheep are vulnerable, and in practice prudence discourages the free expression of hostility' (264). Among limiting factors are the precaution of trespassing only with a secure line of retreat, and fighting with weapons likely to wound but not kill. The individual family is too small a group to afford the loss of a male member. Hence, if a murdered man's brothers are all married, he is unlikely to be avenged (195). Although Sarakatsan families are not economically equal, none is strong enough to gain preponderant power (266). Consequently, the unending struggle after honour, which families believe essential in order to maintain prestige, has to be carried through on a daily basis in ways that are not materially damaging. Successfully to oppose other families in the competition for prestige it is necessary for all concerned to adhere closely to a common system of values; what Campbell calls 'rules of the game' (264–7).

Individual aspects of this lower-key but keenly felt competition strike responsive chords for readers of the *Characters*. Competitive behaviour is to be tempered by a general sociability on the part of heads of families in the public places of the village square and coffee house. Both locations loosely resemble the Agora and symposium as offering scope for maintaining and losing honour. Campbell provides details of etiquette appropriate to public places (283–5): keeping one's end up in sharp-edged conversation, while practising self-assertion without being exposed as an empty boaster (Theophrastus' 'Talker' and 'Boastful Man'). Specifically open to criticism are the tight-fisted who fails to pay for his round of drinks, and the spendthrift, unmindful of responsibilities towards his household ('Penny-Pincher' and 'Conspicuous Consumer'). Heads of families must also know how best to behave when on display at public occasions, such as village festivals and weddings. They should not show any negative effects of heavy drinking, possess a repertoire of songs, have the correct bearing when dancing, and maintain appearances with suitable clothes and grooming (respectively, Theophrastus' 'Repulsive Man', 'Late-Learner', 'Tactless Man', and 'Offensive Man'). These fragments of behaviour bear testimony to what Horden and Purcell label the 'depth' of honour: an 'obsession with apparent trivia' by which honour and shame are expressed on a daily basis. 'That is how honour's depth as a value, its tenacious hold on everyday conduct, is most fully revealed' (505).[192]

Characteristics of the depth of honour and shame demonstrated by the *Characters* are detailed in the following chapters. For the present may be noted the behaviour of the 'Tactless Man' (12.6), who, as guest at a wedding, delivers himself of a tirade against the female sex. In accord with the high profile of female sexuality in ordering values of honour and shame around the Mediterranean, it is with regard to female honour that there occurs the most direct correspondence between the Sarakatsani and the *Characters*.[193] For the Sarakatsani, complementing male *andrismos* is the code of honour appropriate for women: *ntrope* or shame; specifically, sexual shame. Women, through the weakness of their wills and the nature of their sexuality, are open to entrapment by the devil, and so continually threaten the honour of men (31). The most shaming disobedience is adultery (152), death being mandatory for those caught in the act. As the weak link in the human chain, a woman's sexual purity is regarded as symbolic of the family's honour (199). Maidens must be virgins, and even married women must remain virginal in thought and expression. The awarding of honour depends on the opinion of the community, best protected by rigid conformity, outwardly at least, to the code of sexual shame (270). Campbell summarizes the shifting terms of female etiquette, appropriate in turn to unmarried women, wives, and the old (286–91). 'A girl who is seen running risks ridicule and a reputation for shamelessness. If, by evil chance, she were to fall backwards "with her legs in the air" (*anaskela*) she would virtually lose her honour' (287). The worst insult against a man is to name his sister or mother in an unpleasant sexual context (271).[194]

In addition to the terms of reference that Sarakatsan rumour-mongers share with Theophrastus' 'Slanderer', common to both is the technique of gossip. According to Campbell, 'Scandal which falsely questions the virtue of a maiden is believed to be particularly wicked. It may be easily achieved by only a few allusive remarks' (291). Women are particularly vulnerable. Campbell also refers (270) to a woman being 'used' (*metacheirismene*) on the lips of men, and thereby being 'lost' (*chamene*). But gossip could be brought to bear on aspects of anyone's behaviour. Within hours of an incident occurring, small groups of Sarakatsani would be discussing what had been said and done, and whether it accorded with the values of the community (39). 'And since the downfall of one family validates and in some sense improves the status of other families, men attempt by every means of allusive gossip and criticism of conduct to deny each other their pretensions to honour' (272). Related to withdrawal of social recognition are the sentiments of 'self-regard' (*egoismos*) and 'shame' (307–12), which are closely linked to an individual's fear of gossip and ridicule. The prestige of individuals and families is constantly being re-evaluated in the community through gossip about personalities and events (307–12). Gossip consists mainly of adverse criticism, resulting in laughter and ridicule at the expense of the individual under discussion. Knowledge, real or imagined, of this ridicule (seldom made to an individual's face) is a key element in provoking a man's feelings of shame. Gossip is incessant, seizing on the pettiest of details and circumstances (314). Campbell's account demonstrates how for the Sarakatsani gossip and resulting ridicule are the joint medium through which public opinion operates to sanction the prestige values of the community (315).

A possible barrier here is our own tendency to dismiss 'gossip' as too disassociated to function as an effective regulator of communal opinion: 'casual and idle chat; a conversation involving malicious chatter or rumours about other people', says a standard dictionary. But the importance of gossip in classical Athens as a 'social construct', moulding the 'politics of reputation', has been emphasized by Virginia Hunter (1994) in her valuable account *Policing Athens* (96–119). She identifies gossip as expressive of the norms, values, and ideology of the part-community in which it occurs, and of the wider community too. 'For gossip is about reputation. While asserting the common values of the group, it holds up to criticism, ridicule or abuse those who flout society's or the community's accepted rules. Thus gossip functions as a means of social control, attempting, through its sanctions, to ensure conformity with those rules (96).' With reference to other anthropological studies (including Campbell), Hunter explores the scope for gossip in the overlapping series of 'face-to-face' communities and groupings that made up the Athenian polis: demes with their neighbourhoods, the Agora with its stoas and associated shops and workshops; but the possible list is almost endless.[195] Despite the citizen-orientation of the sources, Hunter is able to construct frameworks for gossip among women and slaves, within and between households (99–100, 111–19). The routine deployment of gossip in law-court and Assembly speeches, and on the occasion of *dokimasia* (public scrutiny of citizens offering themselves for office), provided conduits for feeding gossip directly into the public spheres of justice, politics and administration (102–10). The 'Slanderer's' relabelling of his 'evil-speaking' (*kakos legein*) as equivalent to 'free speech and democracy and liberty' now seems not entirely wide of the mark.[196]

The major sources on which Hunter bases her analysis are Attic Oratory, Old and New Comedy; surprisingly absent is the testimony of the *Characters*. In a sense, the whole work is a sustained piece of gossip: a one-sided dialogue in which the author shares with his audience the information needed to undermine the reputations of his thirty-or-so victims.[197] At a detailed level, the *Characters* serves to confirm Hunter's findings. The 'Slanderer' is surely the most single-minded case of a gossip to survive from ancient Athens. Other Characters indulge in gossip more-or-less incidentally, but in ways appropriate to their obsessive personalities. The 'Dissembler' (1.2) attacks people behind their backs, then praises them to their face, commiserating with them when they have lost a lawsuit. 'He forgives those who speak abusively about him and laughs at their abuse.' There is no sense here of turning the other cheek. In his heart the 'Dissembler' feels the opposite, and rightly so. The Character ends up by disclosing something of the stock phrases in his gossiping repertoire: 'But that was not the account he gave me', 'It beggars belief', 'Tell that to someone else', 'I don't know whether I should disbelieve *you* or condemn *him*.' Other Characters provide gossip in the making: the 'Ungrateful Grumbler' (17.2) complaining to the person (possibly a slave) bringing him food from a dinner sent by a friend that he's been done out of the soup and wine; likewise the 'Disagreeable Man' (20.9) telling third parties that his friends are never satisfied with what he does for them.[198]

Gossip has typically been conceived as destructive of reputation, but it suits the interests of the 'Toady' (2.2) to insinuate otherwise. He tells the person he is walking with about all the admiring looks he is receiving, which happens to no one else. He backs this up by saying: 'The esteem in which you are held was publicly acknowledged in the stoa yesterday'; recounting how 'Thirty or more people were sitting there and the question cropped up, who was the best man in the city, and his was the name they all arrived at, starting with the "Toady".' Although the 'Toady' is presumed to have invented the occasion, he supplies plausible circumstantial detail, locating this ranking of reputation in one of the stoas in the Agora. He neatly presents himself as introducing into the discussion the name of the man whom he wishes to flatter, in contrast to the circumspection of the 'Slanderer'. Elsewhere, Characters gossip to further political ends. The 'Oligarchic Man' (26.3) wants to continue his anti-democratic backbiting in private, away from the Agora. The 'Friend of Villains' (29.3–4) demonstrates techniques of breaking and making reputations, saying of honest men that such people do not exist, because people are all the same, adding sarcastically 'What an honest man he is!'. On the other hand, a spin-doctor before his time, he describes a villain as 'a man of independent character' (*eleutheros*), agreeing that some of the things said about him may be true in part, but how he is also 'smart, loyal and shrewd (*euphua kai philetairon kai epidexion*), and he pulls out all the stops on his behalf, insisting that he has never met an abler man'.[199]

Reference has been made to Horden and Purcell's focusing on honour and shame as enabling them to test the arguments of the so-called 'anti-Mediterraneanists' on grounds where the latter are most confident. At the forefront of opposition to the 'honour-shame' approach to Mediterranean anthropology is Michael Herzfeld, objecting to the imposition of what he sees as as an over-simple model on such rich ethnographic diversity. 'Massive generalizations of "honour" and "shame" have become counter-productive; their continued use elevates what had begun as a genuine convenience for the readers of ethnographic essays to the level of a theoretical proposition.' So runs the conclusion to Herzfeld's classic statement of the problems involved in the overall classification of Mediterranean value-systems: (1980) 349. He argues instead for the replacement of 'reductionist generalisation' by 'ethnographic particularism'; that is, the detailed analysis of native categories in their own terms. His objection is that no single model is capable of capturing local subtleties and complexities, which vary so widely between language groups and individual moral communities. This is an extension of Herzfeld's conviction that 'Mediterranean' in anthropological contexts has become a loaded ideological term and even a political weapon, serving to distinguish the advanced north of Europe from the supposedly backward south. 'The nation-state – by its own reckoning, the ultimate symbol and embodiment of modernity – serves as a touchstone against which Mediterranean society and culture acquire their distinctive characteristics, their fundamental otherness, and above all their removal to a more primitive age' (1987a) 11.[200]

As a practical way forward, Herzfeld has suggested displacing 'honour' by 'descriptively simpler and less ambiguous glosses such as "hospitality"', making possible 'more precisely calibrated comparisons' (1987b) 75. He supports this choice with four related points (75–6): hospitality entails social phenomena (reciprocity, proprietary rights) more clearly identifiable than honour; that in turn makes more feasible escape from 'well-worn generalizations about Mediterranean character and values'; hospitality occurs at a range of levels, reaching beyond village ethnography to include even national attitudes; and the position of the anthropologist as a local and national guest forces upon him or her consideration of the role of self in the construction of ethnographic generalizations. Much of this is borne out in the brief study of hospitality that follows, focusing on fieldwork from a mountain village in Crete. Hertzfeld's informants apparently identified honour as hospitality, telling him that *filotimo* was *filoksenia* (87); perhaps prompting others to read his account as 'operationally defining honour in terms of hospitality': Horden and Purcell (2000) 523. In fact, Herzfeld is explicit in proposing not a straight substitution of concepts, but rather the investigation of a 'group of glosses' to yield new insights (75).

Would it do unnecessary violence to Herzfeld's formulation to see in hospitality one of a range of possible components of honour; that is, the variety of institutions through which honour and shame are constructed, demonstrated and evaluated? The *Characters* provides a case in point. We have seen in passing how treatment of *xenoi* confirms or diminishes the host's reputation (56); but there are other, equally powerful ways in which honour might be sought or denied. This harks back to the idea of a polythetic class or 'family resemblance group', explicitly invoked by Horden and Purcell (505–6) to connect different bundles of attributes that give to honour and shame their pattern and depth across the Mediterranean. In the following chapters are explored ways in which honour and shame are expressed and manipulated in the *Characters*.[201]

8

ETIQUETTE FOR AN ÉLITE: AT HOME

Stobaeus attributes a saying to Theophrastus (*Anthology* 3.31.10 = FHS&G 469): 'Have shame (*aidou*) for yourself, and you will not feel shame (*ouk aischuthesei*) before someone else.'[202] The attribution of shame first to self and then to others might seem to support Williams' relating of shame to an 'internalised other'. The sentiment also presupposes a certain amount of self-awareness, a quality routinely absent from the *Characters*. Deliciously so in the case of the 'Man of Petty Ambition' (21), who has already attracted our attention by taking his son to Delphi for a haircut, securing an Ethiopian slave attend on him in public, and memorializing his defunct dog. In fact, attention-seeking is this Character's major concern. Invited out to dinner, he is anxious to sit next to the host as guest of honour. He ostentatiously makes a one-mina payment in newly minted coin, equips his pet jackdaw with a miniature bronze shield (it already has a ladder), nails up outside his house the skull, garnished with ribbons, of an ox he has sacrificed, and every day oils, polishes and garlands the bronze finger he has dedicated in the Asklepieion. But status-seeking in democratic Athens was a tricky business, so that we are to imagine the *time* he so laboriously strives after being withheld. With the Sarakatsani, the inability of families to dominate each other in material terms diverted the struggle after prestige and hierarchy into honour and shame. Although Athens had a far greater spread of wealth (to which the Characters bear witness), the ideology of democracy frowned on excessive personal expenditure, as demonstrated by the implied reputation of the 'Conspicuous Consumer'.

Those ambitious to increase their *time* were better advised spending their wealth on behalf of the community: the liturgies and other public expenditures looming large in several of the Characters. In recognition of the material loss incurred by the donor in benefiting the polis, public opinion responded with appropriate *charis*, resulting in enhanced *time*. The symbolic role of liturgies within the democracy is implied by the stereotypical complaint of the 'Oligarchic Man' (26.5): 'And he says "Compulsory public services and trierarchies will be the death of us – will we never be rid of them?".'[203] The system also operated at a neighbourhood level. When the 'Penny-Pincher' (10.11) entertains his fellow-demesmen to a meal, he short-sightedly misses out on their gratitude by giving them only small cuts of meat. At the opposite extreme are the fantasies of the 'Boastful Man' (23.5–6): 'And he will claim that during the food shortage he spent more than five talents on handouts to destitute citizens – he just could not say no. When he finds himself sitting next to complete strangers he will ask one of them to work the calculator, and then he does an addition, counting from the thousand-drachma to the one-drachma column, and putting a plausible name to each item, and reaches as much as ten talents, and says that these are the sums he has contributed towards loans for friends (*eranoi*) – and he has not included the trierarchies and all his other compulsory public services.'[204] The boasting is carefully conceived, moving from voluntary giving in time of emergency, to loans on a personal basis (supplying spurious detail only when speaking with strangers), to over-fulfilment of civic obligations. The sums involved are grotesquely large, even without including trierarchies and other liturgies (both plural). A working-man might hope to earn one talent every ten or so years.

The *aneleutheros* or 'Illiberal Man' (22) is a minor study in how not to handle public services. Although rich enough to serve as trierarch, he is (as has been seen) sufficiently mean-minded to pull rank on the steersman, appropriating his mattress and stowing away his own (§5). His public services label him as a very wealthy man; but when donations of money are being promised in the Assembly, he quietly slips out (§3), complementing the behaviour of the 'Overzealous Man' (13.2), who stands up and promises more than he can deliver. Although as *choregos* he wins first prize with a tragic chorus, he passes over the opportunity to gain the public recognition he deserves, dedicating to Dionysus only a strip of wood with his name written out in ink (§2). Implied criticism of the muted response by the 'Illiberal Man' to his triumph may be matched against Cicero's denunciation of Theophrastus' praise in his *On wealth* for the 'splendid service involved in public spectacles and his belief that the capacity for such outlays is the fruit of riches' (*De officiis* 2.55–6 = FHS&G 514). Cicero's own preference is for the assistance of specific individuals in need; as he puts it, liberality as opposed to prodigality.[205]

How does this square with the public engagement of the 'Man of Petty Ambition' in his quest for honour? Two of his actions are relevant. After parading with the cavalry (§8), he has his slave take home the rest of his equipment, then strolls through the Agora with cloak thrown back and wearing his spurs. And finally (§11): 'You can be sure that he will arrange with the executive committee of the Council that he should be the one to make the public report on the conduct of religious business, and will step forward wearing a smart white cloak, with a crown on his head, and say "Men of Athens, my colleagues and I celebrated the Milk-Feast with sacrifices to the Mother of the Gods. The sacrifices were propitious. We beg you to accept your blessings." After making this report he goes home and tells his wife that he had an extremely successful day.'

Three strands may be drawn out of these and other aspects of this Character's behaviour. Crucial is the absence of any action calculated to secure reciprocal *charis*. For all his ambition, the *mikrophilotimos* spends money only on himself and never directly for public benefit. His moments of glory are vicarious: sitting next to his host at dinner, and securing the job of publicly announcing, with much cumber and array, the outcome of what was evidently a low-key ceremony. The final, clinching sentence underlines the Character's naivety: sharing with his wife the delusion that he has made a powerful public impression. A late anthology records Theophrastus' warning that excessive keenness presages an unfortunate outcome for the future.[206]

Secondly, the *mikrophilotimos* repeatedly misjudges the situation, contravening rules of etiquette. Three examples may suffice. By insisting on handing over only new coins (quite a lot were needed to make a one-mina payment), he implies that the recipient is a small-minded person, likely to make a fuss over a worn and underweight tetradrachma or two. A cross-reference is supplied by the 'Country Bumpkin' (4.10), who cuts up rough if he receives a coin that seems in some way suspect.[207] By impressing on visitors through nailed-up and beribboned horns that he has borne the expense of sacrificing an ox, the *mikrophilotimos* not only behaves ostentatiously, but also fancifully elevates his house to the status of a shrine or temple. Strolling through the Agora in his spurs he wishes to advertise his élite membership of the cavalry; but his appearance is merely incongruous, combining spurs with a civilian tunic.[208] Etiquette, in its modern guise, resembles gossip as potentially misleading in its apparent triviality. But the concept here relates to the 'depth' of honour described above: how reputations in Athens might be maintained and subverted on a daily basis. The whole Character of the 'Arrogant Man' (24) hinges on his contempt for social convention (below, 74). The presentation of the 'Country Bumpkin' (4) is constructed almost entirely out of the Character's ignorance of social niceties. His shoes are hobnailed and too large, he talks too loudly, he thoughtlessly exposes himself in public, raids the larder, drinks his wine neat, feeds the plough-animals while eating his own breakfast, and even answers the door himself.[209]

Contravention of etiquette ties in with the final strand from the *mikrophilotimos*: the variety of location and circumstance in which he struts his stuff: at home with wife and jackdaw, travelling to Delphi with his son, out on the streets with his Ethiopian slave, dining out somewhere in the city, haunting the Asklepieion, and parading through the Agora. Other Characters substantially expand this list until the overall impression is of Athens as a collection of highly public places, where individuals were perpetually on display and open to assessment. For Horden and Purcell (2000) 90, 'a town is an address, an arena, an architectonic agglomeration: distinctive – sometimes – for the volume and density of its buildings, or the bustle and variety of its population...' All of which marks out the Athens of the *Characters*. The point was appreciated long ago by Jacob Burckhardt in his public lectures on Greek culture, first delivered in Basel in 1872 and published in English as *The Greeks and Greek civilization* (1998). Burckhardt conducts his audience on a rapid tour of almost all thirty Characters (50–5), apparently taking the preface at face value (350) and repeatedly asserting that they are drawn from life (see n. 127). He considers that (351) 'mass observation in the manner of Theophrastus was only possible in the total openness of Attic life. The Athenians were perpetually on show and consorting together, and the habitual attitude of "hail-fellow-well-met" created a social atmosphere quite different from our own...' He goes on to explain how a person like the 'Toady' would find opportunities for his importunate behaviour that no longer exist. Though Burckhardt does not make the connexion explicit, the constant scrutiny to which the Characters – and, by extension, citizens – were subjected, surely ties in with the agonal or competitive ethos he famously identified at the heart of Greek society (160–213, 237–9, 327–8).[210]

The idea of *agon* ('contest') is central to the phenomenon of 'performance culture', already briefly encountered with reference to Theophrastus lecturing to his pupils within the Lyceum, and here seen as central to the Athenian civic experience. Its key features are set out by Goldhill in his 'Performance Notes', which more than introduce the essays in *Performance culture and Athenian democracy* (1999). He details how recent cultural history has found in the idea of performance a crucial analytical category for the construction of social experience. 'When the Athenian citizen speaks in the Assembly, exercises in the gymnasium, sings at the symposium, or courts a boy, each activity has its own regime of display and regulation; each activity forms an integral part of the exercise of citizenship' (1). The chosen examples overlap with the actions of the Characters; others might be substituted. Goldhill singles out four Greek terms that underpin the notion of performance in the context of Athens' democratic culture: *agon, epideixis, schema*, and *theoria* (1–8).

Agon we have already met: Athens as a place where authority and status were endlessly contested. Goldhill's summing-up might serve as a commentary on the *Characters* (2–3): 'The hierarchical pursuit of *time* ('personal honour'), the concomitant elaborate discourse of outrage (*hubris*), the interaction of *philoi* ('friends') and *echthroi* ('enemies') around the injunction to do good/harm in an economics of carefully observed reciprocal treatment, all play an integral role in the social exchanges in which the Athenian citizen's self is enacted. For all of this, the *agon* is a fundamental cultural context.' *Epideixis* or 'display' refers not only to the performance of set-piece speeches, but those institutions of democracy (gymnasium, theatre, Assembly) demonstrating power and status. '*Epideixis* becomes the site where the self-advancement of the citizen is negotiated in the city of words' (4). As will be seen, the Characters exploit a hierarchy of city-locations to their self-detriment. *Schema* is here the appearance that an individual presents, or chooses to present, to his fellow-citizens: his way of walking, attitude and expression. Again, closeness to the *Characters* is apparent: 'The gaze of the citizens, in which honour and status are contested, constructs the citizen's bodily appearance as a *schema* open to evaluation, regulation and scrutiny. It is the gap between *schema* as form and *schema* as appearance that allows for the performance of self – that is, self-presentation, self-regulation, self-concealment which construct or stage the citizen in the public eye' (4). *Theoria* ('spectating') picks up on the idea of 'the gaze of the citizens': how being part of the audience across a range of democratic institutions itself constituted a political act. 'As *epideixis* highlights the function of speech-making in democracy ... and in the construction of the political subject of democracy, so *theoria* emphasizes the role of the evaluating spectator as a key factor in the construction of democratic culture. Both terms show how visual and verbal display become the topic of self-reflexive concern in Athenian democratic discourse' (8).[211]

It is with regard to *theoria* that the *Characters* offers an angle of perspective that diverges from 'Performance Notes' and most of the chapters that follow. As noted in passing by Goldhill (6), *theoria* can also encompass the philosopher's contemplative view of the world, which is arguably the gaze appropriate to the author and intended audience of the *Characters*. Their position is potentially complex. Theophrastus invites his pupils, who constitute a group theoretically beyond citizenship, to contemplate the behaviour of a group of citizens engaged with Athens' resiliently democratic ideology, evaluating their behaviour in terms of shared Peripatetic outlook and also the imagined response of the Characters' fellow-citizens. The Characters also demonstrate a different emphasis in the *epideixeis* of their performance. 'Performance Notes' naturally emphasize the nodal points of display in the Athenian polis, as do the essays that follow: courts, gymnasium, theatre, festivals. Although, as will be seen, there is considerable overlap, the Characters are also prone to a more diffused type of display, through the Agora, in the streets, and even within individual households.[212]

In what follows, location is the principle used to order the shame-incurring performances by the Characters, moving outwards from the household to more-or-less public places in the city. Paradoxically, this means starting with the conventional antithesis of public space: the supposed privacy of the Athenian home, as inhospitably emphasized by the 'Country Bumpkin' (4.8). Having created a minor sensation by answering the door himself, he ostentatiously takes his dog by the snout and tells visitors: 'This fellow guards the farm and the house.' But even at home, the Characters can still be seen. The 'Illiberal Man' (22.8) may stay in his house because his only cloak is at the cleaners, but he remains resolutely on display. Of course, reality has been suspended, as if Theophrastus' audience were invisibly present in the house, but this imagined autopsy may have an element of plausibility. Hunter (1994) 81 wonders whether 'privacy' might not be an anachronistic idea when applied to the domestic circumstances of ancient Athenians. She demonstrates how slaves might act as informants about what went on deep within the *oikos* (70–95). 'They talked, both within the house to fellow-slaves and outside in the streets and marketplaces to the slaves of other households. It would not take long for the details whispered by slaves among themselves to find their way into the grapevine of neighbors and demesmen' (89). Hunter bases her argument on the testimony of the Orators, but Theophrastus also provides explicit examples of how not to do it. The 'Country Bumpkin' (4.3) makes it easy for his slaves, with whom he perversely prefers to discuss his important business. The 'Disagreeable Man' (20.5), 'is prone to ask in front of the slaves, "Mummy, tell me, when you were in labour and bringing me into the world, what […]?"' The slave nurse from whom he takes his baby to feed it is also witness to his tiresome behaviour, chewing up the child's food, 'mouthing "pop-o-pop-o-pop" to it, and calling it "Pop's bun in the oven"'. The news of events outside Attica that the slave of the piper Asteios allegedly passes on to the 'Rumour-Monger' (8.4) suggests how information acquired by slaves might be fed back into the circle of citizens.[213]

Hunter speculates on the extent to which the presence of slaves in the household would have deterred individual citizens from criminal or anti-social behaviour. Certainly, the Characters repeatedly expose their stupidity to their slaves (material for gossip) or make them privy to their deviousness (hostages to fortune). The 'Boastful Man' does it twice over (23.2, 8). In order to impress *xenoi* about the extent of his business interests, he sends off his slave to the bank, even though he has not a single drachma on deposit. When visiting the clothing stalls in the Agora, he chooses clothes amounting to two talents, then feigns anger with his slave for failing to bring any money. Similarly, when at the baths, the 'Shabby Profiteer' (30.8) pretends the oil brought by his slave is rancid so as to borrow someone else's. In his relations with his slave attendant, the 'Coward' (25.2, 4) again displays his split personality (above, 38). On board ship, the slave to whom he hands his clothes is a close witness to his fear. As hoplite, however, he is careful to send his slave outside the tent 'to see where the enemy are', while he hides the sword he claimed to have mislaid. Elsewhere, Characters implicate household slaves in their conspicuously foolish behaviour. The 'Overzealous Man' (13.3) insists on his slave mixing more wine than those present can drink. The 'Obtuse Man' (14.9) berates his slave for failing to buy cucumbers in winter. Tibeios, attending on the 'Shameless Man' at a dinner-party (9.3), would be able to report back how his master fed him straight from the table, without even asking the host. The slaves of the 'Distrustful Man' (18.2, 8) would have a tale to tell their pals: how their master sends out one of them shopping, and then another to find out how much things really cost; how he carries his money himself; and how he makes the slave attending on him walk in front, not behind, so as to watch out in case he runs away. In fact, distrust has clouded this Character's judgment, rendering his actions ineffectual. The two slaves sent off to the Agora are presumably quite capable of colluding over monies spent; the slave attendant, if so inclined, could pick a far better opportunity to abscond.

If no man is a hero to his valet, still less was a master to his domestic slaves. For the Characters, so dependent on the slaves in their households, an issue crucial to their personal honour was the preservation of social distance alongside the physical intimacy inevitable while living cheek-by-jowl. Living shared lives presumably meant that hierarchy had to be all the more rigorously maintained. Here is a regular way in which the Characters as citizens of substance let themselves down. Already identified as a major failing of the 'Country-Bumpkin' is his inability to maintain sufficient distance between himself and the slaves in his household. Practical problems likely to arise are evident in his relationship with the slave-girl who bakes the bread (4.7). Having made secret sexual advances, he then works alongside her helping to grind the grain. It is unclear whether we are to regard this as the price of her silence or his habitual insensitivity to differences in status; perhaps both. The 'Late Learner' (27.12) sacrifices his dignity as a senior citizen by joining with his slave attendant in playing at 'Long Man': an otherwise unknown children's game. Where the slightest gain is at stake, the 'Shabby Profiteer' (30.9, 16) cheerfully sets himself alongside his slaves: 'If his slaves find a few coppers in the street he is liable to demand a portion of the money, saying "Luck's for sharing".' When he hosts a communal dinner for members of his phratry, he goes to extremes in saving money, requesting that his slaves be fed from the common meal, as if members of the group (compare the 'Shameless Man' not even asking before feeding Tibeios). However, he insists that an inventory be made of radish-halves left over, so that the slaves waiting at table will not get them. Presumably, the waiters were a different set of slaves, hired for the occasion; as by the 'Illiberal Man' for his daughter's wedding (22.5), warning them to be sure to bring their own food.

Here is a hint from the *Characters* how social distance might be maintained: reinforcing the slave-as-property idea by hiring out household slaves to third parties. With an eye to the main chance, the 'Shabby Profiteer', while travelling abroad, seizes on the availability of his acquaintances' slaves so as to rent out his own slave attendant (30.17). Testimony is hardly needed to confirm that the hirer of such a slave would have no interest in his or her physical well-being beyond the short-term: the 'Illiberal Man' refusing to take responsibility for feeding the slaves he hires. With a man's own slaves, self-interest might result in a minimum level of care. That presumably lies behind the implied criticism of the 'Penny-Pincher' (10.5) for docking the rations of any slave who breaks a piece of pottery; likewise the 'Shabby Profiteer' (30.7) who, serving on an embassy, loads his slave attendant with more baggage than he can carry and provides him with shorter rations than anyone else. He also has a slave who apparently 'lives apart', paying 'rent' to his master (§17). When he receives a payment (*apophora*) from the slave in copper coins, he over-asserts his authority by insisting on an additional and, to him, presumably trifling sum to cover the cost of changing them into silver. For more than a hint about the preservation of master-slave hierarchy there is the behaviour of the 'Tactless Man' (12.12), who 'stands watching while a slave is being whipped and announces that a slave of his own once hanged himself after such a beating'. Criticism is here levelled at the Character, not for his cruelty in driving his own slave to suicide, but in saying the right thing at the wrong time.

Nothing about the *Characters* suggests that the etiquette of master-slave relations encouraged good treatment of slaves for its own sake; still less for the sake of the slaves. Any sympathy that the audience might feel for the overloaded, underfed slave of the 'Shabby Profiteer' was incidental to the contempt intended towards his master; similarly with regard to the wine-pourer, at whom the pendant to the 'Offensive Man' (19.10) spits across the dining-table. Comparable is the presumed reader-response to Ariston's version of the 'Self-Centred Man' (col. xvii): 'When he buys a slave he doesn't even ask for his name, nor give him one himself, but merely calls him "slave (*paida*)"'. There was presumably nothing remarkable about having the 'Ungrateful Grumbler' (17.6) refer to the slave bought alarmingly cheap not as a person but as 'it'.[214] Theophrastus' 'philosophical slave' Pompylus was a one-off and treated accordingly. In any case, a distinction should be drawn between the household slaves of a wealthy person like Theophrastus, some of whom gained immediate or conditional freedom by his will (Diog. Laert. 5.55 = FHS&G 1.337–43), and those slaves presumably employed on his estates in Stageira and Eresus. Unnumbered and unnamed in the will, they are to be imagined being bequeathed *en masse* as part of the properties.

Not that the slaves Theophrastus owned in Athens were treated as anything other than chattels. The freedwoman identified as the wife of Pompylus was called (more accurately labeled) 'Threpte', meaning 'Homebred' or 'Foundling'. One of the pair of slaves given to Pompylus is not named at all; anticipating Ariston's *authades*, she is simply *paidiske*, 'the young girl' (Diog. Laert. 5.54 = FHS&G 1.336). Aristotle thought it necessary to specify in his will that 'none of the slaves who waited upon me shall be sold' (Diog. Laert. 5.15). According to Theophrastus' instructions, a solitary slave was to be sold on, presumably as a punishment. If so, the delay was in line with Theophrastus' own thinking on punishing slaves and others (Stobaeus, *Anthology* 3.19.12 = FHS&G 526). The man who is prudent (*phronimos*) will never do anything in anger, which is subject to impulses (*hormai*). 'Consequently you ought not to take immediate revenge for misdeeds either from your slaves (*para ton oiketon*) or from anyone else, in order that you may always do what [seems] best to reason, not what is dear to rage.' But the delay is not intended to protect the victim, rather, 'that you might extract a penalty from your enemies, as a result of which you are going to harm them without causing yourself pain... Consequently one ought to seek to defend oneself over a period of time rather than quickly to chasten the enemy in a way not beneficial to oneself.' So errant slaves are here assimilated to *echthroi*.[215]

So far, Characters have shamed themselves through inappropriate interaction with their slaves. But they are also capable of acting independently in ways better suited to slaves. Three do so from different motives, but all at cost to their standing as wealthy members of the citizen-élite. The 'Country Bumpkin' (4) need not detain us further. He is, as has been seen, simply ignorant of the necessity of preserving distance between the actions of slave and free. The 'Toady' (2) is presumably aware of the implications of his degrading behaviour, but regards them as counterbalanced by looked-for benefits. He aims to ingratiate himself with his would-be patron by performing, as a citizen, services appropriate to a slave attendant (*akolouthos*). In fact, his behaviour is likely to cause problems for both of them. Stopping people on the streets until the 'great man' has passed is liable in egalitarian Athens to lower both their reputations. When the man is on the way to visit a friend, he scurries on ahead and says, 'He is coming to visit you', then he hurries back and says 'I have warned him of your arrival'. Attribution of the identical action to a slave of the 'Arrogant Man' (24.10) implies that the 'Toady' unwittingly compromises his patron's standing with the friend he is visiting. He accompanies the man on a shopping expedition, and is also willing to run errands to the women's agora, 'without stopping to draw breath' (see n. 255). As a guest at the man's house for dinner, he takes upon himself something approaching the role of personal attendant or parasite, asking his host if he feels cold and wants to put something on, leaning forward and whispering in his ear. In the theatre the servile behaviour of the 'Toady' is made explicit: it is from the slave that he takes the man's cushions 'and spreads them on the seat with his own hands'.[216]

The obsession of the 'Distrustful Man' (18.3, 8) causes him twice over to take on the role of his slaves. Not only does he insist on carrying his money himself, but in making his slave walk not behind but in front, roles are reversed so that he appears to passers-by in the capacity of slave attendant. Finally, the 'Illiberal Man' (22) or *aneleutheros* (appropriately, 'not behaving like a free man') declines to spend money on what he regards as unnecessaries, ignoring the shame incurred by a person of his status. He runs his household with fewer than the minimum number of slaves needed to maintain respectability; as already noted, he has to hire waiters for his daughter's wedding. Even though his wife brought him a dowry, he refuses to buy a slave-girl to attend on her, but hires a slave from the women's agora to accompany her on outings. Rather than run to an extra slave or two, he does their jobs himself, carrying home in his front pocket the food he has bought in the Agora, and getting up early each morning to sweep out the house and debug the couches.

With reference to free members of the household, the scope for manipulation of honour and shame is more subtle. As is apparent from the observations of the 'Slanderer' (28.3–4), it was the role of the head of the household to promote a lifestyle appropriate to the standing of the family, exerting authority over the women, but without compromising their status as free persons. Theophrastus himself is reported to have said (Stobaeus, *Anthology* 3.3.42 = FHS&G 523) that a man 'ought to take good and humane care (*kalos kai philanthropos*) of his wife and children, for they return the service (*tais therapeiais*) as their father grows old, while she will give back the kindness (*euergesian*) in times of sickness and in the daily management of the household'.[217]

In material terms, the 'Shabby Profiteer' (30.11) and the 'Morally Degraded Man' (6.6) represent opposite ends of inadequacy: the one stinting on grain-rations for the family (above, 39), and the other hyperbolically letting his mother starve. We have just met the 'Illiberal Man' (22.4, 10), refusing to provide a slave attendant for his wife. He also skimps on his daughter's wedding, selling off the meat from the sacrifice (save for the priest's share). There is a scattering of cases where heads of household fall short in offering proper respect to their womenfolk. The 'Chatterbox' (3.2) unthinkingly praises up his wife to a complete stranger; the 'Offensive Man' (19.5) gets into bed with his wife without first having a wash, and his untitled appendage (§7) blasphemes when his mother has gone out to the augur's. The women in childbirth whom the 'Superstitious Man' (16.9) uncharitably refuses to go near are most naturally understood as members of his own *oikos*. As we have seen, the 'Disagreeable Man' (20.7) embarrasses his mother with intimate questions in front of the slaves. Embarrassing from the opposite extreme is the 'Overzealous Man' (13.10), desperately anxious to accord due honour and thereby offending the canons of restrained good taste. 'He inscribes on a dead woman's tombstone the names of her husband, her father, her mother, her own name, and where she comes from, and adds "They were estimable (*chrestoi*) one and all".'[218]

If it is degrading for masters to assimilate themselves to slaves, it is also demeaning to take over the responsibilities delegated to women. The imagined extent of the wife's role within the household may be inferred from the circumstances of the 'Superstitious Man' (16.12). It is envisaged that his wife might be too busy to accompany her husband

and children on their monthly visit to the Orphic ritualists, so their nurse gets to go instead.[219] A handful of texts gives an inkling of Theophrastus' formal attitude towards women's role within the *oikos*. According to Stobaeus (*Anthology* 4.28.7 = FHS&G 661), he stipulated that women needed to be clever (*deinai*) in household management (*oikonomia*) as opposed to politics. Cleverness entailed 'education in letters' (*paideusis ton grammaton*) as far as was necessary for *oikonomia* (*Anthology* 2.31.31 = FHS&G 662). Anything beyond that would make a woman lazy (*argos*), garrulous (*lalos*) and officious (*periergos*). Athenaeus (13.610a-b = FHS&G 564) has one of his diners tell of Theophrastus' implied approval of contests occurring 'in some places' between women concerning temperance and household management. Eustathius (*Commentary on Odyssey* 1.357 = FHS&G 636) illustrates Penelope's direction of her slave-women's labours by citing Theophrastus' approval of wives overseeing the female slaves (*amphipoloi*). He attributes this approval to 'overreaching emulation' (*dia to tou zelou huperopion*), 'because the man does not generally oversee the *douloi*, and she does not closely direct the *therapontes*'.[220]

Several Characters encroach on women's work within the household. The 'Country Bumpkin' (4.7) and the 'Shabby Profiteer' (30.11) from different motives take on the woman's job of measuring out the grain for the family and slaves (above, 39). The 'Distrustful Man' will lie in bed and ask his wife whether she has carried out her appointed tasks: closed the chest, sealed the sideboard and bolted the front door. 'Even if she says "Yes", he throws off the bedclothes anyway and gets up with nothing on and lights the lamp and runs around in his bare feet to inspect everything in person, and so he hardly gets any sleep.' If the wife of the 'Penny-Pincher' (10.6, 13) drops a copper-coin, he takes charge, shifting the kitchenware and couches and chests, and rummaging through the rubbish. He also forbids her to lend out the household goods in her charge (salt, lamp-wick, cumin, marjoram, barley-meal, fillets, sacrificial grain), claiming that 'little items like these add up to a tidy sum in the course of a year'.

From the words of the 'Ungrateful Grumbler' (17.7) may be inferred the conventional response to the birth of an heir: 'To the person who brings him the good news "You have a son" he says "If you add 'And you have lost half your fortune' you will not be far wrong".' His complaint ignores the reciprocal obligation imposed on children to care for their parents in later life; commonplace in drama and philosophy, and acknowledged elsewhere by Theophrastus himself.[221] The affection of the 'Disagreeable Man' (20.5) for the child he takes from its wet-nurse is palpable; the problem for those present being that it is all too palpable (above, 73). The conventional bond between father and child is indicated by ways in which the 'Toady' (2.6) and the 'Obsequious Man' (5.5) fuss over the children of the person they wish to please. The former is ingratiating, complimenting the father *via* his children, bringing to the house presents of fruit bought for the purpose, kissing and praising them in the host's presence as 'Chicks of a noble sire'. The latter comprises a vignette: invited to dinner, he asks his host to call in his children (there are at least four of them); he embraces, kisses, and sits them down beside him. He then plays with some of them, joining in their cries of

'Wineskin' and 'Axe' (some children's game); and lets others fall asleep on his stomach even though they are crushing him. A touching scene, but one lacking in dignity for an adult Athenian out to dinner; likewise for the 'Talker' (7.10), who is the butt of his children's jokes, but couldn't care less.[222]

So far as the Characters' relations with their sons are concerned, the major theme, as befitted the preoccupation of Theophrastus and his audience, is education. According to the *Gnomologium Vaticanum* (no. 336 = FHS&G 472), Theophrastus compared those who are handsome but uneducated (*apaideutoi*) to alabaster perfume-jars containing vinegar. Typically, the Characters let their preoccupations get in the way of providing a settled education for their children. The 'Talker' (7.5) enters schools and palaestras, disrupting the lessons. The 'Late Learner' (27.13) muscles in on his children's teaching in archery and javelin-throwing, telling them to take a lesson from him, because the tutor doesn't have the know-how. He disrupts sessions at the wrestling school by joining in (presumably against the children) with no holds barred (§6), and also inverts the parent-child relationship by having his son teach him military drill (§3). The 'Obtuse Man' (14.10) exhausts his children by forcing them to wrestle and run races with him. When there is a festival of the Muses, the 'Illiberal Man' (22.6) will not send his children to school, but claims they are ill, so that they do not have to make a contribution. The 'Shabby Profiteer' (30.14, 6) deducts school fees for days missed through illness, and won't send his sons to school in the month of Anthesterion, because there are so many shows to be paid for. He takes his son to the theatre only when admission is free.[223] Elsewhere, children are pawns, participating in their father's obsession or as a vehicle for his status-seeking: the 'Superstitious Man' (16.12) taking his children to visit the Orphic ritualists every single month, and the 'Man of Petty Ambition' (21.3) accompanying his son to Delphi for a ritual haircut.

As for relations with women outside the household, shame is not apparent over straightforward attachment to a *hetaira*, but rather over how the relationship is handled. The 'Tactless Man' (12.3) is censured for serenading his girlfriend (*eromene*) when she has a fever. When being kissed by his *hetaira* the 'Ungrateful Grumbler' (17.7) cannot help but ask himself, 'I wonder if your affection for me (*ei me phileis*) really comes from the heart (*apo tes psuches*)?'; thereby implying what might legitimately be expected from a *hetaira*. 'The Late Learner' (27.9) behaves like a young man in falling for a *hetaira*, assaulting her door, and getting into a fist-fight. Against this, explicit involvement with girl pipers seems ambivalent, appropriate to Characters who are immediately unpleasant in their affect. When hosting a dinner, the 'Disagreeable Man' (20.10) 'says over the wine that there is something available to amuse the company and, if they give the order, the slave will go and fetch her right away from the brothel-keeper, "so that she can play for us and give us all a good time".' The 'Repulsive Man' (11.8) buys a meal for himself, hires girl pipers, 'then shows his shopping to people he meets and invites them to join him'. Hospitality here is double-edged. In both cases, the speaker deludes himself into thinking that those being addressed share in his own shamelessness.[224]

The Athenian house with its variety of rooms and services provides a stage on which the Characters act out their belittling behaviour. The 'Distrustful Man' running around barefoot and naked after lights-out (18.4); the 'Obtuse Man' (14.5, 6) unable to find in his house something he has himself stored away, then, on a nighttime visit to the lavatory, being bitten by the neighbour's dog; the larder being raided by the 'Country Bumpkin' (4.6); the bedroom where the 'Overzealous Man' (13.8) tells his father that mother is asleep; the garden from which the 'Penny-Pincher' (10.8) prevents people from eating figs. For the 'Superstitious Man' (16), his house is at the heart of his religious anxieties. On seeing a holy snake in the home, he instantly sets up a hero shrine (§4). He frequently purifies his house, claiming it is haunted by Hekate (§6). If a mouse nibbles through a bag of barley, he consults the expounders of sacred law and, regardless of their advice, performs an apotropaic sacrifice (§7). Twice every month (on the fourth and seventh days), he mobilizes the family to boil up wine, purchases myrtle-wreaths, frankincense and cakes, and spends the whole day garlanding the household statues of Hermaphrodite (§10).[225]

Since the norm in democratic Athens was for relative homogeneity in housing, houses themselves are occasionally deployed in the *Characters* in the scramble after honour.[226] The 'Slanderer' (28.3) personifies his victim's house as a *porne* or prostitute with its legs in the air. Because houses were generally straightforward in design, the 'Toady' (2.12) makes a point of praising his host's house as finely built (n. 216). The 'Conspicuous Consumer' (5.9–10) has a house with unusual appurtenances: 'a little palaestra with a sanded area for wrestling and a room for boxing practice'. Merely possessing a place with these special features is not enough for this Character, who in the quest for maximum publicity has created a thoroughly public space within his *oikos*. 'He goes around offering this arena to sophists, drill-sergeants and music lecturers for them to perform in. And he arrives at these performances after the spectators are already seated, so that they will say to each other, "This is the owner of the palaestra".' The 'Boastful Man' (23.9) lives in a rented house, but tells his unknowing listener that it belonged to his father, and how he intends to sell it as being too small for the scale of his hospitality. Although portraying himself as aspiring to a large house, he cleverly implies that this is not from mere ostentation. Similarly, the 'Disagreeable Man' (20.9) slides across from the excellence of his domestic arrangements to the scale of his entertaining. He tells people about his 'cold water in a cistern at home and a garden with plenty of succulent vegetables and a cook who prepares a good dish, and that his house is an inn (it is always full) and his friends are a leaking jar (however many good turns he does them he can't fill them up)'.[227]

These Characters demonstrate the crucial role of the house (or part of it) as a place for interaction, where people from the outside are invited into what is nominally private space. Doorkeeping was emphatically not a job for wives and daughters (28.3). Within the house itself, Theophrastus is reported as stipulating that women should not enter the men's quarters without their husbands (Eustathius, *Commentary* on *Odyssey* 15.93–4 = FHS&G 644). The nature of the encounter gave plenty of scope for transgressing the rules of hospitality, with corresponding adjustments to honour and shame. Cicero (*De officiis* 2.64 = FHS&G 515) tells of his approval for Theophrastus' praise of hospitality; how it is fitting that distinguished men should make welcome distinguished guests; and how it is a mark of honour for the state that outsiders should not lack this kind of generosity. We have already witnessed the shabby treatment of *xenoi* as guest-friends at the hands of the Characters (above, 56).[228] The 'Country Bumpkin', showing off his guard-dog to the visitors he should be making welcome, repeatedly breaks rules of etiquette through ignorance. The 'Arrogant Man' (24) does so through a misplaced sense of innate superiority. He refuses to accommodate visitors who want an urgent meeting, putting them off until he takes a stroll after dinner. He declines to receive visitors when he is putting on oil or bathing or eating, and those who wish to buy or hire something from him are instructed to present themselves at his house at daybreak. The 'Self-Centred Man' (15.9) will not wait long for people who are delayed. The 'Dissembler' (1.4) acts pointlessly yet inconsiderately in fobbing off people who are pressing for a meeting, pretending he has only just arrived home, or it is too late, or he is ill. People visiting the 'Disagreeable Man' (20.4) are asked to wait while he goes out for a walk.

Those doing the visiting also have etiquette to observe. Philodemus in his *On rhetoric* (*P.Herc.* 1007/1673 col. 13 = FHS&G 689A) cites with approval Theophrastus' advice that harshness ought to be absent from even 'apologetic metaphors', which (as he states) should be 'mild and inoffensive, such as one that does not belong should be, just as when visiting a house'. The advice is ignored by the 'Tactless Man' (12.2), who drops by for a discussion when you are busy, and by the 'Disagreeable Man' (20.2) coming right in when you have just dozed off and waking you up for a chat. As a guest the 'Overzealous Man' (13.9) proves an intrusive liability: 'When the doctor orders him not to give wine to the invalid [he is presumed to be visiting] he says he wants to do an experiment and gives the poor man a good drink.' An additional unwelcome visitor for the sick (though under different circumstances) is the 'Tactless Man' (12.3) serenading his poorly *eromene*; where *komazein* implies something more vigorous than gentle crooning.[229]

The 'Arrogant Man' (24.10) when travelling presumes on his own importance by sending someone on ahead to warn of his arrival. In a striking piece of haughtiness (§9), when giving a dinner for his friends, he does not dine with them but instead details one of his underlings (*ton huph' hauton*) to look after them. In doing so, he breaks one of the fundamental rules of commensality: that the person doing the hosting should actually turn up.[230] Wining and dining were rule-bounded occasions for both host and guests. The onus was on the host to strike the right balance between hospitality and excess. The 'Overzealous Man' (13.4) mixes more wine than can be drunk: presumably to the guests' discomfort, both physical and psychological. The latter is also the imagined reaction of guests at the house of the 'Disagreeable Man' (20.10), obliged to collude as their host shows off the qualities of his parasite (the 'Toady' seen from the host's perspective), and then smirkingly offers to send out to the brothel for a girl piper.

The dinner-party (complete with girl pipers) to which the 'Repulsive Man' (11.8) invites those he meets while out shopping is presumably an impromptu affair. Other Characters introduce a range of formal occasions for eating and drinking, each with its own requirements of etiquette. Already encountered is the 'Illiberal Man' (22.4), who skimps on his daughter's wedding, telling the hired waiters to bring their own food and selling off the meat from the sacrifice. The 'Penny-Pincher' (10.3, 11) takes part in a communal dinner to which those present each make an appropriate contribution. He himself makes the smallest preliminary offering of anyone to Artemis, counts how many cups each guest has drunk and, when asked to settle his own account, claims that every item, however little was paid for it, was too expensive. Apart from improperly mixing money with mutuality, he implies that his fellow-diners are not to be trusted. When entertaining his demesmen to dinner he gives them small cuts of meat. The 'Shabby Profiteer' (30.2, 4) when entertaining does not provide enough bread, but sees himself right by insisting on double helpings as server. Hosting a communal dinner for his phratry, he makes sure his own slaves are fed from the common table, but denies even half-radish leftovers to other slaves waiting at table (§17). When it is the turn of his dining-club to meet at his house he makes a charge for firewood, beans, vinegar, salt, and lamp-oil (§18), so undermining the reciprocity on which the process of rotation depends.

Guests were also under an obligation to conform to rules of etiquette. The 'Toady' (2.10) is embarrassing in his fulsome praise for the host. Having secured the place next to the host (the 'Man of Petty Ambition' would be his rival: 21.2), he is first to praise the wine, complimenting him on the luxuriousness of his entertaining and singling out items from the table with 'How exquisite!' While talking to other guests he rudely continues to gaze at the host, monopolizing his attention with whispered comments. Elsewhere, the norm for the Characters-as-guests is either ingratitude or more-or-less disruptive behaviour. The 'Ungrateful Grumbler' (17.2) is sent food by a friend, but complains about not being invited to dinner; the 'Talker' (7.8) prevents other diners getting on with their meal. When dining out, the 'Shameless Man' (9.3) openly hands his slave bread and meat from the host's table, even though he is well supplied at home, having just completed a sacrifice and salted down the meat. The Characters are also prone to make exhibitions of themselves concerning entertainments. The 'Self-Centred Man' (15.9) flatly refuses to sing or recite or dance. At the age of sixty, the 'Late Learner' (27.2) takes the time and trouble to memorize popular songs and, while performing at a party, forgets the words. The 'Tactless Man' (12.14) seizes as dancing-partner a person who is not yet drunk. When a girl plays the pipes, the pendant to the 'Offensive Man' (19.9, 10) hums and claps, then blames her for stopping prematurely; he also spits across the table, hitting the wine-waiter. At least the victim there is only a slave; but the 'Disagreeable Man' (20.6) when at dinner incommodes other guests, telling 'how he was cleaned out top and bottom after drinking hellebore, and how the bile from his faeces was blacker than the broth on the table'.

9

ETIQUETTE FOR AN ÉLITE: AWAY

As we have seen, dinner and drinking parties established complementary sets of expectations for host and guests. When they emerged from their houses onto the streets and other public places of Athens, a uniform code of behaviour applied to wealthier citizens, judging and being judged. Going for a stroll, seeing and being seen, was a feature of leisured life in the city (2.2; 20.4; 21.8; 24.2). Even before words were spoken, personal appearance and demeanour invited assessment: the *schema* inherent in performance culture (above, 28). Preoccupation with appearance, both clothing and physiognomy, is clumsily manipulated by the 'Toady' (2.3), who removes a flock of wool from the cloak of the man he wishes to impress, or picks from his hair a bit of wind-blown straw, 'adding with a laugh "See? Because I haven't run into you for two days, you've got a beard full of grey hairs, though nobody has darker hair for his years than you"'. As we have seen with housing, so with clothes. Democratic ideology encouraged simplicity and similarity in types of clothing, but plenty of scope remained for differentiation in appearance. Opposites are supplied by the 'Oligarchic Man' (26.4), going out at midday, when he 'struts about dressed in his cloak (*himation*), with his hair trimmed and his nails carefully pared'. The ideological edge he gives to his appearance is reinforced by his telling listeners 'how ashamed he is when he finds himself sitting in the Assembly next to some scrawny fellow who has not used any oil'.

Cloaks and shoes are handy accessories to character, cutting both ways. 'If clothes are a language, individual garments constitute a vocabulary', as Geddes (1987) aptly observes in his unravelling of the costume of Athenian men in the fifth century (315). The *himation* was a relatively cheap and apparently uniform garment (312–3). Yet it could be manipulated (deliberately or unconsciously) to say something about the wearer.

The 'Repulsive Man' (11.2) takes manipulation to extremes; as we have seen, deliberately hitching up his *himation* so as to expose himself to freeborn women. For the 'Late Learner' (27.5), his cloak plays its part in his 'grand gesture', as he throws it off before attempting to get a neck-hold on the bull about to be sacrificed to Heracles. The 'Toady' (2.3–4), apart from grooming his patron's clothing, feigns uncontrollable laughter by stuffing his own cloak into his mouth. The 'Oligarchic Man' (as above) cannot bear to dispense with his cloak at the hottest time of the day. It will be recalled how the 'Man of Petty Ambition' (21.8, 11) incongruously appeared in the Agora wearing spurs with his *himation* flung back; on another occasion, he steps forward to announce a sacrifice, dressed in a shining white cloak, fresh from the fuller's. The 'Distrustful Man' (18.6) appears in a badly mended cloak: the person doing a better repair-job does not offer the best security. The 'Illiberal Man' (22.8) doesn't appear at all, staying at home while his only cloak is at the cleaner's. Apart from having frequent haircuts, keeping his teeth white and using unguents, the 'Conspicuous Consumer' changes his cloak before it gets dirty (5.6). The 'Offensive Man' is seen in the Agora wearing a thin cloak full of stains. The 'Illiberal Man' (22.11, 13) wears no cloak at all; just a tunic, which when sitting down he turns up, so avoiding wear and tear. He sports shoes which have been resoled and is proud of it, claiming they are 'strong as horn'. Likewise the 'Country Bumpkin' (4.2, 4, 13) sits with cloak hitched above the knee, and wears shoes which are too big, into which he hammers hobnails. All very different from the 'Toady's' wealthy patron (2.7), whom he helps in choosing lightweight 'Iphicratids'.[231]

According to Teles the Cynic, describing the unhappy experiences of Metrocles (above, 34), Theophrastus himself insisted that his pupils should dress well, with a *chlamys* or short cloak, wear shoes which were neither stitched nor nailed, and be attended by slaves. He allegedly singled these out as features of an *eleutherios* or liberal lifestyle.[232] The 'Illiberal Man' (22.7) therefore conforms in reverse to alleged Peripatetic type by saving not only on cloak and shoes, but also on slave attendants, doing his own fetching and carrying from the Agora. Other Characters are inappropriate in selecting and handling their slave attendants: the 'Man of Petty Ambition' with his Ethiopian ostentatiously present; and the 'Distrustful Man (18.8) making an exhibition for passers-by, insisting that his slave walk out in front.[233]

These instances of appearance and behaviour on the streets are contributory; part of the pattern making up each Character. But in the case of the 'Offensive Man' (19.1–6), unpleasant physical attributes are the whole picture.[234] Others out of shame might attempt to conceal their defects, but he 'parades about' (*peripatein*) with his scaly, blanched skin and black nails, in which he displays a perverse pride; how these are congenital ailments, inherited from father and grandfather, making it difficult to palm off an illegitimate son on the family. Other disfigurements are a matter of choice: he refuses treatment for the sores on his shins and toes so that they fester. He appears on the streets, his armpits infested with lice, hair extending over his body, with teeth which are black and rotten. He goes out to the Agora looking like this, wearing thick underwear under his dirty, thin cloak.[235]

The 'Offensive Man' is not just an unpleasant sight on the streets; he is disagreeable to associate with, letting himself down by wiping his nose while eating, scratching himself while sacrificing, belching while drinking, and spitting while talking. The etiquette of closely encountering people is underlined by the exaggerated actions of the 'Obsequious Man' (5.2): 'the sort who greets you from a distance, calls you "My dear Sir", and when he has sufficiently expressed his admiration embraces you with both arms and won't let you go, then comes a little way with you and asks you when he will see you again, before taking his leave with a compliment on his lips.' The encounter is visual, oral and excessively tactile. 'Beware of a charming friend whose word is always pleasant', was supposedly a saying of Theophrastus (Walter Burley, *On the life and character of philosophers* 68.7 = FHS&G 546). The 'Obsequious Man' attends on the person he meets only a little way; when people tell the 'Talker' they can no longer stay (7.6), he insists on accompanying them all the way home, but only so as to carry on chattering.

The proper giving and returning of greetings had particular significance, initiating or refusing an encounter. The 'Arrogant Man' (24.8) walks in the street with head down, not speaking to passers-by and looking up only when it suits him. The apparent ideal was an open, even friendly countenance, accompanied by a steady gait.[236] The 'Repulsive Man' (11.5) perversely calls out the name of a passer-by to whom he is a stranger, placing him at a disadvantage as unable to return the greeting. Opposed to the compulsive geniality of the 'Obsequious Man' is the behaviour of the 'Self-Centred Man' (15.3, 6, 8), who will not return a greeting given on the street, nor will he forgive anyone accidentally jostling him or treading on his toes; when he stubs his own toe, he curses the offending stone. The 'Illiberal Man' (22.9), should he spot in the distance a friend whom he knows to be raising a loan, will dodge down a side-street and reach home by a roundabout way. Chance encounters should be managed so as not place people in the awkward position of contriving to respond without giving offence: the 'Shameless Man' (9.6) asking the person he meets for a share in his cut-price purchase; the 'Repulsive Man' (11.8) casually inviting those he meets to share his dinner, complete with girl pipers.

The *Characters* is a work in large part about conversation, on the streets and in other public places, with the Characters themselves repeatedly showing how not to do it. We have already seen (39) how Theophrastus supposedly compared 'disordered speech' to an unbridled horse. Stobaeus (*Anthology* 2.15.31 = FHS&G 521) records Theophrastus' claim that 'We do not make our life trustworthy as a result of cleverness in speech, but our speech is a result of orderliness (*eutaxias*) in our life.'[237] Peter Burke (1993) warns of the need to discover the linguistic rules, explicit or implicit, that underpin all conversation; how 'the medium, code, variety or register employed is a crucial part of the message, which a historian cannot afford to neglect' (19). Specifically, he identifies four characteristics of the conversational genre (91–2): 'the co-operative principle', equal distribution of 'speaker rights', spontaneity and informality, and concern with matters beyond practical business; to which might be added intimacy or privacy (114). Burke immediately refines these qualities by identifying possible tensions between conversational co-operation and competition, equality and hierarchy in speaking, spontaneity and self-conscious concern over performance. How do these considerations match up with conversation in the *Characters*?[238]

Several Characters are primarily concerned with wrong kinds of talk: the 'Chatterbox', 'Slanderer' and 'Boastful Man'. It is the way of the 'Country Bumpkin'

(4.3) to destroy conversational intimacy by talking at the top of his voice. We have just seen how the 'Arrogant' and the 'Self-Centred Man' ignore the principle of conversational co-operation. Others over-exploit conversation as a competitive encounter, illicitly turning the occasion to their advantage. Disruption of equality in speaker-rights might seem all-the-more reprehensible between citizens more-or-less on a level. The 'Rumour-Monger' (8.2–10) has a finely honed technique. He greets his friend with a smile and immediately pitches in with a barrage of questions: ' "Where have you come from?" and "Anything to tell me?" and "How are you?".' But before the other can respond with even a conventional greeting ('Very well, thank you'), he interrupts with 'You ask whether there is any news? Yes there is, and fine news it is too'. Before his friend can reply, he rushes in with 'You really mean to say you have heard nothing? I think I have a treat in store for you...'; thereby establishing his superior role in the exchange of information. If challenged ('Do you really believe this?'), he is ready with supporting evidence, how 'it is the talk of the polis, discussion is intensifying and all are of one voice'; intimating that his friend is one of the few left out of the conversational loop. He also insinuates his closeness to those in power: 'The faces of the political leaders (*ton en tois pragmasin*) support his story – for he has himself seen how changed they are.' He has his ear to the ground: 'He has overheard that they have got someone hidden in a house who has arrived from Macedonia four days ago...' In telling his story, he feigns appropriate emotion, complete with apostrophe: 'Unlucky Cassander! Oh you poor man! Do you see how capricious fortune can be?' Finally, he flatters the listener's sense of importance by concluding 'This is for your ears only'.

The 'Talker' (7) has a battery of techniques for dominating the conversation, bluntly telling the person he meets, no matter what he says, that he is speaking nonsense, and how he will only learn the whole truth if he listens to *him*. Alternatively, he will regain the initiative by interrupting the other's reply with 'Don't forget what you are leading up to', 'Thanks for reminding me', 'You're quick to grasp the point', and 'I was waiting all along to see if you would reach the same conclusion as me'. His insistence on conversation as a minor *agon* is made explicit by the description of his encounters in terms appropriate to military engagements. 'He has such a variety of disruptive tactics in his repertoire that his victim cannot get a breather before the next assault. When he has worn down a few lone stragglers he will march against whole bodies of men and put them to rout...' Success is not always guaranteed. When asked for the latest news from the Assembly, he overreaches himself, tacking on accounts of debates from a generation earlier in Athens, and in Sparta from the generation before that. He then moves on to his own public speeches, adding in abuse of the masses (unwise on the streets of Athens), so that his listeners, according to their disposition, cut him short, doze off, or wander away. The 'Oligarchic Man' (26.3–4) is more circumspect in choosing the venue and the audience to whom he airs his anti-democratic prejudices, concerning sycophants, judicial corruption, and the burden of liturgies.

Between them, the Characters undermine the security of the spoken word; a phenomenon which allegedly provoked Theophrastus elsewhere. On encountering a talker (*lalos*), he is reported as asking: 'Tomorrow, where will it be possible not to see you?' (*Gnomologium Vaticanum* no. 331 = FHS&G 452).[239] The 'Dissembler' (1.5–6) relentlessly and pointlessly conceals his true feelings: 'He pretends not to have heard, claims not to have seen, and says that he does not remember agreeing. Sometimes he says that he will think about it, at other times that he has no idea, or that he is surprised, or that he once had the same thought himself.' He has a wide repertoire of expressions of disbelief: 'I don't believe it', 'I can't imagine it', 'I am amazed', concluding: 'I don't know whether I should disbelieve *you* or condemn *him*', 'Are you sure you are not being too credulous?'[240]

With the 'Toady' (2.3–4) the sincerity of the spoken word is under threat. His attempts to ingratiate himself with the man with whom he is in conversation include the telling of lies, inventing a discussion involving more than thirty men in one of the stoas. He also distorts any collective response by stage-managing the man's conversations, telling those present to be quiet, audibly praising him, saying 'Hear! Hear!' at every opportunity, and stuffing his cloak in his mouth as if he can't control his laughter at every feeble joke. The 'Obtuse Man' (14.7, 13) makes conversation problematic by his bizarre responses. On receiving news of the death of a friend and an invitation to the funeral, he bursts into tears and says 'And the best of luck to him'. If it is raining, he says 'How sweetly the stars smell' (in place of 'the earth'). 'When someone remarks "You can't imagine how many bodies have been taken out to the cemetery through the Erian Gates", he answers "I wish you and I could have such a windfall".'

The 'Self-Centred Man' (15.2) is, as has been seen, a conversational non-co-operator, stifling any possible encounter. Apart from refusing to return a greeting, if asked directly, 'Where is so-and-so?', he responds with 'Don't bother me!'.[241] The 'Country Bumpkin' (4.13) on the way to the city, interrogates a man he happens to meet about the date, the price of hides and salt-fish, then gratuitously adds that he intends to have a haircut, go round the shops, and pick up a kipper from Archias's. But the life of the city is wasted on him; on his arrival his only interest is for livestock he comes across in the streets (above, 36). In his preoccupation he resembles the 'Superstitious Man' (16.15), for whom the city with its temples, fountains, streets and crossroads is simply a sequence of locations for religious happenings: 'If he sees a madman or an epileptic, he shudders and spits into his chest.' Apart from family, the only people he meets intentionally are dream analysts, bird-watchers, Orphic ritualists and priestesses. His sole recorded conversations are with priestesses and expounders of the sacred law, who don't tell him what he wants to hear, advising that he take his mouse-eaten leather bag to the tanner to be sewn up.

Thus far, attention has focused on appropriate behaviour at more-or-less casual meetings, mainly on the streets. The city with its built environment comprised a range of locations offering opportunities for enhancing or diminishing honour. Goldhill (1999) 25–6 cites Pericles' building programme as creating 'monuments and spaces which were meant to do things to the citizen'. The only 'Periclean' building to get a mention is the Odeion (3.3). Less dignified places in the polis had their parts to play.

It is, appropriately enough, in the Deigma or 'Display Area' in the Piraeus that the 'Boastful Man' stands while striving to attract the attention of strangers (23.2). At the opposite extreme of visibility (but still 'doing things' to citizens) is the prison in the Agora, where the 'Morally Degraded Man', conspicuous by his absence, spends more time than in his own home (6.6).[242] Non-civic architecture also offered opportunity for *epideixis*. As has been seen, Diogenes (6.90 = FHS&G 23) tells how Crates, reprimanded by the city-magistrates for wearing linen, told them how he would 'show (*deixo*) even Theophrastus wrapped in linen'. Whereupon he led them to a barbershop where Theophrastus was having his hair cut. The barber's as itself a place for performance is apparently confirmed by Plutarch on Theophrastus, who 'in jest calls barbershops wineless symposia on account of the chatter of those sitting there' (*Quaestiones convivales* 679A, 716A = FHS&G 577A-B).[243] There is a final glimpse of the aged Theophrastus 'on display' in the streets of Athens. According to Diogenes (5.41 = FHS&G 1.61–4), 'Favorinus says that when Theophrastus had grown old, he was carried around in a litter.' He is particularly precise about his source of information: 'and this is stated by Hermippus, who adds that Arcesilaus of Pitane narrated it in his remarks to Lacyades of Cyrene.'

An exemplary location for *epideixis* is the public baths, where individuals were intimately on display to their fellows. Here is where the 'Late Learner' (27.14) practices wrestling 'with frequent buttock-twists, so that he may pass for an expert'. The 'Shabby Profiteer' (30.8) pretends his oil is rancid so as to borrow someone else's; the oil used by the 'Offensive Man' (19.5) really is rancid, so that he stinks. The 'Country Bumpkin' (4.12) lets himself down by singing; the 'Shameless Man' (9.8) by appropriating the supply of hot water, involving himself in an unseemly argument with the bath-attendant, to whom he ends by refusing his gratuity.[244] Elsewhere in the city, at the lower end of the spectrum of public locations, were *thaumata* or street entertainments: conjurers, jugglers, singers and the like. The action of the 'Shabby Profiteer' (30.14), keeping his children off school in the month when shows were most frequent, supports the idea that audiences inclined to the young. Certainly, the 'Late Learner' (27.7) sits through three or four performances of such a show, in an abortive effort to get the songs by heart. They provide a suitable opportunity for the 'Morally Degraded Man' to demean himself, going round the audience, asking for their coppers, and arguing the toss with ticket-holders who claim there is nothing to pay (6.4). Towards the other end of the status-spectrum are the situations sought out by the 'Conspicuous Consumer' (5.7), who 'haunts the banks in the Agora, dallies in the gymnasia in which the ephebes are exercising, and sits near the generals when there is a performance in the theatre.' The gymnasium was, in Goldhill's words (1999) 24–5, 'a prime site for the contests of masculinity, both through competitive exercise and through other status pursuits and displays'. We will return to the Agora (ch. 10).[245]

The device of seeking status through physical proximity to the good and great recurs in Theophrastus' work *Peri kolakeias* or 'On flattery', as cited by Athenaeus (6.254d-e = FHS&G 547). Cleonymus the 'dancer and flatterer', who 'liked to be seen with the eminent men of the city', repeatedly sat himself beside Myrtis the Argive and his fellow-judges. However, 'Myrtis took Cleonymus by the ear and dragged him from the chamber, saying in the presence of many people, "You will not dance here, nor will you hear us".' Here is a heightened version of the situation in the *Characters*: an individual of low status seeking honour-by-association at what look like formal judicial proceedings. The outcome for Cleonymus is shaming in the extreme: full-blooded *hubris* of physical and verbal insult in front of a large audience. For the 'Conspicuous Consumer' at the theatre and elsewhere, contempt remains imagined and internalized. He is the only Character using the theatre with its audience in an attempt actually to increase his honour. All others contrive to incur shame, attracting greater or lesser publicity; notably, the 'Morally Degraded Man' (6.3) willing to dance the *kordax* while sober.[246]

Not only actors but also the audience were on display, and even before the performance started. We have seen how different Characters take their sons to the theatre only when admission is free (30.6), prevail on guests to pay (9.5), and do the slave's job of positioning the cushions (2.11). Once the performance has begun, the 'Talker' (7.8) prevents those around him from watching the play. So far as the 'Repulsive Man' (11.3) is concerned, there is no such thing as bad publicity. He deliberately invites notoriety by applauding when everyone else is quiet, hissing those actors whose performance the audience is enjoying, and 'when silence has fallen raises his head and belches to make everyone turn round and look at him.' The 'Obtuse Man' (14.4) falls asleep and is found in his seat when the audience has left. In the aftermath of the performance, the 'Illiberal Man' (22.2), winner with the best tragic chorus, fails to publicize the honour that is his due.

A better sense of self-publicity is demonstrated by Damippos. At any rate, the 'Chatterbox' (3.3) is suitably impressed with the size of the torch he set up at the Mysteries, presumably as a votive offering. 'Ritual is by its very nature performative', is how Jameson begins his exploration of 'The spectacular and the obscure in Athenian religion' (1999) 321. Religious ceremony provides the Characters with a range of opportunities for attracting honour and shame. Their underlying fault consists of ignoring the proper function of ritual in regulating relations with the gods and within the community. When the 'Penny-Pincher' (10.3) makes the smallest sacrifice to Artemis, he is apparently unmindful that he is likely to receive back from her the least return. The 'Self-Centred Man' (15.11), withholding credit from the gods for blessings received, lessens the likelihood of receiving any in the future. Other Characters participate enthusiastically, but out of a misplaced sense of self-aggrandizement. Ceremonial looms large for the 'Man of Petty Ambition' in his search for honour (21.3, 7, 9, 10–11): taking his son to Delphi, sacrificing an ox, setting up an inscribed tombstone for his Maltese dog, dedicating and paying daily attention to a bronze finger in the Asklepieion, and treating public sacrifice as a personal ego-trip. Religious gatherings provide audiences for the 'Late Learner' to impress with his prowess (27.4, 5, 8), joining in the young men's torch-race team for the hero-festivals. If invited to a shrine of Heracles, he will try to lift the bull so as to get it into a neck-lock. At his initiation into the cult of Sabazios, he is anxious that the priest should judge him the handsomest of the initiands. It may be recalled that he is introduced as being sixty years of age.

The 'Superstitious Man' (16) proclaims religion on a personal and domestic level, apart from the wider community; other Characters incidentally subvert the communal aspect of religious ceremonial. Theophrastus' thoughts on sacrifice, as preserved by Porphyry *On abstinence from eating animals* 2.15.3 (= FHS&G 584A.151–3), are only indirectly concerned with the communal aspect of sacrifice, but regarding the cost of sacrifice he comments on the way 'the divinity looks more to the character of those sacrificing than to the quantity of the things sacrificed'. Sacrifice, ostensibly an opportunity for confirming solidarity, tends to bring out the worst in the Characters. Rather than share round the sacrificial meat, the 'Shameless Man' (9.3) salts it down for his own use. Even worse, the 'Illiberal Man' (22.4, 6), having given the priest his share, sells off the sacrificial meat from his daughter's wedding; he also denies his children the opportunity of attending the Festival of the Muses. It is when people are engaged in sacrifice involving heavy expense that the 'Tactless Man' (12.11) turns up, not offering to help out, but demanding payment of interest on a loan. The solemnity of the occasion is disrupted by the out-of-place addition to the 'Offensive Man' (19.5, 7–8) who scratches himself while sacrificing; during a prayer and the pouring of a libation, he drops his cup and laughs, as if he had done something clever. Tempting the gods, he deliberately blasphemes while his mother is at the augur's.[247]

The Assembly and the law-courts are obvious locations for seeking honour and suffering shame; in Goldhill's phrase (1999) 25, 'the paradigmatic agonistic arena[s] especially for élite competition', where citizens contend for success or failure in front of a large audience with a collective memory. The 'Talker' (7.7), it will be recalled, before relating his own triumphs in the Assembly, harks back to a debate 'in the time of the orator Aristophon'. Direct competition in the Assembly might arise out of public donations: the 'Overzealous Man' (13.2) carried away by the occasion and promising more by way of a contribution than he can deliver, the 'Illiberal Man' (22.3) slipping quietly away. Concerning conventional political debate, we have seen the 'Slanderous Man' (28.5) talking to his neighbours, running down the speaker. When the Assembly is concerned with religious ritual, debating the relatively minor matter of assistance for the archon in organizing the procession at the Great Dionysia, the 'Oligarchic Man' (26.2) attracts adverse attention by injecting into the discussion his own, divisive ideology. He incongruously proposes that whoever is appointed should possess plenipotentiary powers: 'One is enough; but he must be a real man.' Presumably, the appointee he has in mind is himself. We have already heard about the shame he feels in the Assembly, when some underfed and unwashed citizen sits next to him. That is only his version of events, but proximity is also an issue for the 'Country Bumpkin' (4.2–3). Before attending the Assembly, he drinks a bowl of pungent gruel, and then, as if on the defensive, asserts that 'garlic smells as sweet as any perfume'.

The 'Oligarchic Man' is naturally much concerned with the political arena, seen from his own perspective. He combines a strong sense of reciprocal obligation with the honour he considers due to persons of his status. He finds it intolerable that, by courting office, he and his like place themselves at the mercy of the mob (*ochlos*) in inflicting *hubris* or granting *time*: 'It's either them or us; we can't both live in this polis' (26.3). He advises his cronies: 'You must not expect thanks from the common people: they soon forget where the handouts come from' (§4).[248] The sentiment is reminiscent of advice attributed to Theophrastus (*Gnomologium Vaticanum* no. 324 = FHS&G 524): 'Treat the masses neither well nor badly; "for if they are ill-treated they remember forever, but if they have been done a service, they forget immediately".' It might be expected that Theophrastus and his audience, given their wealth and status, might share at least a selection of political views appropriate to the 'Oligarchic Man'. It may be that distance is deliberately created (how *not* to promote oligarchy) by turning him into a comic figure with his melodramatic delivery (*tragoidon*), all dressed up, but alone on the streets during the midday siesta. Moreover, he is conceived as intellectually deficient, knowing by heart only one line of Homer: ' "Multiple rule is not good: so let there be one single ruler", and he is completely ignorant of the rest.' He creatively rewrites early Athenian history, blaming Theseus, through his synoecism of the polis, for the misdeeds of contemporary demagogues.[249]

The 'Friend of Villains' (29.2, 5, 6) is represented as supporting the same wrongdoer both in the Assembly and in the law courts. Theophrastus claims to reproduce the Character's rhetorical tricks: 'You must judge the case, not the man', implying the importance otherwise of reputation, which the litigant in question evidently does not possess. He describes him as the 'watch-dog of the people, because he barks at offenders', and claims 'We shall have nobody willing to trouble their heads on our behalf if we throw away people like this'. But at odds with this democratic stance is his own taste for acting as patron (*prostates*) over the lowest citizens (*phauloi*), 'sitting with them on the jury to see that villainy is done, and his judgment is warped by a propensity to put the worst possible construction on the arguments advanced by the opposing parties.' There is further evidence for obsession overcoming self-interest in his tendency to team up with those who have actually been defeated in public cases (*demosiai dikai*), 'supposing that if he associates with them he will learn the tricks of the trade and become a man who is not to be trifled with'. The courts provide a suitable setting for the 'Morally Degraded Man' (6.8) to display his indifference to opinion about his lack of integrity, playing equally well the parts of plaintiff and defendant, sometimes swearing that he should be excused attendance, or going to the opposite extreme, 'arriving with a boxful of evidence in his coat pocket and strings of little documents in his hands'.[250]

The shame of being worsted in a court case is a recurring feature in the life of the Characters. Theophrastus himself, it will be recalled, was supposedly made to look foolish before the Council of the Areopagus (25). The 'Oligarchic Man' (26.4) makes stereotypical complaints to his associates about sycophants and judicial corruption.

Law courts located in the Agora were liable to attract an audience, adding to the element of display. The 'Overzealous Man' (13.11), if correctly understood as a witness in court, weakens his credibility by stopping to tell the bystanders (*hoi periestekotes*) that he's an old hand at oath-taking.[251] Directly involved in the courts are the 'Obtuse Man' (14.3), who, having a lawsuit to defend, forgets all about it, and spends the day on his farm; and the 'Rumour-Monger' (8.11), who loses a lawsuit by being busy talking elsewhere. The 'Overzealous Man' (13.3) over-presses his case when he has virtually won and goes on to lose it. But the case need not necessarily be lost for the Characters to show themselves to disadvantage. The 'Ungrateful Grumbler' (17.8) wins a unanimous court victory and then, instead of showing gratitude as appropriate, complains that his speechwriter left out many arguments in his favour. Although the 'Late Learner' (27.9) conceivably wins his case against his attacker, he shames himself in the process (above, 63). The 'Talker' (7.8) when on a jury prevents the others from reaching a verdict.[252]

The Characters find openings for their preoccupations in the defeats of others, contriving to add to their own shame. The 'Repulsive Man' (11.7) deliberately congratulates a person emerging from the court after losing an important case, while the 'Dissembler' (1.2) attacks people behind their backs, and then commiserates with them for losing a lawsuit. The 'Tactless Man' (12.4, 5) asks a person to stand bail who has just forfeited a security deposit, and arrives to act as a witness after the case is closed. Other Characters cause disruption before cases reach court. The 'Arrogant Man' (24.4), when asked to arbitrate, does so walking down the street. The 'Tactless Man' (12.13) as arbitrator sets at loggerheads parties who are on the point of agreement. When called in to arbitrate, the 'Obsequious Man' (5.3) unaccountably wants to appear impartial, and therefore tries to please both sides, to the presumed dismay of the man who appointed him.

10

FACE TO FACE IN THE AGORA

After describing the appearances of the 'Morally Degraded Man' in the courts, the characterization continues (6.9): 'He does not think it beneath him, either, to manage (*strategein*) a mass of market-traders and lend them money on the spot and charge a daily interest of one-and-a half-obols to the drachma, and do the rounds of the butchers, the fishmongers, and the kipper-sellers, and pop the interest from their takings straight into his mouth.' The scene is the Agora, drawing to a close this account of the world of Theophrastus more-or-less where it began, though under changed circumstances. In the case of Theophrastus' encounter with the little old woman, she as seller had the better of it, at least in the verbal exchange. Here, stallholders are being exploited by a citizen, who, ignoring the proprieties of his status, plays the part of the petty usurer, charging and exacting in person a rate of 25% per day for his overnight loans.[253]

Here is the Agora at the heart of a city-wide network of interpersonal relations involving citizens and others, open to constant renegotiation with consequent adjustments in honour and shame. The Athenian Agora with its public buildings, open spaces and fringe of houses, shops and workshops may be identified as a zone of intense and visible interaction, frequently but by no means exclusively focused on the process of exchange.[254] Citizens and others were here on display for their own good or ill; in the case of the Characters, wealthy and well connected, overwhelmingly to their disadvantage. It is in the Agora that the 'Offensive Man' (19.6) exhibits his physical defects and shoddy, stained clothing. The 'Man of Petty Ambition' (21.8) parades there in his spurs, presumably with his Ethiopian in attendance. It would have been noted how the 'Illiberal Man' (22.7), having gone shopping, chose not to have a slave to carry his purchases. Apart from passers-by, there were plenty of bystanders, including the shopkeepers themselves. A shop in the Agora was presumably the scene for the 'Toady's' toe-curling flattery of the man buying Iphicratids (2.7): how his foot is more shapely than the fashionable shoe. The Agora is also a natural setting for the 'Conspicuous Consumer' (5.8) to 'tell everyone in the polis' about his prestige purchases.

One of the stoas in the Agora is chosen by the 'Toady' as the location for imagined mass-gossipping (2.2), which is also where the 'Rumour-Monger' (8.11) holds forth about battles by land and sea. The 'Repulsive Man' (11.8–9), having bought food and drink for dinner in the Agora, invites passers-by to join him, 'then stops by the hairdresser's or perfumer's and announces his intention to get drunk'. Frequenting different parts of the Agora carried connotations for a person's reputation. By 'haunting' (*prosphoitao*) the bankers' stalls, the 'Conspicuous Consumer' (5.7) gave out a message about his aspirations, if not his actual status. It was, however, apparently demeaning for the 'Toady' (2.9) to run an errand to the women's market.[255] The 'Boastful Man' (23.7–8) wants to be seen at the right places in the Agora, pretending to spend two talents on clothes, and approaching the sellers of fine horses as a prospective buyer. At the other extreme, the 'Penny-Pincher' (10.12) might appear to bystanders to be seeming to shop for *opson* (meat or fish), and then being judged accordingly for buying nothing to go with his dry bread. It is presumably in or near the Agora that the 'Country Bumpkin' (4.13) intends to have his haircut and do his shopping for salt-fish, patronizing the particular stall belonging to Archias.[256]

Interaction between buyers and sellers, involving the detailed etiquette of exchange, has ramifications for the wider relations between citizens and friends. When the 'Shameless Man' (9.4) goes shopping, 'he reminds the butcher of any favours he has done him, then stands by the scales and throws in some meat, if he can, otherwise a bone for his soup; and if he is allowed to have it, well and good; if not, he snatches up some guts from the counter and makes off with them laughing.' This deceptively subtle vignette demonstrates something of the interplay of status, exchange, reciprocity, and personal relations. The 'Shameless Man' mixes reciprocal obligation with marketing, challenging the butcher to respond to alleged services in the past with some free food, opening the bidding with a request for meat, but offering to settle for a bone. If the butcher holds out, he simply takes something, using laughter to disguise the theft as a joke, relying on the cheapness of the stolen offal and his presumed status as a wealthy citizen to get away with it. In the accepted terminology of reciprocity, he substitutes Negative for Balanced Reciprocity, theft in the place of mutual exchange. The technique of the 'Repulsive Man' (11.4) is more refined. He goes to the stalls selling nuts, myrtleberries or fruit, 'and stands munching away while chatting idly to the stallholder'. His chosen time is when the Agora is at its busiest, the stallholder most easily distracted from his pilfering, and also least likely to make a fuss in front of bystanders. In both cases, the formal, fleeting exchange-relationship between buyer and seller is combined with an element of personal involvement. Though slight in the case of the 'Repulsive Man' (merely chatting), with the 'Shameless Man' reciprocity and ongoing expectation are made explicit.[257]

Reciprocity in the regulation of relationships has already occasionally surfaced with the *Characters*: between *xenoi*, offering reciprocal favours (56); the return of *charis* to those performing services for the community (69); grudging the gratitude owed to those helping out with contributions (66); even the 'Shameless Man' refusing *charis* to the bath-attendant with whom he gets into hot water (88). Theophrastus makes an independent observation on the centrality of reciprocity within the polis (Stobaeus, *Anthology* 4.1.72 = FHS&G 517): 'When Theophrastus was asked by someone what holds together the life of men, he said, "Kindness and honour and vengeance (*euergesia kai time kai timoria*)".' That is to say, preserving one's honour by helping friends and harming enemies.[258] Empirical evidence bears out Theophrastus' response. The Characters repeatedly shame themselves and incidentally threaten the community of relations by undermining the ideology of reciprocity on which personal relationships depended. At the heart of *philia* or friendship was mutual and ongoing benefit, confirming and reinforcing the connexion.[259]

'If the possessions of friends are in common (*koina ta philon*)', Theophrastus is supposed to have advised, 'it is especially necessary that the friends of friends be in common' (Plutarch, *On brotherly love* 490E = FHS&G 535).[260] The 'Shabby Profiteer' (30) may be taken as paradigmatic, repeatedly compromising friendship in the quest for gain, however trivial and shameful. We have already encountered a range of his actions: providing insufficient bread for fellow-diners, but securing a double-helping for himself; measuring out household rations with a Pheidonian measure; taking his son to the theatre only when admission is free. But it is with respect to exchange relations that his cozening is most reprehensible. Dining-clubs depended on the concept of Generalized Reciprocity; that is, with expenditure evening out over time as the venue rotated. The principle is undermined by the 'Shabby Profiteer', who insists on charging his guests for sundries (above, 91). He threatens the reciprocal basis of friendship by leaving town so as to avoid the purchase of a wedding-gift for a friend or his friend's daughter. Even more disgraceful, he sells (not gives) a friend wine which he has watered down; again, Negative in place of Balanced Reciprocity. It is from an acquaintance that he borrows a cloak while his own is at the cleaner's, keeping it for several days until the embarrassed lender is forced to ask for it back. Here, at least, he misjudged the situation.[261] In general, his technique in lending and borrowing may be summed up by the concluding comment: 'He borrows from acquaintances (*ton gnorimon*) the kinds of thing which nobody would demand back or be in a hurry to take back if offered.' Such is his expectation behind borrowing oil at the baths, on the pretence that his own is rancid. In repaying a debt of thirty minas, he pays it back four drachmas short; that is, 749 tetradrachmas in place of 750. Either he disguises the underpayment or (in line with his tendency as borrower) presumes on the goodwill of the creditor to 'let him off' the missing coin. When on an embassy, he borrows for his daily expenses from fellow-ambassadors; then asks for his share of the presents, which he sells off, shamefully combining gifts with monetary gain. Analogous is the action of the 'Illiberal Man' (22.4), selling not sharing the meat from the sacrifice at his daughter's wedding (above, 77).[262]

Other Characters fill in by contraries the detailed etiquette of reciprocity and friendship. Again, Theophrastus himself has a pertinent comment, following on from his earlier remarks regarding reciprocal relations between father and children, husband and wife (Stobaeus, *Anthology* 3.3.42 = FHS&G 523): 'If it is necessary to loan money to someone, try to put it on a solid basis (*meta tou bebaiou*), for it is characteristic of the wiser man to put out money wisely and regain it on friendly terms (*philikos*), rather than to contract with benevolence (*philanthropos*) and then recover the loan with hostility.' This may be tied in with his often cited observation on friendship (FHS&G 538A-F): people should be judged before being admitted to friendship, and not afterwards.[263] The fundamental principle of helping friends and harming enemies is subverted by the 'Dissembler' (1.2–3), who actively seeks out the company of his enemies, pretends affability with them and apparently forgives their abuse. Nor is he over-anxious to help his friends, fobbing off those looking for an *eranos*-contribution (see below). The 'Shameless Man', as described above, breaks with approved convention by actively reminding the butcher in the Agora of previous favours. The breach of etiquette is confirmed by the 'Arrogant Man' (24.3, 6), who does not hesitate to say how he never forgets a good turn that he has done. By the same token, he declines to take the initiative in performing a service, waiting for others to engage with him. In this way he avoids the risk of reciprocity being refused. The corresponding extreme is supplied by the 'Toady' (2), altogether excessive in his approaches, in anticipation of a still better return.[264]

The 'Tactless Man' (12.8, 10) is anxious to perform the part of a good friend, and 'enthusiastically tries to secure what you don't want but haven't the heart to refuse'; similarly when he brings along a higher bidder after the sale in which you are the seller has just been completed. Both actions place the recipient (who has not materially benefited) under an obligation to reciprocate. We have seen the 'Ungrateful Grumbler' (17.2) sent food by a friend, but far from showing gratitude, complaining how he would rather have been invited to dinner. When he finds a purse in the street, the equivalent of a 'free gift' with no need to reciprocate, he bemoans that it is not a hoard of treasure.[265] The 'Disagreeable Man' (20.9) implies that his friends are all take and no give, complaining to third parties that his friends are like a leaking jar: for all the good he does them, it is never enough. This piece of gossip may be designed to heighten his own reputation for generosity; but it also lessens the likelihood that those listening will want to engage with the friends whose reputations he is running down.

The role of reciprocity within friendship is highlighted in the institution of *eranos* loans: interest-free contributions collected from friends and acquaintances in time of need.[266] In alleging that his *eranos* contributions run to ten talents, the 'Boastful Man' (23.6) promotes not only his capacity for generosity, but also the extent of the network of his friends and acquaintances. His converse is the 'Illiberal Man' (22.9). Though obviously wealthy, he strenuously avoids making an *eranos* contribution to his friend, seen approaching in the distance, by ducking down a sidestreet and hurrying to the safety of his home. Behaviour of other Characters supplies the detailed ideology. The 'Self-Centred Man' (15.7) strikes at the reciprocal basis of friendship, fulfilling his obligation, but still implying that the would-be borrower is not to be trusted. 'When asked by a friend for a contribution to a loan, he at first refuses, then comes along with it, saying that this is more money wasted.' When the friends of the 'Ungrateful Grumbler' (17.9) collect a loan for him and tell him to 'cheer up', he answers, 'How do you mean? When I have to refund every one of you and on top of that be grateful for the favour?' His response, if taken seriously, threatens the element of gratitude essential to ongoing personal relations. 'A good friend when hurt is more grievously angered', as Theophrastus is said to have warned.[267]

The sphere of informal, personal transactions is easily disrupted by scorning etiquette, so subverting the underlying ideology. The 'Penny-Pincher' (10.13) forbids his wife to lend out the household goods central to reciprocal relations between neighbours and friends. If he is right in his claim that over a year these items 'add up to a tidy sum', that demonstrates the degree of interdependence. The 'Distrustful Man' (18.7, 9) will not lend items to friends or acquaintances (so calling the relationship into question) and, given the choice, would prefer not to lend out even to relatives. Unable to resist the strength of the prevailing ideology, he meets a request from a member of his immediate family for the loan of gold or silver cups by checking the quality and weight of the metal, and practically getting someone to guarantee the cost of replacement. When a person buys something from him and asks him to put it on account until he is free, he replies: 'Don't trouble yourself. I'll keep you company until you are'; inconveniencing himself and also implying that the buyer is not to be trusted. Other aspects of exchange-etiquette are flouted by the 'Shameless Man' (9.2, 6, 7), who twice over ignores the principle of reciprocity, deliberately withholding money from a creditor, from whom he then seeks a further loan. He borrows straw and barley from a neighbour, and makes the lender deliver it to his doorstep, treating him like a slave. Coming across a person carrying home goods bought at a bargain price, he cheekily asks for a share, rather than waiting for it to be offered. The 'Country Bumpkin' (4.11), being with all his faults a good neighbour, has lent out a plough, a basket, a sickle and a bag; but he calls this to mind as he lies awake, and goes to ask for them back in the middle of the night.[268]

Even where impersonal transactions are involved, there are still rules of the game for the Characters to transgress. Here and elsewhere, what is striking is the extent to which money is manipulated in the regulation of status. Whatever the degree of monetization of the Athenian economy (perhaps the wrong question), the Athenians themselves were certainly 'money-minded'.[269] So the 'Penny-Pincher' (10.2, 7, 13) contrives to make an exhibition of himself when both selling and lending at interest. In formal loan transactions, he breaks with accepted practice by coming to the house before the end of month to ask for a half-obol of interest; he also harries overdue debtors and charges compound interest: exploitative tendencies which verge on the usurious behaviour of the 'Morally Degraded Man'. When selling anything, the 'Penny-Pincher' inevitably pitches the price so high that the buyer is bound to lose out. The implication is that between citizens the bargaining process ought ideally to act to everyone's advantage, at least over time. From the opposite side, the 'Ungrateful Grumbler' (17.6) as buyer drives such a hard bargain that he tricks himself into wondering whether the slave he has purchased so cheaply can be in good health.[270]

Like Theophrastus' little old lady, the Characters know how to introduce power-play into the process of exchange.[271] The 'Dissembler' (1.5) keeps people guessing as to whether he has anything for sale or not. When selling something, the 'Self-Centred

Man' (15.4) seizes the advantage, opening the bargaining process by asking what the buyer will give rather than naming his price. The 'Arrogant Man' (24.7, 12–13) emphasizes his power by insisting that those wishing to buy or hire from him present themselves at his house at daybreak. In closing the deal, he also makes clear who has the upper hand, instructing his slave to do the calculation, work out the total, and then prepare a written invoice. Insistence on a written record, prepared by a slave, emphasizes the impersonal nature of the transaction, the absence of goodwill ensuring that no enduring relationship should arise. Similarly, when the 'Arrogant Man' sends a written request, he dispenses with language appropriate to reciprocity: 'It is not his style to say "I should be obliged (*charizoio an moi*)", but rather "I expressly desire" and "My agent is on the way" and "No alternative" and "Without delay".'[272]

11

CONSPICUOUS CO-OPERATION?

'From the days of the Greek philosophers to the present, a degree of leisure and of exemption from contact with such industrial processes as serve the immediate everyday purposes of human life has ever been recognized by thoughtful men as a prerequisite to a worthy or beautiful, or even a blameless, human life. In itself and in its consequences the life of leisure is beautiful and ennobling in all civilised men's eyes.' The sentiment is Thorstein Veblen's, the quixotic North American political economist and sociologist, in the chapter on 'Conspicuous Leisure' from *The theory of the leisure class* (1899) 37–8.[273] The thinking might seem unexceptionable: everyone needs 'time off' from their work. But the idea of leisure is developed by Veblen into a powerful and controversial indictment of what he saw as a crucial weakness of contemporary capitalist society: how the 'direct and subjective value of leisure' is largely secondary and derivative. That is to say, leisure is valued chiefly as a means of gaining the respect of others. By the same token, 'The performance of labour has been accepted as a conventional evidence of inferior force; therefore it comes itself, by a mental short-cut, to be regarded as intrinsically base.' The quest for 'Conspicuous Leisure' is reinforced by the phenomenon of 'Conspicuous Consumption', already identified as characteristic of the behaviour of the untitled supplement to Theophrastus' 'Obsequious Man' (5.6–10).

In his sympathetic introduction to *The leisure class*, C. Wright Mills portrays Veblen in terms fancifully reminiscent of Theophrastus of the *Characters* (viii): 'an idle, curious man, watching bustling citizens'; though the figure with which he explicitly identifies the iconoclastic Veblen is Socrates (xi), 'in his own way as American as Socrates in his was Athenian'.[274] Briefly, Veblen's hypothesis opposes the productive and useful in society with the ostentatious and honorific. As in the quotation above, labour has become undignified, in contrast with leisure in the sense of everything not associated with the world of everyday work (43). To this extent, Veblen's concept of leisure approximates to Greek *schole*: time spent in not getting a living. As he puts it (92), 'The early ascendancy of leisure as a means of reputability is traceable to the archaic distinction between noble and ignoble employments.' Conspicuous leisure (in the sense of mere idleness) might within a close-knit group signal an individual's superior power and wealth. However, in wider, less compact communities, it is necessary to find ways of advertising leisure in more tangible forms (86–7). These might be, as Veblen suggests (44–5), the 'lasting products of the labour performed for the gentleman of leisure by handicraftsmen and servants in his employ'. But there are plenty of non-material alternatives. Such 'trophies' might encompass systems of rank, titles and insignia; alternatively, it might mean acquisition of arcane knowledge relating to dead languages, occult sciences, domestic music, or 'the latest proprieties of dress, furniture, and equipage; of games, sports, and fancy-bred animals, such as dogs and race-horses'. Such, then, is conspicuous consumption: the high-profile waste of valuable resources in the competition for respectability.

Veblen's exposition is understandably focused on the psychological basis of contemporary North-American economy and society. His analysis is critical, exploring how leisure is associated with exploitation: unnecessary expenditure at the upper end of society implies privation further down. There is, however, a rudimentary sense of historical development along the lines of 'staged' theories of the evolution of economy and society. In 'primitive barbarian' culture (17; cf. 246–7), ' "honourable" seems to connote nothing else than the assertion of superior force. "Honourable" is "formidable"; "worthy" is "prepotent".' Over time, however, accumulation of property comes to replace the prestige of predatory exploits as the basis of esteem; what Veblen terms 'pecuniary emulation' (22–34), eventually extending across into a variety of forms of competitive consumption. The motive is rivalry: 'the stimulus of an invidious comparison which prompts us to outdo those with whom we are in the habit of classifying ourselves' (103). How this process of change relates to representative historical societies is only lightly sketched.[275] There is an opening statement to the effect that the clearest development of a leisure class is found (1–2) 'at the higher stages of the barbarian culture; as, for instance, in feudal Europe or feudal Japan'. Passing references follow to Brahmin India, Polynesian islanders, and the Icelandic sagas. A triad of later references locate 'Homeric times' in the earlier stages of competitive development: Homeric heroes with their 'exuberant truculence' (392) exhibited the 'ideal of predatory culture' in their seizure of women (146), who served as a unit of value (45). Apart from a smattering of classical allusions (and most of them Roman; see n. 281), *The theory of the leisure class* apparently has little to do with the ancient Greek world. In this, it resembles Mauss's *The gift*, making its measuring against Greek experience potentially the more fruitful.[276]

In Veblen's own summary (74): 'The quasi-peaceable gentleman of leisure … consumes freely and of the best, in food, drink, narcotics, shelter, services, ornaments, amulets, and idols or divinities.' Some of this overlaps directly with the activities of Theophrastus' 'Conspicuous Consumer', as we have been calling him. More so, with Veblen's addition of the acquisition of costly items from abroad, characteristic of conspicuous consumption (152–3): 'the remarkable feather mantles of Hawaii, or the well-known carved handles of the ceremonial adzes of several Polynesian islands'. Beautiful though these may be, 'at the same time the articles are manifestly ill-fitted to serve any other economic purpose'. These are equivalent to the 'Conspicuous

Consumer's' possession of luxury items from overseas: ornaments, household adornments and (above all) pets. His ape, oriental pheasant and Sicilian pigeons are effective twice over as objects of display. Also deeply implicated is the 'Man of Petty Ambition', providing a shield for his jackdaw to carry up its ladder and supplying a funeral monument for a pet dog. Domestic pets, 'which ordinarily serve no industrial end', are singled out by Veblen as standard items of conspicuous consumption (139–46).[277]

Veblen highlights the advantage of expenditure on dress as being (167) 'always in evidence', affording 'an indication of our pecuniary standing to all observers at first glance'. Veblen on clothing as satisfying a 'spiritual need' is cited by Geddes (1987; above, 83) in his exposition of changing trends in Athenian clothing (309–10). He demonstrates how, in the course of the fifth century, increasing prosperity was para-doxically associated with a shift to more modest clothing: the ubiquitous *himation* being both cheap and impractical as a work-garment (312–14). Geddes associates the trend to conformity with other material aspects of democratic ideology, including housing (325–31; see my n. 226). Veblen himself comments with approval on the relative stability in the costume of the peoples of antiquity, including the Greeks (175); but both he and Geddes pass over the ingenuity with which the Characters manipulate clothing as part of their appearance. Apart from changing his cloak before it needs washing, the 'Conspicuous Consumer' (5.6) has frequent haircuts, whitens his teeth and uses unguents. He may also be presumed to carry with him his 'twisted walking-stick' from Sparta. Veblen has plenty to say about the sociological implications of walking-sticks (265), which are carried by women only if infirm, but for men indicate leisure combined with a hint of truculence appropriate to 'barbarian man'.[278]

But what marks out Theophrastus' 'Conspicuous Consumer' as such is his blending of economically unnecessary expenditure with maximum publicity; exemplified by the luxury goods he purchases for *xenoi* overseas, 'while telling the whole polis what he is doing' (5.8). Other Characters engage directly in conspicuous consumption, notably the 'Man of Petty Ambition', through his appearance, expenditure and unnecessary travel; likewise the 'Boastful Man' romancing (though in his imagination) about the jewelled cups he has brought back from the East, lauding Asian over European craftsmen, and pretending to buy expensive clothes or a thoroughbred horse (94, 74). The 'Superstitious Man' may also be included, with his 'myrtle-wreaths, frankincense and cakes', as analogous to the 'amulets, idols, divinities' enumerated by Veblen above. Elsewhere (119–26), he characterizes cult expenditure by the individual as 'devout consumption'.

Similarities might be multiplied; but more revealing with regard to the behaviour of the Characters is the divergence of views between Veblen and Theophrastus. For Veblen, the whole process is reprehensible as a shocking waste of material resources. As Wright Mills discerns (xi), 'He wholeheartedly accepted one of the few un-ambiguous all-American values: the value of efficiency, of utility, of pragmatic simplicity.' According to Veblen the fault was embedded in society, an innate feature of the class of consumers (198): 'The leisure class is the conservative class.' For Theophrastus, however, inappropriate consumption arose out of individual moral failure, the result of avoidable deviation from the mean, bringing shame on the person concerned: 'spending money where it is not needed', as he describes the *salakon* or 'swaggerer' (see n. 12).

Forms of conspicuous consumption which are stigmatized by Veblen, meet with Theophrastus' implicit approval. Fundamental to the positive lifestyle of the Characters is the seemingly perpetual enjoyment of *schole*. Ironically (at least in our eyes), the only Character actually shown working for his living is the 'Morally Degraded Man', as inn- and brothel-keeper, tax-collector, auctioneer, hired cook, gambler, usurer and thief.[279] In the world of the Characters there is nothing reprehensible about leisure in itself. Singled out for criticism is the high-profile time-wasting of the 'Conspicuous Consumer' (5.7), already seen illicitly attempting to enhance his status by frequenting gymnasia where ephebes exercise and haunting the bankers' tables in the Agora.

Essential to the Characters' pursuit of legitimate leisure is the possession of household slaves and (presumably) the economic exploitation of slave labour. Slaves are highlighted by Veblen as the chief form of wealth during the 'predatory stage' of society, and 'especially during the earlier stages of the quasi-peaceable development of industry that follows the predatory stage' (38–9); which seems broadly equivalent to the ancient world. As a result, the benefits of wealth and power 'take the form chiefly of personal service and the immediate products of personal service', so that the gentleman of leisure may live 'in manifest ease and comfort'. Hence, abstention from labour was established as the 'conventional mark of superior pecuniary achievement and the conventional index of respectability'. This has its downside in that: 'Habits of industry and thrift, therefore, are not uniformly furthered by a prevailing pecuniary emulation. On the contrary, this kind of emulation indirectly discountenances participation in productive labour.' Whatever the plausibility of the argument, the assumption that wealthy citizens should have slaves to wait on their wants is never questioned in the *Characters*. Elsewhere (above, 35), Theophrastus cites by way of analogy the commendable practice of having slave stewards to supervise other slaves; as has been seen, individual Characters are censured for taking on the roles proper to their slaves.

The divergence may be taken further, if Veblen's negative observations on domestic servants are set against the presentation of slaves in the *Characters*. The economically unnecessary labours frequently performed by servants count as 'vicarious leisure', indirectly enhancing the respectability of the head of the household (57–60). By the same token, it is seen as degrading to possess personal servants whose general incompetence suggests that they have to double-up as (say) agricultural labourers. 'The possession and maintenance of slaves employed in the production of goods argues wealth and prowess, but the maintenance of servants who produce nothing argues still higher wealth and position' (63). Although the Characters are to be imagined as possessing productive slaves, none in fact puts in an appearance; presumably they are to be taken for granted. In the case of the 'Country Bumpkin', his domestic slaves are mentioned separately from the hired men he employs on the farm (n. 121). For Veblen, one of the peaks of conspicuous consumption was the possession of specialized servants to attend on the person (56). Two of the *Characters* straddle what for Theophrastus was the acceptable mean. The 'Man of Petty Ambition' is at fault for ostentatiously exhibiting an Ethiopian as an attendant, but the 'Illiberal Man' is criticized for their conspicuous absence.[280]

Wining and dining present a similar pattern. For Veblen (74–5), the giving of presents and feasts (meat and drink to the Characters) represents, in addition to straightforward ostentation, an opportunity to call upon one's friends to witness and assist in the consumption of valuable goods. By a neat turn, competitors may be invited along to participate in the host's enhancement: 'He consumes vicariously for his host at the same time that he is a witness to the consumption of that excess of good things which his host is unable to dispose of single-handed, and he is also made to witness his host's facility in etiquette' (75). The 'Toady' is most obliging in this regard (2.10): 'How luxuriously you entertain! ... How exquisite!' But there is a sting in the tail. Veblen has earlier set out at some length (45–53) 'manners and breeding, polite usage, decorum, and formal and ceremonial observances' as 'required evidences of a reputable degree of leisure'. This is on the ground that manners (like clothing) are immediately observable. Although he does not doubt that the origin and derivation of manners lies elsewhere, possibly as an expression of the relation of status, an 'ulterior, economic ground is to be sought in the honorific character of that leisure or non-productive employment of time and effort without which good manners are not acquired' (45–8). Thus does he call into question the extended system of etiquette that underpins the positive behaviour implicitly attributed to the Characters.

Crucially absent from Veblen's analysis of the Leisured Class is an appreciation of the dual function of etiquette, present in the *Characters*, simultaneously promoting and circumscribing competition. The tension was appreciated by Gordon (1912) 61: 'Mixed with the rivalry of household with household, there is a strange community in their lives. They are always borrowing things from next door.' The Characters provide detailed instruction about the danger inherent in distorted or uncontrolled emulation, pecuniary or otherwise. The 'Conspicuous Consumer' displays only one possible deviation; others include concealment of competitive feelings ('Dissembler'), wilful ignorance of the rules ('Country Bumpkin'), insufficient emulation ('Obsequious'), misdirected emulation ('Petty Ambition'), excessive acquisition ('Shabby Profiteer' and others). Overall, the message to be taken from the *Characters* is that conflict, though essential to the pursuit of honour, ought to be kept under control.

Finally, and closer to home, is Veblen's labelling of classical learning as a distinct form of conspicuous consumption. We have already encountered in passing the cultivation of the dead languages alongside occult sciences as evidence of past leisure (45). The idea is developed at length in his final chapter: 'The higher learning as an expression of the pecuniary culture' (363–400). The tenor of Veblen's arguments can be anticipated, leading to his conclusion that domination of higher education by the

Classics and their reputation as the most honorific of all learning stems from their 'utility as evidence of wasted time and effort, and hence of the pecuniary strength necessary to afford this waste' (396–7). The recondite element in scholarly learning constitutes 'a very attractive and effective element for the purpose of impressing, or even imposing upon, the unlearned' (366). Worse still, the grip exercised by the Classics over higher education has served to 'shape the intellectual attitude and lower the economic efficiency of the new learned generation' (394–5). This has been achieved by combining an inspired aversion to what is useful with consumption of the learner's time and effort in acquiring knowledge which of itself is no use. Not that Veblen wishes to seem to disparage the cultural value of the Classics or 'the bent which their study gives to the student'. Although that bent admittedly seems to be of 'an economically disserviceable kind', that need not concern anyone 'who has the good fortune to find comfort and strength in the classical lore'. What, he asks, does the loss of the learner's 'workmanlike aptitudes' count in comparison with the 'cultivation of decorous ideals'? The argument is clinched with an unattributed quotation from Horace: 'Iam fides et pax et honos pudorque/ Priscus et neglecta redire virtus/ Audet' (*Carmen saeculare* 57–9). It is hard to avoid the suspicion that Veblen is playing with the reader.[281]

The quotation returns us to the world of Theophrastus, though from a different perspective. We have already encountered, with reference to imitators of the *Characters*, the unattributed classical quotation as a nineteenth-century equivalent of allusion in antiquity to unspecified but identifiable philosophical doctrines (31). Here is the phenomenon writ large: Veblen's insists on modern-day immersion in the Classics as indicative of élite status, corresponding in antiquity to the leisured discipline of learning philosophy. The analogy may be taken further. The time-consuming aspect of classical learning, highlighted by Veblen, echoes the bitter complaints attributed to Theophrastus on shortage of time needed for philosophical learning. Diogenes Laertius (5.40 = FHS&G 1.44–5) reports as one of Theophrastus' favourite sayings the Veblenian sentiment that 'time is a costly expenditure'. According to Cicero (*Tusculan disputations* 3.69 = FHS&G 36A), Theophrastus on his deathbed bemoaned the injustice that nature had given long lives to stags and crows who did not need them, but men, who had perfected all the arts and could benefit from polishing their lives by learning, lived only a short time. 'Therefore he was complaining that he was dying just when he had begun to understand these things.' The insatiable pecuniary emulation identified by Veblen as characteristic of North American capitalism meets its match in the Peripatetics' limitless appetite for learning.[282]

Veblen closes his book with hard words about extension of the concept of 'Classic' to denote (398) 'the obsolete and obsolescent forms of thought and diction in the living language, or to denote other items of scholarly activity or apparatus to which it is applied with less aptness. ... Elegant diction, whether in writing or speaking, is an effective means of reputability.' He highlights (389) as 'an instance of futile classicism as can well be found', correct English orthography. Since it is 'archaic, cumbrous, and ineffective', time-consuming to master and its absence readily detected, 'conformity to its ritual is indispensable to a blameless scholastic life'. It is therefore fitting that *scholastikos* should be a term explicitly associated with Theophrastus; used, according to Diogenes (5.37 = FHS&G 1.21), in his letter to Phanias. Nothing is known of the context (Theophrastus characterizing himself?), but the sense is surely positive: 'free from the distractions of business and politics', rather than 'pedantic'.[283]

It is time to establish limits to the analysis supplied in this and the preceding chapters. Any attempt directly to recreate the 'realities' of interpersonal relations from fourth-century Athens would need to incorporate a mass of material from a range of texts with different registers.[284] What emerges from the *Characters* alone is necessarily restricted but significant in its specificity. Theophrastus has created for his audience an implied code of conduct: a perspective on honour and shame, co-operation and conflict, as they might impinge on upper-class citizens with reference to the civic society peculiar to democratic Athens. The picture is internally consistent and incidentally agrees with scattered observations directly attributed to Theophrastus. The notional model which emerges has already been tentatively labelled 'Theophrastus' Man'. Its essential practicality as a guide to conduct may be confirmed by comparison with the Peripatetic ideal as arguably exemplified by Aristotle's *megalopsuchos* or 'Great-Hearted Man'.[285]

The process is not straightforward, given the dispute over the intended status of the Great-Hearted Man. Central to the problem is his apparently unappealing personality: 'that irritating paragon' is Fisher's phrase (1992) 12, which is milder than many. One response has been to treat the concept of the Great-Hearted Man as *endoxa* or received opinion, appropriate to contemporary cultural ideals. According to John Burnet, this 'ideal of the average Hellene' proved unacceptable to Aristotle, and is therefore undercut in the *Nicomachean ethics* through a presentation that is essentially ironic. Alternatively, the unpleasant side of the Great-Hearted Man may be dismissed as culturally specific, appropriate to a society dominated by an aristocracy or otherwise privileged upper class, within which his perceived smugness and condescension might seem unexceptionable. If so, being the product of a particular form of society, hostile to democracy or egalitarianism, he becomes peripheral to ethics in the sense of human goodness. In what follows, I adopt with slight modifications Michael Pakaluk's revisionist reading of the Great-Hearted Man (2004b), which is his preferred translation for *megalopsuchos* (246–7).[286]

In his 'Meaning of Aristotelian magnanimity' Pakaluk argues, initially through Plato's Socrates, that Aristotelian *megalopsuchia* aims at 'a person's acquiring a settled disposition to consider as relevant, in deliberation and action, above all else the moral character of an action' (244). To do so it is necessary to dismiss all goods competing with what is required by virtue. Thus the contempt felt by the Great-Hearted Man is not for people but for things, specifically external goods. 'This attitude of idealistic moral aspiration, implying the capacity to dismiss competing goods as of no account, is what, I maintain, Aristotle means by *megalopsuchia*' (245). As a virtue, it is to be understood not as a possession but an aspiration, in which superiority is not to be smugly enjoyed, but sought after on a daily basis. It therefore has ethical significance reaching out beyond contemporary Greek culture. Moreover, Pakaluk argues that the presentation of the Great-Hearted Man is constructed so as to substantiate Aristotle's identification of *megalopsuchia* as a *kosmos* or adornment of the virtues, enhancing their greatness (1124a1–4). The portrait covers the virtues in the order in which they appear in the *Ethics*, arguing in each case 'that *megalopsuchia* disposes someone to realize that virtue in an exemplary way' (246).

That is the barest summary of a subtle and challenging paper: 'These matters are difficult and perplexing' is Pakaluk's own conclusion (275); but sufficient to support a reading of the Great-Hearted Man against Theophrastus' 'model man' implicit in the *Characters*. In fact, Pakaluk himself supplies a list of seven ways in which Aristotle's conception of the *megalopsuchos* differs from a typical Theophrastan Character. What should emerge from the analysis that follows is support from a different perspective for Pakaluk's well-founded scepticism.[287]

Book 2 of the *Nicomachean ethics* offers an early glimpse of the Great-Hearted Man. Aristotle's aim is to establish moral virtue as a disposition to observe the mean in appropriate areas of behaviour, 'as a person with practical wisdom (*phronimos*) would determine it'. Error takes many forms, whereas success is possible in only one way. Aristotle quotes a verse of unknown origin (1106b2–36): 'Goodness is simple, badness manifold', which might almost serve as an epigraph (or epitaph) for the *Characters*. In his preliminary listing of individual virtues with their negative co-ordinates, he includes, as we have seen, a selection of negative qualities recurring as Theophrastan Characters (29). Among the virtues cited is 'Greatness of Heart' (1107b22–08a4): 'In respect of honour and dishonour, the observance of the mean is Greatness of Heart, the excess a sort of Vanity (*chaunotes*), as it may be called, and the deficiency, Smallness of Heart (*mikropsuchia*).' As with the *Characters*, then, honour and shame are perpetually at stake. This loose association may be taken a stage further, in that aspects of negative behaviour eschewed by the Great-Hearted Man regularly recur in the *Characters*. This becomes apparent when *megalopsuchia* resurfaces in Book 4, where key virtues are examined in greater detail. 'Now a person is thought to be Great Hearted if he claims much and deserves much; he who claims much without deserving it is foolish, but no one of moral excellence is foolish or senseless' (1123b1–4). This might seem to have a bearing on the behaviour of several Characters: the 'Boastful Man' with his fantastic claims about his generosity, public and private, or even the 'Coward', falsely claiming recognition for having rescued a comrade-in-arms. Aristotle continues (1123b26–9): 'The Small-Hearted Man (*mikropsuchos*) falls short both as judged by his own deserts and in comparison with the claim of the Great-Hearted Man; the Vain Man (*chaunos*) on the other hand exceeds as judged by his own standard, but does not however exceed the Great-Hearted Man.'[288] Again, the negative co-ordinates find broad equivalences in the *Characters*: the 'Illiberal Man' selling himself short in claiming honours; the 'Man of Petty Ambition' exalting over comparative trifles.[289]

But from this point, divergence seems to set in: 'Honour is clearly the greatest of external goods. Therefore the Great-Hearted Man is he who has the right disposition in relation to honours and disgraces.' (1123b20–22). As Pakaluk points out in his conclusion (274–5), according to Aristotle, *megalopsuchia* is the outcome of imparting a rational form to the near-universal motivation of 'aspiring to honour'. What 'Theophrastus' Man' lacks is that crucial element of reason that would lead him to reject ultimately unhelpful external goods. The Great-Hearted Man looks in a measured way (*metrios*) on wealth, power, and good and bad fortune in general, as they may affect him, not rejoicing or grieving overmuch in prosperity or adversity. This relentless application of reason causes the Great-Hearted Man to behave in ways which at first appear puzzling or paradoxical. Though, as has been established, his especial concern is with honour, 'he does not care much even about honour, which is the greatest of external goods; ... he therefore to whom even honour is a small thing will be indifferent to other things as well.' (1124a12–20). But the implication of the detailed behaviour of the *Characters* is that honour and associated virtues ought to loom large for 'Theophrastus' Man'. The 'Arrogant Man' (24.5) supplies a specific example: criticized for begging himself off the public office to which he has been appointed by popular vote. Here is another case. According to Aristotle: 'Honour and dishonour then are the objects with which the Great-Hearted Man is especially concerned. ... Honour rendered by chance persons and on trivial grounds he will utterly despise, for this is not what he merits' (1124a5–11).[290] To be sure, the 'Man of Petty Ambition' is condemned for revelling in trivial honours, but the 'Oligarchic Man' is implicitly criticized for scorning honours bestowed by the common people (above, 91).

Aristotle seems to offer a way forward in the distinction he draws between true and assumed greatness of heart; how the 'gifts of fortune' (wealth and high birth) are erroneously thought to indicate *megalopsuchia*, because they might seem to indicate superiority. 'But in reality only the good man ought to be honoured, although he that has both virtue and fortune is esteemed still more worthy of honour; whereas those who possess the goods of fortune without virtue are not justified in claiming high worth, and cannot correctly be called great-hearted, since true worth and greatness of heart cannot exist without complete virtue.' (1123b20–29). This seems to provide an appropriate category for 'Theophrastus' Man', enjoying relatively high status, but without the superabundance of virtue that distinguishes the Great-Hearted Man. Theophrastus is said to have pointed out elsewhere that wealth, not having its own life, is not able to seek out good men and therefore falls also to men who are bad (scholion to Plato, *Laws* 1.631C = FHS&G 507). Between them, the 'Oligarchic', 'Arrogant' and 'Self-Centred' Men show the 'wrong type' of contempt; that is, for individuals rather than things. 'It is true that even those who merely possess the goods of fortune may be haughty and insolent; because without virtue it is not easy to bear good fortune becomingly, and such men, being unable to carry their prosperity, and thinking themselves superior to the rest of mankind, despise other people, although their own conduct is no better than another's. ... For the Great-Hearted Man is justified in showing contempt – his estimates are correct; but most proud men have no good ground for their pride' (1124a29–24b7). Purging the Characters of their contempt would not leave them with the virtue that marks out Greatness of Heart. For a hint of what is missing there is the motivation in battle of the Great-Hearted Man, who 'will face danger in a great cause, and when doing so will be ready to sacrifice his life, since he holds that life is not worth having at every price' (1124b7–9). Resolving the behaviour of Theophrastus' 'Coward' produces something different: battle as a potential source of honour rather than furthering a cause (above, 29).

Reference has been made to the seemingly idiosyncratic behaviour of the Great-Hearted Man. This is present in his attitude to reciprocity, where his behaviour overlaps with, but does not entirely conform to, norms implicit in the *Characters*. On occasion, his preferences seem calculated to hinder the smooth operation of reciprocal relations within the community. 'He is fond of conferring benefits, but ashamed to receive them, because the former is a mark of superiority and the latter of inferiority. He confers greater benefits in return, since this will put the original benefactor into his debt in turn, and make him the party benefited' (1124b10–13). There is no suggestion in the *Characters* that receiving deserved benefits was in any way shameful. The 'Illiberal Man' (22.2) is criticized for failing adequately to memorialize his victory as *choregos*. Moreover, returning every service with interest would effectively remove the Great-Hearted Man from the normal network of giving and taking. The 'Shameless Man', it will be recalled, was censured for seeking a second loan from an existing creditor (97).[291] Additionally: 'The Great-Hearted are thought to have a good memory for any benefit they have conferred, but a bad memory for those they have received (since the recipient of a benefit is the inferior of his benefactor, whereas they desire to be superior); and to enjoy being reminded of the former but to dislike being reminded of the latter' (1124b13–17). The mechanism, somewhat sketchily illustrated by examples from myth and history, seems the reverse of approved behaviour implied in the *Characters* (and elsewhere): recipients should always be mindful of their obligations. By the same token, the 'Arrogant Man' (24.3) is censured for claiming never to forget a favour he has done.

The apparent divergence may be explained in terms of motivation. Whereas the Great-Hearted Man is exclusively concerned with preserving his own exemplary virtue, reflected in his preoccupation with benefits received and their origins, what ought to concern the Characters is the practical problem of their reciprocity-rating within the community. Those around them should feel comfortable in their presence. Again: 'It is also characteristic of the Great-Hearted Man never to ask help from others, or only with reluctance, but to render aid willingly; and to be haughty towards men of position and fortune, but courteous towards those of moderate station, because it is difficult and distinguished to be superior to the great, but easy to outdo the lowly, and to adopt a high manner with the former is not ill-bred, but it is vulgar to lord it over humble people (*tois tapenois*): it is like putting forth one's strength against the weak' (1124b18–23). Presumably, his haughty behaviour is towards those (like the Characters) who have position and fortune without the necessary virtue; but 'rendering aid willingly' at first seems to contradict his 'bad memory for benefits received'. In fact, the Great-Hearted Man is not bothered about balancing out reciprocity, being ready instead to 'give without counting the cost'. This unconventional attitude is apparently confirmed by his abandonment of the principle of 'helping friends and harming enemies': 'He does not bear a grudge, for it is not a mark of greatness of soul to recall things against people, especially the wrongs they have done you, but rather to overlook them' (1125a3–5).[292]

The distinctive behaviour of the Great-Hearted Man suggests a location for the *Characters*. What emerges from Characters' actions is not how to be a good man; nor even necessarily how to be a good citizen. Rather the message is how to be good at being a citizen in the context of a democratic polis.[293] There is a framework for articulating this distinction in Aristotle's approach to justice and citizenship in Book 3 of the *Politics*. The virtues highlighted by Aristotle (and Theophrastus) are naturally those appropriate to citizens of a polis. In an ideal polis, where all citizens possess a full measure of virtue, being a good man and a good citizen will coincide. But in reality, the relationship is blurred. Aristotle draws the analogy of sailors as members of the crew of a ship (1276b20–35). Each has his own different function and virtue (pilot, rower, lookout), but all aim at the preservation of the ship. Similarly citizens share the common function of preserving their community, which is the constitution. 'For this reason the virtue of a citizen is necessarily relative to the constitution. Since there are many forms of constitution, it is clear that there cannot be a single and complete virtue of the excellent, but we do say that a man is good by having one virtue, which is complete. It is clear then that it is possible for someone to be an excellent citizen without possessing the virtue in accordance with which he would be an excellent man' (1276b20–35). The final sentence seems to match the discrepancy between the Great-Hearted Man and Theophrastus' Man derived from the *Characters*. Does the fact that Aristotle classified democracy as a 'deviant' constitution, on the ground that the poor rule in their own interests, mean that being a good citizen in a democracy entails acting contrary to virtue? Or does he envisage the possibility of a good citizen in a deviant constitution possessing genuine virtue? Does Theophrastus in the *Characters* provide a guide to the best that can be hoped for? How far Aristotle's analysis of citizenship and justice in the *Politics* can be mapped onto the Theophrastan account of citizenship remains problematic.[294]

12

THEOPHRASTUS NONESUCH

'What an incomparable work!' (*Che incomparabil opra!*) is how, as in the epigraph to this essay, the *Characters* are acclaimed by Ofelia, joint-heroine of Salieri's opera 'The grotto of Trofonio' from 1785. All ends happily when, after various twists of fortune, she finally marries Artemidoro, her equal in studiousness and keen reader of 'divine Plato'.[295] Readers over the centuries have generally echoed Ofelia and reacted enthusiastically to the *Characters*, endorsing its description by Casaubon as *aureolus libellus*.[296] Inevitably there have been dissenting voices.

But, Theophrastus, it is difficult to meet in one's life men who are exempt from such vices and are total strangers to the wickedness which is shown here. Even a person who is not in every regard wicked stands excluded, however, in a majority of ways, from the chorus of virtuous people. And so, to obey you, it is necessary for us to flee from the sight of all humans; or if we participate in their words and actions, to imitate the spirit of each one of them. But in the latter case, there follows on a swarm of vices and an aversion to virtue; in the former, misanthropy and the reputation of a Timon. In these circumstances it is certainly difficult to take the better part, and on both sides the slope is dangerous.

The same criticism [lack of originality] applies to the tract known as the *Characters* of Theophrastus, a book far more praised than it deserves. In the form now extant it gives a series of portraits of various social vices – all of them forms of littleness or meanness such as are the characteristics of a shabby and idle society. Moreover, the drawing of these characters is not psychologically subtle, as is often asserted. The features brought out are rather those intended for stage characters than those drawn from a careful observation of real life. The book has to me the air of a treatise not copied from the New Comedy, as has been suggested, but rather composed as a handbook of characters for a young author intending to write such comedies. ... In the *Characters* it is the nature of man as shown in an idle and decaying provincial society – the passions and pursuits of people with no public spirit or interests; the virtues are omitted, even the stronger vices, and all the changes rung upon the foibles and vulgarities of everyday life.

The first passage is from a MS of the *Characters* (*Parisinus* 1639), an explicit inter-polation, written in indifferent Greek ('verba semidocti Graeculi' is Casaubon's phrase), in which the author is moved to take Theophrastus to task for seeming to set impossibly high standards of behaviour.[297] The second is by J. P. Mahaffy in his *Greek life and thought from the age of Alexander to the Roman conquest* from 1887 (117–18). Both assessments demonstrate an idea underlying this study: how, in the absence of any explicit guidance from its author, readers of the *Characters* need to construct their own frame of reference. As we have seen, an obvious strategy has been to relate the text substantially to the reader's present, illustrating how 'people don't change'. We know nothing of the circumstances of the anonymous commentator, but he plainly takes the *Characters* as a serious call to proper behaviour in his own present. Arguably, he misreads the message, interpreting it as an injunction to shun all people at fault rather than avoid in oneself the faults they display. An Arabic source attributes to Theophrastus the saying, 'Sometimes there is need to resort to evil people for mutual benefit'.[298]

Mahaffy's verdict is more open to investigation. His criticism of the *Characters* appears in an innovatory attempt to stake out a claim to the Hellenistic period for English readers. He begins by describing, amusingly and ironically, how (xxxiii), 'By a sort of tacit consent the Battle of Chaeronea is considered the minor limit of all that was good and perfect in Greek thought and life.' Schoolboys are therefore doomed to study, in place of the excellent Plutarch (xxxv), 'the intricacies of Demosthenes, the subtleties of Plato, or the contortions of Thucydides'. Mahaffy summarizes the undeniable achievements of the Hellenistic Age in international politics, art, and philosophy (xxxvii–xxxviii). Shattering events in Asia Minor are compared with the 'magnificent fooling' between Demosthenes and Aeschines in Athens after Chaeronea (1–2): 'What matter whether a golden crown was voted to Demosthenes rightly or not? What matter whether a broken-down politician had been honest or not? The world had moved on a century in these eight years.' Such is the context for Mahaffy's assessment of the *Characters* ('This tedious itching to describe types', 118) as the product of decadent Greek particularism. For Mahaffy the solution should have been simple (3): 'An amalgamation therefore of Greek and Macedonian interests was the policy which every true and reasonable patriot should have adopted.'

The reading may be taken further. John Pentland Mahaffy, Fellow and eventually Provost of Trinity College Dublin, and leading conservative member of the Anglo-Irish community, provides for his readers plenty of illustrative parallels of Greeks and Macedonians drawn from contemporary Ireland (6–7). 'But we are quite accustomed in our day to this Home Rule and Separatist spirit, while the very complainants are profiting signally by the greatness and the resources of the empire which they revile and profess to hate.' He goes on to compare opposition to Macedonian rule with 'the outrageous prints circulated in Ireland in our own day that show a ruler may be the soberest, the most conscientious, the most considerate, and yet have terrible things said of him by mere political malcontents.' It is difficult to avoid reading all this (and much more) not as illustrative but rather as formative of Mahaffy's opinions on post-classical Athens and the *Characters* of Theophrastus.[299]

Such a reader-based approach might seem unavoidable. In the absence of any expression of authorial intent or other obvious vectors of composition, the *Characters* in isolation can hardly be read as a 'tract for the times', unless it be the reader's own times. At the other extreme, the *Characters* as a text has been literally 'deconstructed'; dismantled and used as a quarry for the more-or-less sophisticated reconstruction of aspects of contemporary Athenian society. 'Stylish back-up' is Lane Fox's phrase (1996) 128; 'mining' is the term introduced above (40). A more negative metaphor is preferred by Susan Lape with respect to modern uses of Menander (2004) 21–2. She argues that 'the plays cannot be pillaged as a direct source of information for "the way things were" in either the classical or the Hellenistic periods, for the comedy dramatizes the citizenship law in action using its own conventions, themes, plot devices, and formulaic narrative patterns'. An overlapping but not identical set of considerations applies to the *Characters*. In the absence of any plot in the conventional sense and with a set of formulaic patterns unique to the *Characters*, what alternative strategies can the reader to bring to bear, and with what consequences?

A substantial part of this essay on the world of Theophrastus has been concerned with trying to recreate, however speculatively, an alternative range of contexts within which the *Characters* might be read. Of course, there is nothing new about contextualizing the *Characters*. Every commentary marks a fresh attempt to embed the text in appropriate linguistic and cultural settings. As has been seen, there have been repeated attempts to slot the *Characters* into the narrative of events in Athens after Alexander, and also to relate its content to the philosophy of Aristotle or the comedy of Menander. In so far as the approach offered here is different, it aims to supply a range of settings that move beyond the usual literary or philosophical backgrounds. Most immediate is the attempt to establish a context of performance for the *Characters*; notably the Lyceum itself, incorporating intellectual and even physical characteristics. The notion of performance culture, with its emphasis on audience and display, may be extended to the actions of the Characters themselves, and thence to Athenian citizens.

The other key contemporary context is Theophrastus' collected writings; now made accessible through the labours of 'Project Theophrastus'. As well as the botanical and other scientific works (confirming Theophrastus' independent and normative approach as a philosopher-scientist), there are also the extensive fragments and other testimonia. Their use raises questions of method: what about their credibility (are they really from Theophrastus?), the criteria for their survival (are they a typical sample?), and their intellectual coherence (written over perhaps half a century?). Even so, it does seem possible to detect congruence between a significant sample of thoughts and actions attributed to Theophrastus, and a set of values seemingly implicit in the *Characters*.[300] Other Greek texts play their part in locating the *Characters*: Aristotle's Great-Hearted Man (in Michael Pakaluk's interpretation) indicating by contraries the practical side of the *Characters*; Menander (in Susan Lape's revisionist reading) arguing for the continued existence in earlier Hellenistic Athens of democratic, egalitarian values.[301]

A range of non-classical texts has been read against the *Characters*, helping to establish its distinctive qualities. An obvious part is played in this by imitators within the character-genre, from Ariston down to Canetti. Invaluable here is the work of J. W. Smeed (1985), surveying the whole genre of the Theophrastan Character, and simplifying immeasurably the process of identifying significant differences. Between them, Theophrastus' successors help to highlight absence from the *Characters* of overt self-reflexivity, its restricted range of character-types, and the coherence of its values.

It would be fascinating to try to take the comparison further, matching the *Characters* against character-sketches from totally different traditions. Japanese literature offers the possibility in 'Tales of the Floating World'. These are texts intended to accompany woodcuts of members of the 'café society' from early eighteenth-century Kyoto, Osaka and Edo: 'a spendthrift', 'a swaggerer', 'a rake', 'a worthless trio' all from *Characters of worldly young men* by Ejima Kiseki (1715). Superficially, these and other characters seem Theophrastan: brief, witty, and with a moral purpose. But as Howard Hibbett notes in his brilliant study *The Floating World in Japanese fiction* (1959) 63, Kiseki's figures 'lack the precise focus of the Theophrastan genre', with a single character-trait reflected in a range of actions. They are moulded instead by satirical tendencies, tending away from the typical towards individual eccentricities. Interestingly, Hibbett compares Kiseki's sketches with English characters from the seventeenth century in their divergence from the Theophrastan model. All this reinforces Boyce's verdict (1947): 'The pleasure obtained in an attentive reading of Theophrastus is so distinctive that, once having enjoyed it consciously, the reader is not likely to mistake other pleasures for it' (177).

A further selection of non-classical texts provides orientation. The General Prologue to the *Canterbury Tales* clarifies the difference between character-types and individuals; while, in Jill Mann's reading, it indirectly emphasizes the Characters' alienation from the world of work and the visible impact on others of their bad behaviour. Unlike Chaucer, Theophrastus does not ask his audience to suspend moral judgment. 'Know what remains (*ta loipa gnothi*)' in the sense of 'be aware of the consequences' is a saying attributed to Theophrastus, quoted from his *Ethics* by Fulgentius (*Mythologies* 2.1 = FHS&G 468). Peregrine Horden's and Nicholas Purcell's *The corrupting sea* highlights the profile of Mediterranean connectivity in the *Characters*, which has regularly been described as 'parochial'. But more importantly, *The corrupting sea* raises the issue of honour and shame as characteristically Mediterranean values, which can be identified as decisive factors in articulating the Characters. Bernard Williams in *Shame and necessity* demonstrates from a philosophical angle how shame has its part to play in establishing an individual's sense of identity. The testimony of the *Characters* incidentally contributes to countering the view that value systems based on honour and shame are essentially rural phenomena.[302] From their different perspectives on ancient and modern Greece, Virginia Hunter and J. K. Campbell provide frameworks for assessing the role of gossip in linking behaviour within the *Characters* to the values of the wider community. Thorstein Veblen's polemic against late-nineteenth-century 'pecuniary emulation' illuminates the characteristics of leisure and the importance of etiquette for Theophrastus and his audience in establishing and controlling competition.

Against Veblen's predominantly negative view of etiquette (and prevailing views of its irrelevance) may be matched Norbert Elias' influential study of evolving manners as a crucial aspect of what he terms *The civilizing process* (2000).[303] His analysis demonstrates something of the sociological significance of the *Characters* within the tradition of written codes of appropriate behaviour.

Elias' argument starts from the premise that: 'No society can survive without a chan-nelling of individual drives and affects, without a very specific control of individual behaviour' (443). Controlling of these individual impulses, potentially hostile to the wider community, is a function of socio-political institutions, which are in turn directly reflected in the accepted code of etiquette or manners. The English translation of *The civilizing process* is subtitled 'The history of manners'. Standards of conduct correspond to distinctive social structures (59), paving the way for a dynamic analysis. The question Elias seeks to answer is nothing less than: 'How did the extremely decen-tralized society of the early Middle Ages, in which numerous greater and smaller warriors were the real rulers of Western territory, become one of the internally more-or-less pacified but outwardly embattled societies that we call states?' (xii). This involves investigation of the 'sociogenesis of the state': lengthening chains of social interdependence combined with Weber's concept of the 'monopoly of force'; one of the defining features of the state is a monopoly in the exercise of physical coercion (xiii). Acquisition of absolute power is associated with 'restraint and moderation' in the behaviour of individuals; courts became 'style-setting centres' (188). Rulers deployed etiquette to express their own dignity, to make manifest hierarchy within society, and to 'make all others, first and foremost the courtly nobility themselves, aware of their dependence' (189).[304]

There is much here that might seem alien to the context of *Characters*: notably, Elias' emphasis on identifying change through time (how apparently fixed codes of conduct actually evolve); and on the crucial role of the court in centralizing authority, as exemplified through the dissemination of etiquette. But aspects of Elias' method correspond to our current concern with the *Characters*. Not least, there is his close reading of 'manners books' to demonstrate the process whereby actions, apparently trivial in themselves, may acquire far broader social significance. Elias presents as one of his case-studies changing attitudes towards spitting (129–35): from medieval warnings against spitting over the dining-table, to Edwardian advice about concealing the spittoon. The pendant to Theophrastus' 'Offensive Man' (19.10) is surely criticized for spitting across the dining-table; not for spitting in general, or specifically for hitting the wine-waiter. The actual 'Offensive Man' (19.5) seems to spit unthinkingly as he speaks, but his habit of wiping his nose while eating falls foul of advice on etiquette from the thirteenth century onwards (121–9). Comparison might also be drawn between 'the invisible wall of affects which now seems to arise between one human body and another' (60) and criticism of the 'Arrogant Man' (24.12) for refusing to receive visitors while putting on oil, or bathing, or eating.[305] More generally, Elias emphasizes the central position in social life of eating and drinking (53; 72–109); he quotes as illustrative of the new, scholarly literature of manners, Erasmus' own comment on his *Colloquies* (145): 'As Socrates brought philosophy from heaven to earth, so I have led philosophy to games and banquets.'

It is Erasmus' best-selling manner-book *De civilitate morum puerilium* from 1530 that Elias takes as paradigmatic of his analysis of codes of conduct (47–68). The treatise focuses on outward manifestations of posture, gesture, dress and facial expression as external affirmations of the inner person. Elias' presentation of *De civilitate* is reminiscent of our exposition of the *Characters*, save that (as befitted an imagined audience of boys) Erasmus makes the behavioural imperative explicit: 'Clothing, he says now and again, is in a sense the body of the body. From it we can deduce the attitude of the mind' (67). Moreover, Elias infers from the text and its context a character for Erasmus that (with one obvious anachronism) intensifies our appreciation of Theophrastus from the *Characters*. Erasmus manifested (64) 'in a particularly pronounced form, the characteristic self-confidence of the intellectual who has ascended through knowledge and writing, who is legitimized by books, the self-assurance of a humanistic intellectual class who was able to keep his distance even from ruling strata and their opinions, however bound to them he may have been'.[306]

The bearing of Elias' work on the Greek world and even on Theophrastus has occasionally been acknowledged.[307] It is, however, paradoxical that the most revealing text about the *Characters* in the sense of prompting fruitful questions, has regularly been seen as barely relevant. But Nancy Henry has succeeded in reclaiming Eliot's *Impressions of Theophrastus Such* as a crucial item in the character-genre; not least, by virtue of its location right on the boundary. The 'loving laughter in which the only recognized superiority is that of the ideal self' (13) hints at the reading into the *Characters* of 'Theophrastus' Man'. Her description of *Theophrastus Such* (xii) as 'a book about what defines moral character, about how fictional characters are created, and about how the author survives as his or her written text is inherited by successive generations' might be applied directly to the *Characters*. The role of literature in forming rather than merely reflecting and preserving contemporary culture may be open to dispute.[308] But beyond doubt is the way in which the *Characters* has over recent centuries moulded perceptions of Athenian culture both classical and early Hellenistic. That is why it seems important for historians to continue to explore the world of Theophrastus.[309]

What emerges from this inquiry is the simultaneous habitation by the *Character*-writing Theophrastus of at least three worlds: as a natural scientist locked into the wider Mediterranean world of knowledge; as a leading member and then head of the Lyceum; and as a metic-member of Athens. We have seen how a variety of texts disassociates

116 PAUL MILLETT

Theophrastus from the community of citizens. Apart from his non-Athenian origins and the Macedonian connexions of the Peripatetic school, the anecdotal tradition (or a significant part of it) emphasizes his status as an outsider, unable to compete not only with members of the Council of the Areopagus, but even with Athenian women of low social standing. It has been suggested that Theophrastus' monograph 'On piety' (*Peri eusebeias*) was intended as a retrospective defence against the formal accusation of impiety in an Athenian court. The argument is based on the range of respectful references to Athenian religious practices in the surviving sections of 'On piety'.[310] To make out a similar claim for the *Characters*, as an exercise in (re)habilitation, seems simplistic. Rather the text might be read as a practical commentary on living, according to Peripatetic principles, in a democratically oriented polis, with behaviour calculated to reinforce its positive values. It is striking that, as Lane Fox has pointed out (132), the *Characters* contains no overt criticism of democracy nor pokes fun at the *demos*.[311] Overall, such a reading of the *Characters* seems in accord with the broad Peripatetic approach, as summarized by pseudo-Plutarch in *On the opinions of the philosophers* (847F-75A = FHS&G 479): 'Aristotle and Theophrastus and almost all the Peripatetics divided philosophy as follows: the perfect man must be one who both contemplates realities and engages in right actions. ... Again, he investigates how one lives in a fitting manner and how one guides children and how one legislates. For all these subjects are investigated for the sake of action, and such a person is a man of action.'

It would be naïve to imagine that this study, although approximately one hundred times the length of the text it tries to address, constitutes any kind of final or even definitive word on the *Characters*. In spite of all efforts to ground the text in the Lyceum and contemporary Athens, the evolving perceptions of readers will continue to prove decisive. It is salutary to find Steinmetz closing his astute 'Nachtrag' (103) to the *Characters* from 1970 by wondering whether growing interest in ancient Greek society will suggest a new direction for investigation. I decline to speculate about future lines of enquiry, save to suggest that the direct and near-universal appeal of the *Characters* (not just to historians) remains largely unexplained. I do not believe that the literary artistry of Theophrastus-in-the-*Characters* lies entirely or even mainly in apposite choice of concrete detail, crucial though that undoubtedly is. That is possibly why translators and imitators struggle to recapture the engaging qualities of the original. Anderson (1970) remarks feelingly on the 'heavily additive nature' of Theophrastus' descriptions, singling out repeated use of *kai* as a connective as 'extremely bad style by the standards of earlier Greek prose' (vii). Smeed provides a framework for further consideration (5): 'Theophrastus' manner of proceeding seems simple at first, but as one comes to know these short pieces better, one sees that each detail chosen, each habit of speech recorded, each episode related is telling and appropriate, one more significant piece in the design. The art is of the kind that conceals art (and the plain writing conceals it still further).'[312]

Through the blurring of textual corruption can be discerned Theophrastus' skill in guiding the listener or reader through each sketch by subtle variation in the narrator's and the subject's voices: the description of the 'Toady' (2) alternating between reported action and direct speech; the reported speech of the 'Chatterbox' suddenly interrupted by the very direct statement, 'I threw up yesterday' (3.3). There is the way the narrator in his descriptions supplies words appropriate to the Character concerned: the slave bought by the 'Ungrateful Grumbler' referred to as *andrapodon* and then by the Character himself as 'it' (above, 75); the description of the 'Arrogant Man' detailing 'one of his underlings' to act as host as embodying his own view of their inferior status (n. 230). There is added variety in the changing perspective on the Characters as they are viewed in turn by narrator, third parties, and themselves. The 'Talker' (7) is a case in point, doing the talking to others, addressing himself, just occasionally being talked to, ignored, and finally being kept up late by his children. The self-awareness exhibited by the 'Talker' ('It's hard for me to keep quiet') hints at further variation. Are the Characters conscious of their failings? Certainly so with the 'Repulsive Man' (11); possibly with the 'Toady' (2) and 'Self-Centred Man' (15); emphatically not in the cases of the 'Disagreeable Man' (20) and the 'Man of Petty Ambition' (21). Apparently on the defensive at least part of the time are the 'Country-Bumpkin' with his garlic-laden breath (4.2), the 'Offensive Man' (19.2) with his 'congenital ailments', and the 'Illiberal Man' (22.11) over his patched-up shoes.[313]

For historians, approaches to the *Characters* will respond to changed perceptions of Athens in the late-fourth century alongside developments in historical method. There is nothing in the least authoritative about the choice of modern texts against which I have tried to read the *Characters*. On several occasions through this essay there have surfaced the late Keith Hopkins' writings on the practice of ancient history: his creative use of ideas from other disciplines (n. 158); his demonstration of the need for clear 'rules of evidence' in the writing of history (n. 139); the use of literary fiction to write social and cultural history (n. 158). Let him have (almost) the final word: 'I used to think that further research and learning would fill the gaps in our knowledge. And sometimes that happens. But filling all the gaps in the historical record is a positivist delusion – or nightmare. Behind the deceptive veil of a partial source there is no solid reality to be discovered – only more veils.' In the case of the *Characters* we are fortunate in possessing such an attractive and apparently unending collection of veils.[314]

ENDNOTES

1. FHS&G 7A (Cicero); 7B (Quintilian). The translation from *Brutus* has been altered to express the force of *percontaretur*: 'press' rather than 'ask', justifying the woman's pointed response. Although neither text identifies her as a market-trader, the assumption is defensible. *hospes* presumably stands for *xenos* in the Greek original, if there were one. The linguistic phenomenon is familiar, introduced by Maria Edgeworth in chapter 1 of *The absentee* (1988) 5: 'The extraordinary precision of her London phraseology betrayed her not to be a Londoner, as the man who strove to pass for an Athenian was detected by his Attic dialect.' (I owe this reference to James Diggle.)

2. Though Mejer (1998) 15–16 thinks that, given its attribution solely to Theophrastus, the anecdote is probably 'more than just biographical fiction'. As suggested below (25–6), it may be constructed to coincide with an aspect of Theophrastus' perceived persona.

3. For possible implications of Theophrastus' (new) name, see below, 26. Does Cicero intend a close correspondence in relative status between Tinca and Granius, and Theophrastus and the old woman? The ambivalent status of Granius as a prominent *praeco* is well brought out by Rauh (1989) 455–6: descended from a Campanian family, but an associate (albeit unequal) of prominent senators, including Caius Marius. The position of Tinca is difficult to locate; presumably of high status in his own community of Placentia, which however remained a colonia Latina until 89 BC. Quintilian (1.5.12) has Hortensius also refer to Tinca's non-standard Latin.

4. References throughout are to the *Characters* as newly divided by Diggle (2004), whose translation is also adopted, with minor alterations. All those working on the *Characters* tend to have their treasured renderings. For the *aponenoemenos* (6), I favour the 'Morally Degraded Man' (for Diggle, the 'Man Who Has Lost All Sense'). My labelling of the second half of the *areskos* or 'Obsequious Man' (5.6–10) as the 'Conspicuous Consumer' is explained below, 99.

5. Millett (1991) 5–6 with 244 n. 7. For use of material concentrated within specific Characters, see n. 160.

6. The best text of Diogenes' *Life* (with commentary) is by Sollenberger (1985), with Sollenberger (1987); reprinted (with translation) in FHS&G vol. 1, 20–47. For ancient materials relating to the life of Theophrastus: Mejer (1998) 8–28, with Dorandi (1998), Sollenberger (1992) 3852–5 and Fortenbaugh (1998) on the reliability of Diogenes' catalogue of Theophrastus' writings.

7. Details of Project Theophrastus in FHS&G 1 vii–viii, 1–14, with up-to-date information on the Project Theophrastus website. 'Monographs' means Opuscula, preserved independently in MSS (but excluding the botanical works and *Characters*); 'Fragments' includes testimonia. It is intended that coverage should in time extend over the entire 'School of Aristotle'. For the reader's convenience, titles appearing to date (with six further volumes promised) are as follows:

> Fortenbaugh, W. W., Huby, P. M., Sharples, R. W., Gutas, D. (1992–3) (eds.) *Theophrastus of Eresus: sources for his life, writings, thought and influence*, 2 vols., Leiden.
> Sharples, R. W. (1998) (ed.) *Sources on physics*, commentary vol. 3.1, Leiden.
> Huby, P. M. (1999) (ed.) *Sources on psychology*, commentary vol. 4, Leiden.
> Sharples, R. W. (1995) (ed.) *Sources on biology (human physiology, living creatures, botany)*, commentary vol. 5, Leiden.
> Fortenbaugh, W. W. (2005) (ed.) *Sources on rhetoric and poetics*, commentary vol. 8, Leiden.
>
> Comparable in scope are two independent publications:
> Szegedy-Maszak, A. (1981) (ed.) *The* Nomoi *of Theophrastus*, New York.
> Fortenbaugh, W. W. (1984) (ed.) *Quellen zur Ethik Theophrasts*, Amsterdam.
>
> New editions of Opuscula appearing to date:
> van Raalte, M. (1993) (ed.) Theophrastus of Eresus, *Metaphysics, with an introduction, translation and commentary*, Leiden.

Fortenbaugh, W. W., Sharples, R. W., Sollenberger, M. G. (2003) (eds.) Theophrastus of Eresus, *On sweat, On dizziness*, and *On fatigue*, Leiden.

Collected papers published in the companion series, Rutgers University Studies in Classical Humanities:

vol. 1, Fortenbaugh, W. W. (1983) (ed.) *On Stoic and Peripatetic ethics: the work of Arius Didymus*, New Brunswick, NJ.

vol. 2, Fortenbaugh, W. W. (1985) (ed.) *Theophrastus of Eresus: on his life and work*, New Brunswick, NJ.

vol. 3, Fortenbaugh, W. W., Sharples, R. W. (1988) (eds.) *Theophrastean studies: on natural science, physics, ethics, religion and rhetoric*, New Brunswick, NJ.

vol. 5, Fortenbaugh, W. W., Gutas, D. (1992) (eds.) *Theophrastus: his psychological, doxographical, and scientific writings*, New Brunswick, NJ.

vol. 6, Fortenbaugh, W. W., Mirhady, D. C. (1994) (eds.) *Peripatetic rhetoric after Aristotle*, New Brunswick, NJ.

vol. 8, van Ophuijsen, J. M., van Raalte, M. (1998) (eds.) *Theophrastus: reappraising the sources*, New Brunswick, NJ.

vol. 12, Fortenbaugh, W. W., White, S. A. (2004) (eds.) *Lyco of Troas and Hieronymus of Rhodes: text, translation, and discussion*, New Brunswick, NJ.

W. W. Fortenbaugh's many contributions to the better understanding of Theophrastus are collected in his *Theophrastean studies* (2003).

8. Also of prime importance is Robin Lane Fox's study 'Theophrastus' *Characters* and the historian' (1996), which deals authoritatively with key aspects of the *Characters* and the writing of history. As will be seen, I rarely disagree with his analysis. It might seem testimony to the historical richness of the *Characters* that, so soon after Lane Fox, things remain to be said. The pioneering study by Schnayder (1962) on sociology in Theophrastus has the virtue of encompassing other works by Theophrastus, but perversely insists that the Characters are depicted 'in einer anonymen Stadt' (22). Giglioni (1980) has comment on interpersonal relations between the Characters and detailed discussion of their notional social status (below, 44). Leppin (2002) complements my analysis at a number of points (below, n. 307). 'The world of Theophrastus' as recreated by P. M. Fraser (1995) overlaps with a small though crucial corner of my own conception of his world (see below, 54).

Earlier literature on all aspects of Theophrastan studies is surveyed in the entry in Pauly-Wissowa by Regenbogen, 'Theophrastos von Eresos' (1940); supplemented by 'Theophrastus' in *Der neue Pauly* (vol. 12.1, cols. 385–93).

9. Substantial reviews appearing to date: Hinz (2005), Parker (2006), Halliwell (2006). Selected material appearing in the 'Introduction' to Diggle's commentary was presented in his earlier 'The *Characters* of Theophrastos' (2002).

10. The titles *ethikoi charakteres* and *charakteres ethikoi* are preserved by Diogenes (see FHS&G 436.4a-c); persuasively defended by Diggle (4–5) against the bare *charakteres* of the MSS. Fortenbaugh (2005) 87–8 speculates that the double entry in Diogenes' list represents the purchase by the Library at Alexandria of two copies with differently ordered titles. The development of *charakter* from the physical imprint on a coin to the metaphorical stamp of distinguishing features is briefly traced by Diggle. The presentation by Euripides of *charakter* as type (*via* the metaphor of money), in contrast to the idea of an individual, is analysed by Seaford (2004) 152–5. For Theophrastus' likely contribution, see Körte (1929); Milbradt (1974) esp. 1419–22.

11 According to Diggle (2004) 20, 'probably the corruptest manuscript tradition in all of Greek literature'. 'It may almost be said that our book has been written by the critics', is how Mark Pattison (1870) opened his lukewarm review of Jebb's edition. Problems of proemium, definitions, interpolations and moralizing conclusions (1, 2, 3, 6, 8, 26, 27, 28, 29) are summarily dealt with by Diggle in 'Authenticity and integrity' (16–19), and in detail in the commentary; cf. Diggle (2002) 58–61. The final blow to the definitions was delivered by Stein (1992), who supplies detailed commentary on substantial parts of the text.

A conspectus of possible interpolations has been compiled by Navarre (1924) xxviii–xxxiv on the basis of Diels' Oxford Classical Text (1909).

12. *P. Herc.* 1457; detail in Diggle (2004) 50. The brief tailpiece to the 'Offensive Man' is not particularly striking; there have been unconvincing attempts to assimilate the Character's vaguely tasteless behaviour to that of the *bdeluros* (11). More significant is the extensive addition to the 'Obsequious Man', suggestive of a publicity-seeking spendthrift. Suggested titles include *apeirokalos, banausos, megaloprepes,* and *philotimos*; detail in Diggle (222–3), who notes the overlap between 5.6–10 and Aristotle's *banausos* and *chaunos* (*Nicomachean ethics* 1123a19–27, 1125a27–32). In neither case is correspondence quite complete: the *banausos* spends money on 'public' occasions (providing a sumptuous dinner for his *eranistai*; extravagantly equipping a comic chorus); *chaunoi* are said to 'undertake honourable responsibilities of which they are not worthy'. The supplement to the 'Obsequious Man' (as it survives) is concerned exclusively with personal expenditure.

We can only guess at the original title; here is another guess. Hesychius (no. 100 = FHS&G 449B) glosses *salakoniasai* (to behave pretentiously): 'They used to call people who give themselves airs *salakones*, from stepping delicately and with daintiness. But Theophrastus says that the man who spends money where it is not necessary (*hopou me dei*) is *salakon.*' The passage in question is very likely preserved in a long quotation or paraphrase from Stobaeus (*Anthology*, 2.7.20 = FHS&G 449a), where Theophrastus argues about ethics along Aristotelian lines, with *salakoneia* (extravagance) and *mikroprepeia* (shabbiness) as the outlying co-ordinates of *megaloprepeia* (magnificence). 'Neither the man who is *lampros* (splendid) on all occasions, even when it is not right, nor the man who never is, is *megaloprepes*, but the man who in accordance with *kairos* adapts himself to the individual case.' Three passages from Aristotle help fill out the sense of *salakoneia*. Most of the details fit the fragment from Theophrastus, to whom Hesychius does after all attribute a different emphasis for *salakon. Magna moralia* (1192b2–5): 'He who is lavish in the wrong place is *salakon*. A man, for example, who entertains the members of his club with all the lavishness of a wedding feast is *salakon*; such being the name we give to one who displays his wealth on the wrong occasion.' *Eudemian ethics* (1221a35–6): 'Likewise the *mikroprepes* and the *salakon*, the one oversteps what is fitting, the other falls below what is fitting.' *Rhetoric* (1391a3): 'The characters which accompany wealth are plain for all to see. ... They are luxurious and swaggerers (*trupheroi kai salakones*), luxurious because of their luxury and display of their prosperity, swaggerers and ill-mannered because all men are accustomed to devote their attention to what they like and admire, and the rich suppose that what they themselves are emulous of is the object of all other men's emulation.' The passages from Stobaeus and Hesychius and the relationship between them are discussed in detail by Fortenbaugh (1984) 167–75.

My detailed reasons for labelling the part-Character 5.6–10 as the 'Conspicuous Consumer' are given in chapter 11.

13. Bibliographical detail and critical estimates by Diggle (2004) 52–7. Missing from my list is the consortium of eight scholars (Bechert, Cichorius, Giesecke, Holland, Ilberg, Immisch, Meister, Ruge) from the Philological Society of Leipzig which published in 1897 a text and commentary that still has much to offer the historian.

14. The idea is borrowed from Edmonds and Austen (1904) xxxv–xxxix, who include in their tabulation titles from Needham's Latin version of 1712 and Howell's English translation of 1824. There are no entries under 29 and 30 for Healey and La Bruyère as the MS containing those Characters had yet to be rediscovered. Rusten (2002) offers a North-American perspective ('Sponging', 'Chiseling'), with brief 'Additional notes' (145–59) on Greek trait-names and his own colloquial titles. There are also English translations by Eustace Budgell (1713; reprinted as late as 1929), Henry Gally (1725), prefaced by an extensive 'Critical essay on characteristic-writings', and Richard Aldington (1924) 27–51. To the German translation by Klose (1970) is appended a wide-ranging 'Nachtrag' (87–103) by Steinmetz.

15. For *aponoia* the Leipzig edition (1897) suggests (in English) 'Moral Insanity'; for Leppin (2002) 41 he is a 'Desperado'; for Janko (1984) 199 the 'Desperately Reckless Man'. Zimmern (1961) 313 n. 1 writes enigmatically: 'The Greeks called him Reckless (though we should not).' For a personal preference, see n. 4.

16. Clausen (1946) makes out a strong case for Casaubon's 1599 edition (newly incorporating *Characters* 24–8) as the inspiration for English imitators. The argument for Hall's *Characters of Vertues* as the first work of literature to be translated from English into French is set out in Kirk's edition (54–7).

17. In a remarkable preface, Navarre deplores the 'snobisme' which has caused scholars to defer to German learning. While not denying 'les mérites éminents de l'érudition d'outre-Rhin', he reckons there are areas where French scholarship is at least equivalent. He singles out for special mention the *Dictionnaire des antiquités* by Daremberg and Saglio: 'precieux recueil qui ... peut soutenir victorieusement la comparison avec n'importe quelle publication de l'étranger'; concluding that the time has at last come for France to assert her proper rights, in philology, 'comme en tout autre domain'. Two years later, the French occupied the Ruhr.

18. The *Characters* imaginatively, if tendentiously, prefaced Vellacott's translation of Menander. It is a pity that the later Penguin *Menander* (translated by Norma Miller) dropped the *Characters*, which is therefore no longer easily acquired by non-specialist readers.

19. Innovative as including (apart from the tabulation of translated titles) a still helpful thematic index and more than twenty apposite illustrations. We perhaps take for granted the ease with which illustrations of ancient 'everyday life' are now available. But not inevitably; compare the strictly utilitarian text and commentary from 1991 by Elizabeth Bobrick.

20. The phrase occurs in Momigliano's review (1965) of Hignett's book.

21. In his account of censoring the *Characters* (vii–viii), Jebb is apologetically on the defensive. For the record, his omissions are: 4.7, 6.5, 11.2, 13.8, 15.5, 19.3–5, 20.6, 27.9. Far less revealing of the man is Jebb's *Life and letters* (1907), compiled by his wife; more forthcoming about 'poor Uncle Dick' is Gwen Raverat's *Period piece* (1952) esp. 67–70. See Diggle (2004) 318 n. 64 for Jebb's misinterpretation of the *bdeluros*'s behaviour through his own attitude to parcel-carrying in public (cf. 370 n. 84). Jebb's *Characters* is located in the context of his other editions by Stray (forthcoming). Easterling (2005) 31 gives a favourable verdict on Jebb's efforts at producing a translation of the *Characters* attractive to non-classicists. The success of Jebb's edition may be indicated by its having apparently served as the model for the only explicit imitation of the *Characters* across 150 years of *Punch* magazine: 20 March (1901) 216 (here reproduced as Appendix 2).

22. The most convenient source for the character-collections by Hall, Overbury, Earle, La Bruyère (in translation) and others remains Richard Aldington's *Book of 'Characters'* (1924); though his version of La Bruyère is abridged and the information that (2) 'a short leader in the Times of the 11th October, 1923, contained a neat *Character of a Plain Man*' is incorrect. The field of characters down to the seventeenth century is rapidly surveyed by Ussher (1966). Details of editions of individual collections are given by Smeed (1985) 339–81. Citations in text and notes are from: Joseph Hall, *Heaven upon Earth* and *Characters of Vertues and Vices*, ed. R. Kirk (1948), including as an Appendix (199–303): 'A Description of A good and Faithfull Courtier'; Thomas Overbury, *The Overburian Characters*, ed. W. J. Paylor (1936): only a minority of the characters attributed to Overbury is by him; John Earle, *Microcosmography*, ed. W. H. D. Rouse (1899), handily including Healey's translation of the *Characters*; Jean de La Bruyère, *Les Caractères*, ed. R. Garapon (1962); William Thackeray, *Book of Snobs*, ed. 'L. M' (1895); Elias Canetti, *Earwitness*, trans. J. Neugroschell (1979). A catalogue of translations and possible imitations of the *Characters* in English down to 1941 has been compiled by Greenough (1947).

There are brief discussions of Theophrastus in light of his imitators in the editions of the *Characters* by Jebb (1909) 22–3, Anderson (1970) xxi–xxxii, and Ussher (1993) 27–31. Navarre unfolds the relationship between 'Théophraste et La Bruyère' (1914). Gordon's early essay on 'Theophrastus and his imitators' (1912) has plenty of good ideas. Kapsalis (1982) introduces otherwise unfamiliar examples of modern Greek character-collections (Dimitrios Darvaris, Charisos Megdanis, Andreas Laskaratos), but the differences he identifies between ancient and modern are not illuminating.

23. So Sandys in his preface to the second edition of Jebb's *Characters* (1909) x–xi; Bennet and Hammond (1902) xix n. 1; Ussher (1993) xiv, as an epigraph.

24. Theophrastan allusions from the opening pages of *Theophrastus Such*; references are to the edition by Nancy Henry (1994): (1) 'a dead philosopher' is presumably Theophrastus himself; (1) singing an exquisite passage out of tune: the 'Offensive Man' (19.9) hums the accompaniment causing the flute-girl to stop playing; (1) foreign accent in ears of native speaker: Cicero-Quintilian anecdote, see above, 1–2; (2) persevering in behaviour distasteful to a woman being pursued: the 'Tactless Man' (12.3) serenades his *eromene* who has a fever; (2) ostentatiously dancing the hornpipe: the 'Late Learner' (27.15) practises dance-steps with women nearby.

25. Stange (1980) 327–8 offers persuasive arguments that Eliot models Theophrastus Such's childhood experiences on her own provincial origins. Henry (1994) viii–ix highlights Eliot's isolation from London society and estrangement from her own family.

26. Summary of content by Henry in Rignall (2000) *s.v. Impressions of Theophrastus Such* (174–5); cf. Haight (1968) 521–2.

27. Subsequent Theophrastan touches: 'freedom of observation as an exceptional case of evil-speaking' (6): the *kakologos* (28.6); 'the loudest grumbling at the heaviest war-taxes' (14): the *oligarchos* on liturgies and trierarchies (26.5); Theophrastus Such 'clad in the majestic folds of the himation' (16): Characters repeatedly described through their *himatia* (below, 83); 'Lentulus' walking in the Mall (46): the *oligarchos* (26.4) in the Agora; 'A Too Deferential Man' (48) cognate with Theophrastus' *areskos* (5); description of Touchwood via accumulated actions in the manner of Theophrastus (56–7): notably, his resentful compliance to a request for benevolence echoes the *authades* (15.7); 'The Watch-Dog of Knowledge' (67): the watch-dog of the people' (29.5); 'The excessive talker' (113): the *lalos* (7). Might Merman's 'miscellaneous periodical writing and multifarious study of moral and physical science' (29) hint at Theophrastus himself?

28. See also Henry's entry on *Impressions of Theophrastus Such* in Rignall (2000). She places *Theophrastus Such* in its political context with regard to Eliot's other writings in 'George Eliot and politics' (2001) and *George Eliot and the British Empire* (2002) 109–40. The edition by D. J. Enright (1995) is disappointing. Apart from placing Theophrastus in the wrong century (xix), misidentifying the 'Aeolic lyrists' (157–8), and misplacing the River Strymon (158), he invariably misquotes the title as '*The Impressions…*'. Ironically, a much earlier occurrence of this error in a publisher's advertisement caused alarm to Eliot herself (*Letters*, vol. 7, 144, from 1 May 1879).

29. Stephen's words are quoted ninety years later by McSweeney (1991) 143, who adds, 'The overall impression made by the *Impressions* is one of tediousness'; for Bennet (1962) 52, they are 'disappointing essays'. Against the trend, Stange (1980) seeks to relate *Theophrastus Such* to Eliot's earliest work and locate it in the tradition of English essay-writing.

30. 'Hep! Hep! Hep!' is an anti-Semitic cry of uncertain origin which caused some bafflement to Eliot's publishers (*Letters*, vol. 7, 94, from 14 Jan. 1879). The chapter as a whole criticizes Christian hostility towards Jews and supports the idea of a modern Jewish nation, reflecting implicitly on English nationality, in which the heritage of language forms a crucial part. Theophrastus Such compares his response to the murdering of Shakespeare in after-dinner readings with the reaction of an ancient Greek 'resuscitated for the sake of hearing Homer read in our universities' (159).

31. These apparent allusions to Theophrastus are identified by Henry (1994) xxx–xxxi; 171 nn. 9–10.

32. On 2 Jan. 1873 Eliot wrote to Sidney Colvin, Fellow of Trinity: 'I was very glad to see Mr. Jebb, for I had a pre-established respect for him, and should willingly have invited him' (*Letters*, vol. 5, 359); for Jebb's own impressions, see his *Life and letters* (1907) 154–7. According to Haight (1968) 448, it was while wintering in Geneva in 1849 that she became interested in Isaac Casaubon, 'and knew his fine edition of Theophrastus'. The context is Haight's discussion of the alleged identification of Rev. Casaubon in *Middlemarch* with Mark Pattison (448–9, 563–5). Haight comes down forcefully against the association, which is cautiously resurrected by Nuttall (2003) 72–83: a fascinating study of perceptions of scholars and scholarship, encompassing Browning, both Casaubons, Pattison and Housman.

   Eliot's knowledge of classical literature was extensive; the range of her reading in Greek and Latin is summarized by Haight (1968) 195, and in 'Classical Literature' in Rignall (2000). Selected classical allusions in her novels are briefly examined by Rendall (1947); her construction of 'a new Antigone' in *Romola* and *Middlemarch* is explored in detail by Laura McClure (1993). Eliot's 'fervency of enthusiasm' for the Greeks is traced by Jenkyns (1980) 112–32, who regards *Daniel Deronda* as her last novel and does not discuss *Theophrastus Such*.

33. *Letters*, vol. 7, 130, from 9 April 1879. The quotation from Phaedrus (Prologue to Book 3, 45–50) refers to the danger of appropriating for oneself what belongs to everyone, and the author's desire not to single out any particular person for analysis, but rather to show the truth about life itself and the behaviour of mankind.

34. The sentence-long quotations are from Virgil, *Aeneid* (6.663), itself embedded in a French quotation from Sainte-Beuve, and from Phaedrus (2.5.3). More direct (but not necessarily straightforward) are references to the Delphic Sibyl (51), the schools of Magna Graecia (73), Dido (74), Circe's herd (83), Scaliger (91), Antinous (100), and Augustus (164).

35. The complaint is from a review in the *Athenaeum* by Joseph Jacobs; details of this and similar reactions are given by Henry (1994) xiii–xiv. Bulwer Lytton caught something of the book's problematic character in a letter to Eliot: 'Theophrastus is a great book, eminently wise. I wonder how many of the exquisite subtleties have by this time penetrated the coarse cuticle of that snorting Behemoth the British public. To me it is a tantalizing book only from what is perhaps one of its chief merits – as a work of art. It opens and indicates so many avenues of reflection which one would wish to penetrate further in the company of and under the guidance of its author...' (*Letters*, vol. 9, 297–7, from 22 Feb. 1880).

36. As indicated by the scope of the endnotes in Henry's edition. She argues elsewhere (1997) 45 that *Theophrastus Such* is 'decipherable in full only when seen as a dialogue with Lewes, which, reflecting both their careers, consistently yokes art and science'.

37. Eliot's 'special devotion' to La Bruyère is detailed by Stange (1980) 314 n. 6, who sees the influence of his *Caractères* as 'the guiding spirit' of *Theophrastus Such* (324–6).

38. I do not understand how Enright (1995) can write of *Theophrastus Such* that (xxi): 'There is no fashionable ambiguity or irony, no "subverting" shifts of perspective or authorial stance, no dodging about between different levels of discourse.' Quite the reverse, and without the need for Enright's pejorative tone.

39. Henry (1994) 179 connects Eliot's Euphorion with the Hellenistic poet and also with the son of Achilles and Helen. But given the context, a more likely model might seem to be Euphorion, son of Aeschylus, who allegedly won four prizes by producing his father's unperformed plays (*Suda* s.v. *Euphorion*).

40. Nancy Henry suggests to me that Eliot's assumption of the role of editor would have put her in the place of Casaubon, further blurring the boundaries between author and character.

41. Smeed (1985) 121 identifies *Theophrastus Such*, with its more extended psychological analysis, as 'not so much an attempt to resuscitate character-writing as an unwitting demonstration of what happens to the "character" in the hands of the novelist'. He briefly analyses elsewhere (284–8) the evolving relationship between theories of character, the humours and personality. Jebb (1909) 22–3 makes commonsense comments on the differences between a Character or Portrait and the development of character in the hands of a novelist: connected actions with scope for authorial comment. In a collection of essays assessing *Characterization and individuality in Greek literature*, Gill (1990) discusses 'The character-personality distinction' with reference to Homer and Tragedy. Theophrastus puts in a brief appearance in Halliwell's 'Traditional Greek conceptions of character' (1990) as representative of the literary line (less elevated than Homer and the earlier tragedians) embracing iambus, parody and comedy, which offers scope for (57) 'precisely the everyday, even the sordid, detail which higher genres consciously exclude'.

42. For an explicit interpolation, addressing Theophrastus directly and taking him to task, see 110.

43. Survival as precarious in that the part we possess of Ariston's *Peri tou kouphizein huperephanias* exists by virtue of being quoted by Philodemus in his *On vices*, which in turn survives as a papyrus from Herculaneum; text and translation conveniently in Rusten (2002) 166–75. Not only form, also content of the sketches is thoroughly Theophrastan, with much to say about etiquette and reciprocity. An earlier

description of a drunkard by Lycon, Theophrastus' successor-but-one as head of the Lyceum, is preserved in a Latin translation (*De figuris sententiarum* 2.7) by Rutilius Lupus, a rhetorician of the first century AD: translation in Boyce (1947) 22–3. Its form, narrating the drunkard's experiences through a single day, is not obviously Theophrastan; nor is its overt moralizing, opening with: 'What hope remains for him who spends all his life in a single, despicable habit?'

44. Hall as the 'Christian Seneca' (alternatively the 'English Seneca') is a theme of the introductory essay (1–65) to Kirk's edition of *Heaven upon Earth* and *Characters of Vertues and Vices*. Kirk persuasively reads *Characters* as the 'literary sequel' (published two years later) to *Heaven upon Earth*, giving practical application to its neostoical ideas.

45. For Aldington (1924) 14, Hall is 'an Anglican divine commending and reproving as a Christian, not without point and wit, sometimes with a flourish of the ornate prose of the age... The defects of Hall's *Characters* are that they are not sufficiently exact; they tend to be allegorical personifications; that he pursues wit and does not always find it.' Müller-Schwefe (1972) 246–7 leaps to Hall's defence: how he enriches his *Characters* with a wealth of concrete elements, detail based on observation, and allusion to topical events. He was, after all, quite a man of the ecclesiastical world. After leaving Cambridge, where he studied and lectured on rhetoric, Hall held two livings and a deanship, before becoming Bishop of Exeter and, as the twelve volumes of his collected works bear witness, taking part in contemporary religious debates. Smeed (1985) 20–4 locates Hall stylistically mid-way between Theophrastus and the remainder of character-writers from the sixteenth century; which is more-or less the position adopted in my text. He also reminds the reader of Hall's assumption that proemium, definitions and moralizing conclusions were from the pen of Theophrastus. The impulse felt by English character-writers to imbue their imitations with moral comment rather than satiric observation is examined by McCabe (1995).

46. Smeed (1985) 48–63 identifies as distinctive to the French tradition of character-writing the blurring of 'portrait' and 'character'. In England, the portrait was reserved for depictions of famous individuals; for a good sampling, including 'John Earle' by Clarendon (168–70), see Smith (1918). La Bruyère combines the two genres, shifting seamlessly between individuals and types. It is from the French portrait tradition that he derives his practice of giving his subjects classical names.

　　Closeness of literary relationship between La Bruyère and Theophrastus is asserted by Navarre (1924), who includes a list of correspondences (421–26). Cazelles (1922) demonstrates the extent of La Bruyère's dependence in arriving at his French version on the Latin translation by Casaubon. The care with which La Bruyère adapted his translation and commentary to the requirements of his readers is defended in a sequence of articles by van de Woestijne (1933, 1934a, 1934b).

47. As originally published in *Punch* there were fifty-four chapters. Given the number of reprints with different paginations and the shortness of each chapter, I refer to chapters in addition to page numbers. Early reprints of *The Snobs of England* in book form omitted at Thackeray's request seven chapters (17–23). These are restored in later editions, as cited in my text and notes.

48. There may be a faint echo of the *Characters* in the satire on name-changing and social advancement: Muggins – Mogyns – de Mogyns (ch. 7, 31–2; cf. *Char.* 28.2: Sosias – Sostratos – Sosidemos), and less faint in recurring Theophrastan descriptions *via* concrete actions: Sir George Granby Tufto (ch. 9, 42); Dinner-giving Snobs (ch. 26, 105); the English Snob abroad (ch. 29, 121). It was believed that the search for accurate local colour concerning 'Club Snobs' led Thackeray to consult the complaint-books of leading London clubs: Thackeray (1895) xiii–xiv. 'As ever,' notes Taylor in his study *Thackeray* (1999) 240, 'it is Thackeray's eye for detail that gives the acid little sketches their bite.' Unlike Theophrastus, but reminiscent of La Bruyère, certain figures in the *Book of Snobs* are identifiable as individuals. The 'Snob Royal' (ch. 3, 2) is plainly George IV; 'On Literary Snobs' (ch. 17, 72) lightly disguises Frances Trollope as 'Mrs. Wollop' and Babington Macaulay as 'Mr. Macau'. There is additional scope for interplay between the text and Thackeray's own drawings. For nineteenth-century illustrations to the original *Characters*, see n. 100.

49. *Punch's* early 'radical years' and concern with the 'Condition of England' are documented in detail by Altick (1997). Thackeray's own political allegiances were mixed; as diagnosed by Peters (1987) 118–42,

apparently more concerned in much of his work with the consequences rather than the causes of flaws in society.

50. Responding to alleged correspondence: 'Having received a great deal of obloquy' (ch. 6, 27); 'Of the many indignant remonstrants who have written' (ch. 17, 71); '"Give us private Snobs," cry the dear ladies' (ch. 25, 99); '"very much obliged to you," says my old school and college companion' (ch. 43, 179). Douglas Jerrold, *Punch's* editor, added to the fun by concocting and printing a letter (signed 'Slaverly Fitztoady') urging the instant dismissal of the unpatriotic author of the 'Snob Papers'; detail in Taylor (1999) 240.

51. While Thackeray was at Cambridge, he contributed to *The Snob*, an undergraduate publication, of which eleven issues appeared in 1829: Taylor (1999) 53. The meaning of 'snob' seems to have evolved from 'shoemaker' to include any tradesman. In Thackeray's Cambridge it apparently referred to townsmen in general, but also acquired the restricted sense of a poor but dedicated scholar (see the *Book of Snobs*, ch. 15, 63–4). The shifting meaning of 'snob' in the *Book of Snobs* (aspiration from below as opposed to contempt from above) is traced by Phillipps (1978) 86–8.

52. It seems inconceivable that Eliot, who described Thackeray in a letter of 1857 (*Letters*, vol. 2, 349) as 'on the whole the most powerful of living novelists', had not read the *Book of Snobs* (or their originals in *Punch*). The evolving relationship between Lewes, Eliot and Thackeray is briefly surveyed in Rignall (2000) *s.v.* 'Thackeray'. It is perhaps significant that whereas *Theophrastus Such* closed Eliot's career as a novelist, the *Book of Snobs* heralded the beginning of Thackeray's.

53. Thackeray's knowledge of Greek and his deployment of classical motifs in the *Book of Snobs* and elsewhere are briefly discussed in Appendix 3.

54. Henry remarks how *Theophrastus Such* 'even when situated in the character-writing tradition, goes so far beyond that genre in its attempt to show the gradual emergence of an author/character who is known only through his own words, that critics still rarely know what to do with it': Rignall (2000) *s.v. Impressions of Theophrastus Such*. Something of the sense of challenge, shared with *Daniel Deronda*, is conveyed in McDonagh's concluding chapter (1977), 'The Shadow of the Coming Age: Modernity and the Limits of Realism'.

55. There is a brief assessment of *Earwitness* by Smeed (1985) 129–31. Here and elsewhere (267) Smeed explains how 'Canetti, in my opinion, shows the boundary beyond which it is impossible to proceed without annihilating the "character".' But he is surely right in identifying as novel in *Earwitness* the absence (crucial for me) of discernible norms, which precludes the dispensing of praise or blame (131): 'We all seem to be on board the same Ship of Fools and it is up to each of us to pick out his or her obsession, vanity or folly.' It is unclear how far Smeed wishes to press the motif of the 'Ship of Fools'; a literary tradition early displaced, as he notes (16), by characters along Theophrastan lines.

56. The sentiment should not be pressed as the attribution to Theophrastus is late and far from secure: Maximus Confessor, *Loci communes* 46 (= FHS&G 519). The translation is also open to argument: 'manner and charm' or 'association and favour'? Theophrastus' preoccupation elsewhere with rules of reciprocity might seem to support the latter; but see the comment by Fortenbaugh (1984) 251.

57. To be precise, the occasion of West's comment was no more than an aside (121 n. 29) in a paper on 'Near Eastern material in Hellenistic and Roman literature' (1969). For earlier assessments of the *Characters* as a compilation, see Diggle (2004) 13 n. 40.

58. For details of the various theories and their leading proponents, see Diggle (2004) 12–16; Lane Fox (1996) 139–42; Fortenbaugh (2005) 89–92; Matelli (1989) 329–35. Included here *exempli gratia* is only a representative and relatively accessible sample. Ethical connexion: Stark (1960); Steinmetz, (1959), defending the Peripatetics against philosophical rivals: how ordinary people don't change. Rhetorical models: Gordon (1912) 54–6; Furley (1953); Fortenbaugh (1994); Trenkner (1958) 147–54. Handbook of characters for Comedy: Ussher (1977); Steinmetz (1960a); Fortenbaugh (1981). The attempt by Bingen (1980) to develop the philosophical significance of the introductory definitions fails by reason of subsequent research by Stein (above, 3).

59. Diggle highlights stylistic qualities of the *agroikos* (4), *aponenoemenos* (6), *mikrophilotimos* (21) and

opsimathes (27): 'What an ancient biographer said of Sophocles could equally be said of Theophrastus, that he can create a whole personality out of half a line or a single word' (22–3).

60. The view is deeply entrenched. Gordon (1912) 57: 'It is a simple method; plain black and white. The author is out of it.' Aldington (1924) 6: 'They are scientific; plain notes of an impartial moralist.' He notes the coincidence (4–5) that Sainte-Beuve, inventor of the 'literary Portrait', likened himself to 'a botanist of minds'. For Navarre (1914) 384, 421: 'la nudité austère de l'exposition y dénonce une oeuvre de science plutôt que d'art'; by avoiding (in contrast to La Bruyère) all that is picturesque and dramatic, 'il se montre avant tout homme de science, très peu littérateur'. For Capelle (1958, 1959), writing from an admittedly scientific perspective, the appropriate, overall label is 'Theophrast der Beobachter' (170, 40); likewise, from the perspective of the social sciences, Schnayder (1962) 20, 38. The image of the recorder of characters as untouched and untouchable is perpetuated by Canetti in his 'Earwitness' (1979) 43–4 (above, 15).

61. Darwin's words are from a letter to Henry Fawcett, 18 September 1861. The issue is rightly revisited by Lane Fox (1996) 126: 'Nowadays our notions of objectivity and scientific fact are more subtle; ... subjective participants collect and isolate statistical "data"; it is we who interpret them to give us facts.'

62. For a conspectus of references to predecessors in *Inquiry* and in *Causes*, see Einarson and Link (1976) xix–xxii. Theophrastus' engagement with Aristotle's incidental comments on plants is drawn out by Regenbogen (1937). The solitary occasion on which Grote refers to Theophrastus in his *History of Greece* (1846–56) 1 325 n. 1 concerns his role as 'phytologist', rejecting the religious explanations of his predecessors in favour of early scientific rationalism (e.g. *Inquiry into plants*, 2.3, 4.16, 5.3).

63. Sorabji (1998) is in part a response to Algra (1992), who also argues for Theophrastan originality, but differs from Sorabji's earlier paper (1988) in questioning whether Aristotle was his point of departure. Here and elsewhere, the relationship between Theophrastus and Aristotle as thinkers emerges as a complex issue to which there can be no straightforward answer; see the introductory comments to van Ophuijsen and van Raalte (1998) vii. The debate is reflected in microcosm through shifting attitudes towards Aristotle and the *Characters*; for a subtle treatment, see Fortenbaugh (2005) 90–2.

64. Views on the relationship of Theophrastus' *Metaphysics* to Aristotle's work are gathered by van Raalte (1993) 23–5, who herself argues for composition in the first generation after Aristotle.

Mejer's 'A life in Fragments' (1998) was originally delivered at a 'Project Theophrastus' Conference (1993), which collectively considered whether the then new collection of Theophrastus fragments added up to a novel whole. The published papers reflect the range of possibilities. Gottschalk (1998) inclines to the traditional view of the Aristotle-Theophrastus relationship (287–8), though stressing their inter-dependence. Mignucci (1998) concludes that 'his work as a logician is not the humble achievement of a commentator, but the result of a profound and original insight' (64). Barnes (1985) esp. 137–9 argues for Theophrastus as likely inventor of the hypothetical syllogism; compare his brief restatement (2005). Sharples (1998), in a programmatic paper, traces the claims about Theophrastan dependence and orig-inality back to antiquity (267–9), as represented respectively by Boethius (FHS&G 72A) and Quintilian (FHS&G 694). After assessing more recent work, he argues cogently that 'how much Aristotle?' may be the wrong approach; rather, it is sufficient for Theophrastus' reputation as a philosopher that he carried on asking questions and raising difficulties (279–80).

65. Further discussed below (n. 35). The so-called *De nuptiis* attributed to Theophrastus by Jerome (*Against Jovinian* 1.47–8 = FHS&G 486) comes close to supplying a version of the character of a married woman; but her behaviour is captured in terms of words and thoughts rather than through actions. For Webster (1950) 214–16, *De nuptiis* is closer to Menander than is the *Characters*. The fortunes of the *De nuptiis* through time are traced by Schmitt (1971) 259–67, who accepts Theophrastus as the likely author of the Greek original. Fortenbaugh demurs (1983a) 215–16, arguing that its tone is at odds with more positive thoughts on marriage attributed elsewhere to Theophrastus.

66. The allusion is to Virginia Hunter's brilliant characterization of Thucydides as *The artful reporter* (1973). The detailed dissimilarity between *Characters* and the General Prologue is summed up by Smeed (1985) 14–15: the latter introduces vivid but untypical descriptive details (the wart on the Miller's nose),

tending away from the representative towards the particular (see 15). The only mention of Theophrastus by Chaucer refers to the *De nuptiis* ('The Wife of Bath's Prologue' 669–85; cf. 'The Merchant's Tale' 1310).

67. The *philologos* issued by the Leipzig Consortium (1897), allegedly from a papyrus in the Egyptian Museum at Plagwitz ('Jokestone'), is helpfully accessible in the version, complete with translation and commentary, by Fortenbaugh (1978); alternatively, Marcovich (1974). For a more recent and less successful parody, see Marcovich (1976). It may be noted that philosophers find no place in the *Characters*; not if Diggle is correct in ejecting the performing philosophers of 5.10 as an interpolation (supported by *P.Herc.* 1457). By contrast, Theophrastus' seventeenth-century imitators do not exclude their own milieux of church, court and university.

The point about the 'Character' of Theophrastus himself was raised some twelve years ago in an Oxford seminar by Daniel Ogden. It is only recently that I have come to appreciate the significance of his suggestion.

68. See respectively, Fairweather (1974) and Saller (1980). Rusten (2002) 11–12 ingeniously ties in aspects of the *Characters* with what is said elsewhere about Theophrastus: anecdotal evidence for Theophrastus and his pupils dressing and living well, and the absence of any Character criticized for extravagance; his reputation for 'elegant manners and sophistication' related to those Characters lacking in social graces or making themselves foolish in society; his extensive writing on sacrifice (FHS&G 584A-585) and his father's connexion with fulling (Diog. Laert. 5.36 = FHS&G 1.1–2) associated with the relatively high profile of both activities in the *Characters*. But in no case is complete consistency possible. Isn't the 'Conspicuous Consumer' criticized for extravagance? Aren't there anecdotes elsewhere about Theophrastus' asceticism? Don't all the Characters behave foolishly in society? Doesn't attending the Assembly (from which Theophrastus was barred) also figure prominently in the *Characters*? It seems safer (though hardly conclusive) to base comparison on writings and sayings directly attributed to Theophrastus.

The fulling connexion has some history. For Edmonds and Austen (1904) xix, 'His father was a fuller, and in the references to this trade in the Characters we may perhaps see reminiscences of his humble youth.' The implication of rags to riches is to be resisted; Einarson and Link (1976) vii–viii are surely right to assume his father Melantas was the owner: 'un riche industriel' according to Navarre (1921) 13. Alternatively, the fuller-father may be understood as part of an upper-class attempt at denigration. Fairweather (246) observes how ancient biographies are 'full of statements about people's ignoble origins and scandalous conduct'. For the latter, there is the allegation attributed to Aristippus in his *On ancient luxury* (Diog. Laert. 5.39 = FHS&G 1.31–2), that Theophrastus 'was erotically attached to Aristotle's son Nicomachus, even though he was his teacher'. The phenomenon of 'philosophical invective' as it impinged on the Peripatetics is investigated by Owen (1983).

69. I must therefore disagree with Diggle's assessment of the *Characters* (2004) 12, that 'the work lacks all ethical dimensions'. Rather, the ethical elements, so laboriously recreated by Byzantine readers, are implicit in the understanding common to author and original audience. Diggles's verdict on Theophrastus' 'economy of language', prompting the reader to 'supply the thoughts at which he only hints' (21–2; above, 16) may be extended to include ethical concerns.

70. In what follows, 'Lyceum' refers to the philosophical school, 'Lykeion' to the shrine of Apollo and, by extension, the gymnasium there.

71. Sollenberger's translation of the will from FHS&G has been slightly adapted, dropping his parenthetical addition: 'And those who hold [title to] these things'; see below (n. 83) for the reason why. I have also altered his translation of the words *kai pros allelois oikeios kai philikos chromenois* (21). The will is carefully analysed with full bibliography by Sollenberger (1992) 3864–9.

72. Some significances of the terminology are discussed in Millett (1991) 148–9, where Demaratus is missing from the list of *hoi koinonountes*. Possible implications of the Lyceum as constituting one of the *koinoniai* that comprised the polis are discussed by Jones (1999) 227–30.

73. Pompylus reappears as a 'slave-philosopher' in Diogenes' *Life* (5.36 = FHS&G 1.7–9) and in Aulus

Gellius' *Attic nights* (18.8). Hipparchus may put in an earlier appearance in Aristotle's will as acting executor (Diog. Laert. 5.12). The reference to possible 'agreements made in my name in Chalcis' by Hipparchus (5.56 = FHS&G 1.354–5) may conceivably, in light of the striking imagery of his 'ship-wrecked affairs', refer to trading contracts.

74. Brief reports of the excavations by Blackman (1997, 2002); for their precise location (down Rigillis Street, between the Sarogleion Megaron and the Athens Conservatory; opposite 'Hodos Lykeiou'!): Rupp (2002) 81–2. At time of writing (April 2006), the site was emphatically sealed off behind welded metal plates; there was a three-inch squint at the Sarogleion end. Evidence for the traditional location is discussed in detail by Lynch (1972) 16–31. No deduction about ancient Greek topography ever seems entirely secure. Does the new location for the Lyceum square with Socrates' account of his route (Plato, *Lysis* 203a): 'I was on my way from the Academy, making straight for the Lyceum, along the road which runs outside the city wall, close under the wall itself'? Quicker to skirt round the city rather than cut across country?

75. For what is known of the detailed evolution from shrines to gymnasia to places of learning, and their likely physical configuration, see Wycherley (1961, 1962) with (1978) 219–35 and Lynch (1972) 9–16. Forbes (1945) explores 'Expanded uses of the Greek gymnasium', beyond exercise and education. Damage to the Lykeion inferred from Theophrastus' will may reflect its enforced military function: Lynch (1972) 104–5. 'The elementary and informal arrangements of an old gymnasium cannot altogether have sufficed for the encyclopaedic programme for the organization of knowledge on which the Peripatetic school presently embarked', warns Wycherley (1961) 10. Aristotle's book collection is well attested (Athenaeus 5.214d; Strabo 13.1.54 p. 608); but Lynch points out (97–8) that space was also needed for storage of specimens gathered on expeditions in the field. The idea had already caught the middle-class imagination. *Punch* for 6 November 1912 (264) prints a cartoon in the series by George Morrow, 'Episodes in the Lives of the Great'. A collection of exotic animals is led before an astonished Aristotle; the caption reads: 'Alexander the Great sends Aristotle a few specimens of the fauna of Asia to assist him in his great work on natural history.'

76. On the mixing of Agora activities and the philosophic response, see Millett (1998) 211–18. There is an obvious contrast here with the practice attributed to Socrates. Although he is depicted as visiting on occasion all three of the philosophical gymnasia, everything we are told about him suggests his preference for the city. In the *Phaedrus*, this is made explicit. Phaedrus, having invited Socrates to accompany him on a walk in the country, along the River Ilissus, comments on how his companion, once outside the city, resembles a visitor being shown the sights by a guide. Socrates responds that the people in the city have something to teach him; not so fields and trees (230C-D). For Socrates' association with people in the Agora, see Wycherley (1961) 157–8. Closest to my position is Jones (1999) 230–4, who sees the fate of Socrates as prompting the removal of the philosophical schools away from the potentially hostile Agora. He sees this modest distancing (accepting the traditional location of the Lyceum) as discouraging casual visitors.

77. For naming of the 'Conspicuous Consumer', see n. 12. Johnson (1957) 300 reckons that perhaps forty persons are to be imagined as present in the house of Callias, listening to the three sophists. As befitted one of Athens' wealthiest citizens, Callias' place would presumably have been on the large side.

78. 'It is an old story that the philosophical schools of Athens ... bore a notable resemblance to our own Colleges' is how Jackson (1920) 191 begins his classic paper (originally delivered in a Cambridge college) on 'Aristotle's lecture room'; Gordon (in a chapter that began life as a lecture given in Oxford) supplies the imagined detail (1912) 50: 'The School of the Peripatetics was much like an Oxford college. It had its chapel, its cloister, its hall, its garden, its library, its walks and its president's lodgings.' But see below (n. 83) for a recent defence of the Lyceum-as- *thiasos* thesis.

79. The distinction is drawn (and earlier bibliography noted) by Sollenberger (1992) 3865 and by Lynch (1972) 99–103.

80. The Spring-House decree: *IG* I^3 49: translated by Fornara (1983) n. 49; brief discussion by Podlecki (1998) 86–7. It is the case that a century later (333/2), one Pytheas was awarded a gold crown worth 1000 drachmas for having personally paid for piping water to the shrine of Ammon; but he was acting

as Water Commissioner and presumably first sought formal approval from the Assembly for his private expenditure (*IG* II^2 338).

81. For the traditional view of the grant of *enktesis*, see Sollenberger (1992) 3822–3. The debate over Aristotle or Theophrastus as founder of the Peripatetic school is discussed by Lynch (1972) 106–8.

82. The extent of the influence of Theophrastus' teaching over Demetrius of Phalerum is disputed, as is the character of his régime (tyranny or philosophically-minded republic?). The reaction against Ferguson's attribution (1911b) of a new code of laws to Demetrius, moulded by Theophrastus' thinking, as set out in detail by Gehrke (1978), is endorsed by Gottschalk (2000). He points out that the only specific piece of Demetrius' known legislation expressly advised by either Aristotle or Theophrastus was his abolition of liturgies (but see below, n. 203). He concludes that Demetrius was concerned with perceived practical needs rather than preconceived philosophical doctrines (378). Gottschalk's essay appears as one of the discussion-papers accompanying the helpful text and translation of Demetrius' surviving fragments, edited by Fortenbaugh and Schütrumpf (2000). A second essay by Tracy (2000) takes a more positive view both of the influence of Theophrastus (*via* the *Nomoi*) and of Demetrius' style of government. 'The evidence suggests that during his ten-year regency the Athenians probably had in Demetrius a leader whose primary aspiration was to be their philosopher-king' (341). But in a third essay, Michael Gagarin (2000) persuasively questions the role attributed to Demetrius as framer of a comprehensive law-code. 'In addition [to sumptuary legislation] it seems likely that Demetrius created or more likely reconstituted … the boards of *Gynaikonomoi* to oversee women's activities and the *Nomophylakes* to oversee religious and political activity. And that's about it' (352). Gagarin also accepts Gehrke's minimalist approach to Peripatetic influence on the general tenor of Demetrius' régime (354–6). Williams (1987) may demonstrate parallels between Demetrius' legislation and broadly oligarchic ideology, but direct connexion with Theophrastus can be no more than speculative (see 93 for a classic 'must have' argument).

83. My admittedly tentative position is close to that of O'Sullivan (2002), who links Demetrius' favouring of Theophrastus with the subsequent attempt by the restored democracy to control philosophical schools (below, 25). Blurring of public and private avoids Lynch's awkward conclusion (1972) 101 that the Lyceum/Lykeion contained two *peripatoi*: one as attached to the gymnasium, the other being part of Theophrastus' private *kepos*. There is a part-parallel for citizen-associates operating on behalf of non-citizens in the use of citizen-agents by metic and possibly by women money-lenders: Millett (1991) 224–9; Harris (1992). Chroust (1972) suggests, without foundation, that Aristotle used a similar device to acquire possession of the *kepos* in the Lykeion. Grayeff (1974) 50 assumes that Demetrius *altered* the law on land-ownership for the benefit of Theophrastus, which seems unlikely. Whitehead (1981) 228–9 envisages Demetrius as enabling the Lyceum to own real property 'as a *thiasos*, an organized corporate body', harking back to the thesis of Wilamowitz, opposed at length by Lynch (106–34). Whitehead draws an analogy with the grant of land in the Piraeus to merchants of Citium for a temple to Aphrodite, to be held as their collective possession. In a recent, balanced survey of the 'Organization and structure of the philosophical schools', Dorandi (2005) concludes that the schools shared '*thiasos* characteristics' (56), but continues to envisage the Peripatos as a permanent, educational foundation 'much like a funeral association'. 'Ownership and possession are bundles of rights which we package together in particular ways; Athenians may have packaged them differently', is how Stephen Todd closes his account 'Possession and ownership' (1993) 236–43. Familiarity with modern legal concepts makes it difficult to conceive present-day equivalents to ancient ambiguities. Perhaps appropriation and possible conservation of buildings by squatters ('possession is nine-tenths of the law'); or popular uncertainty over ownership of Lord's Cricket Ground: Thomas Lord (owner in name), Middlesex Cricket Club (most frequently in possession), Marylebone Cricket Club (in law).

84. So ranging Theophrastus alongside (in Whitehead's formulations) 'Aristotle the metic' (1975) and 'Xenocrates the metic' (1981); for Dinarchus the metic, see below, 25. Whitehead cautions against unfounded exaggeration (notably on the part of Chroust) of Aristotle's sufferings in Athens by virtue of being a metic, arguing instead for the 'cool objectivity' of his own treatment of metic status in the *Politics*. Alongside misguided attempts to attribute to Aristotle privileged status as a metic (noted by Whitehead)

may be placed Edmonds and Austen's fanciful identification of Theophrastus as an Athenian archon (1904) x: 'The design for the cover [of their book] is taken from a Vase-painting ... which bears the inscription *Theophrastus archon*: but since it was prepared Mr. G. F. Hill has kindly informed us that there is not sufficient evidence to identify him with the author.' On the relative frequency of the name in Athens, see 26.

85. *Suda* 1687 *s.v. sustomoteron skaphes* = FHS&G 654, with a cross-reference from Harpocration, *Lexicon of the ten Attic Orators s.v. skaphephoroi* = FHS&G 653.

86. Whatever the relevance of Aristotle's metic status for his treatment in Athens, his Macedonian connexions, including ongoing correspondence with Antipater, were well established. Düring (1957), in his exhaustive treatment of *Aristotle in the ancient biographical tradition*, collects material on both 'Relations with Philip and Alexander' (284–99) and 'Early invectives against Aristotle' (373–95). According to Grayeff (1974) 13, 'the life of Aristotle ... was determined and formed, more perhaps than that of any philosopher, by the events of the day, by intrigues and political upheavals.' The Athens he left in 347 was apparently in the grip of anti-Macedonian feeling following on the fall of Olynthus. This hostility, rather than Speusippus gaining headship of the Academy, has been offered as Aristotle's motive for quitting Athens; detail in Owen (1983). Grayeff argues (21, 37) that Alexander instigated Aristotle's return in 335 in order to establish a new philosophical school to surpass the Athenian-orientated Academy. Certainly, the Peripatos flourished under Macedonian protection, and suffered when it was withdrawn; witness Aristotle's indictment for impiety in 323, possibly part of the reaction to the reported death of Alexander. He fled to Chalcis, where he enjoyed the protection of a Macedonian garrison, wrote complainingly to Antipater of life in Athens, and died soon after. Lynch (1972) 94–6 traces the further vicissitudes of the Peripatos down to 307 and the decree of Sophocles.

87. For the Macedonian angle as never far from Athenian minds, there are the topics of conversation attributed to the 'Rumour-Monger' (8.6–10) and the 'Boastful Man' (23.3–4). Lane Fox (1994) contrasts the private letters from Antipater claimed by the 'Boastful Man' with the public communications characteristic of the developed democracy (cf. Aeschines 3.250). I cannot, however, see how Peter Green (1990) 38 reads Theophrastus as enjoying through these passages sly digs at the expense of anti-Macedonian aristocrats. Nor do the 'Boastful Man's' claims to familiarity with Alexander and Antipater obviously add up to 'scenes of urban life where the insiders were on very comfortable terms with their Macedonian overlords': Green (2003) 6. In fact, the Character goes on to explain (§4) how he has ignored the right granted to him to ship duty-free timber from Macedon, so as to avoid the attentions of sycophants. He seems to add that the Macedonians would need to be cleverer to compromise him, but Diggle here detects deep-seated corruption: (2004) 437–8.

88. Though Marasco (1984) 42–6 sees Demochares as representative of a generalized antipathy towards philosophers. Demochares' speech, from which hints and one direct quotation survive (Athenaeus, 5.215c, 11.509a-b), apparently attacked philosophers in general and Aristotle in particular for having betrayed both Athens and Stageira to the Macedonians. For his reported jibe at Theophrastus' expense, delivered before the court of the Areopagus, see 25–6. Jones (1999) 227–30 identifies the *koinonia* of the Lyceum and of the other philosophical schools with the range of associations explicitly permitted in the polis by a law attributed to Solon (*Digest* 47.22.4). He suggests that this formed the basis of Philon's successful indictment of Sophocles for making an illegal proposal. Philon himself may reappear as Phil(i)on of Alopece, one of the witnesses to Theophrastus' will (Diog. Laert. 5.57 = FHS&G 361–2).

89. Mari (2003) identifies impiety as a stock charge brought by those promoting Athenian independence against intellectuals held to be pro-Macedonian: Demades (324/3), Aristotle (323/2), Demetrius of Phalerum (c.318), Theodorus of Cyrene (309–5); for Theophrastus (c.318), see 86–8. Green (1990) 68 suggests that the prosecution for impiety hinged on Theophrastus' declaration of the sovereignty of Tyche over human affairs (Cicero, *Tusculan disputations* 5.24–5 = FHS&G 494). Demochares and Hagnonides are compared by Green in his 'Occupation and co-existence' (5) to Gaullist Free-French (Phocion and Demades he likens respectively to Pétain and Laval). Their Free-Athenian credentials are displayed by Habicht (1997) 49, 54, 59, 70–3, 79.

90. What is known of the life of 'Dinarchus the metic' is summarized by Worthington (1992) 3–12, who confronts the problem of this non-citizen addressing an Athenian court.

91. Compare the implication for 'justice for metics' of the behaviour of Theophrastus' 'Obsequious Man' (5.4), criticized for assuring *xenoi* that they have a case that is more just than that of his fellow-citizens; though the context is not necessarily a law-court. For the metic as routinely disadvantaged in court through lack of citizen-support networks ('a peculiarly isolated and thus vulnerable figure'), see Patterson (2000) 94.

92. The story (or a version of it) was known to Proclus (*On Plato's first Alcibiades* 114B-D = FHS&G 32B), who significantly envisages Theophrastus as being disadvantaged by unfamiliar circumstances: 'Therefore objectors ought not to say, "Then how was Theophrastus, who was the most persuasive in his private conversations, unable to persuade the members of the Areopagus?" For those persuaded in private were not part of the unpersuaded many, nor were they unpersuaded in matters in which Theophrastus was knowledgeable, but in matters in which he was inexperienced.'

93. A philosophical niche has been carved for Leontion: the *hetaira* of Epicurus, who continued in her old ways even after becoming a philosopher (Athen. 13.588b); maker of witty comments at symposia (Athen. 13.585d); introduced into the writings of those wishing to make shameful allegations against Epicurus (Diog. Laert. 10.4–6). Leontion is only one of several women reported as active members of the Garden: Dorandi (1998) 58.

94. Coincidentally, Aldington (1924) 22–3 points out the different way in which La Bruyère was an 'outsider'; prevented by his non-noble birth from mixing as an equal with the French aristocracy, he instead chose closely to observe them.

95. David Sedley points out to me that other philosophical name-changes seem plausible enough: Clitomachus (né Hasdrubal) and Porphyry (né Malcos). He has speculated elsewhere about the plausibility of Plato's change of name: (2003) 21–3. Einarson and Link (1976) xxiii–xxiv interpret *theophrastos* as having the sense of 'indicated by a god'. Noting that the name is apparently not common outside Athens, they complicate the issue by suggesting that its 'Attic sound' was chosen not by Tyrtamus himself, but by Aristotle as a teasing allusion to Tyrtamus' preference for Attic speech. They go on to assess at length the relatively high degree of Atticism in the *De historia* and *De causis*: 'more precious and at times more Attic than Aristotle' (xxv). For what it is worth, Strabo (13.2.4) tells the story that Aristotle opted to rename Tyrtamus because of the unpleasant sound of his original name. A further variant (*Suda s.v.* 'Theophrastos', no. 199 = FHS&G 2.1) has Aristotle arrive at 'Theophrastus' via 'Euphrastus'. Against Aristotle's involvement is his citing in the *Poetics* (1457a12–14) of 'Theodoros' as a compound noun of which the second part 'does not signify'. (I owe this reference to the anonymous reader.)

96. Lynch (1972) 93–4: 'Not only Aristotle himself, but almost all the known members of his school were non-Athenians.' He quotes Philochorus, as cited in the *Vita Marciana* (12): 'It is not at all likely that Aristotle, since he was a *xenos*, could do this to Plato, who happened to be a citizen and had great influence because Chabrias and Timotheus, the *strategoi* at Athens, were related to him by blood.' For practical implications of the Peripatetic scholarchs as metics, see Sollenberger (1992) 3804–5. Opposition to the idea of the 'metic character' of the Lyceum as a factor in its decline comes from Glucker (1998) 312–14, who points to an extensive non-Athenian membership of the flourishing Stoa. He prefers to explain Peripatetic decline in terms of the shift of science and research, characteristic of the early Peripatos, to Alexandria.

97. The quotation in the text is from the Aristotelian *Metaphysics, Alpha elatton* (993a30–b3), read by Grayeff (1974) 64–8 as a quasi inaugural lecture, 'guiding students to the theoretical study-programme of the Peripatos' (67). Grayeff accepts the traditional attribution of *Alpha elatton* to Pasicles of Rhodes, a pupil of Aristotle who continued to work under Theophrastus. The distinctive nature of philosophical research carried out in the Lyceum, by experts, empirically across a wide range of fields, is emphasized by Glucker (1998) 312: 'In many ways, Aristotle's school was the precursor of our modern university.'

98. *Agon, schema, epideixis* and *theoria* are identified by Goldhill (1999) 1–29 as key elements in

'performance culture'. The concept, touched on only lightly here, will later be applied in more detail to the circumstances of the Characters themselves.

99. Fraser (1995) 168–9 notes how Theophrastus' categorization of plant life (and also stones: *De lapidibus* §48) is based on identifying significant differences (*diaphorai*). The botanical association is made explicit by Green (1990) 69–9: 'It is very tempting to regard his ... *Characters* as an essay in the same genre, an attempt to apply the principles of botanical classification to human beings, to typologize men as one would flowers.' He goes on to detect in the *Characters* a tension, peculiar to the later fourth century, between the tendency to mimetic realism and the drive to abstract and generalize, 'leading directly to the stock characters of New Comedy'. van Raalte in the introduction to her monumental edition of the *Metaphysics* (1993), after remarking on how Theophrastus combined in the *Characters* 'a watchful eye with a sensitive ear', continues: 'This most famous, and at first sight somewhat curious work by a serious scientist such as Theophrastus certainly was, offers a fine example of how the particular combination of observer and subject-matter determines the level of generalization' (28 n. 2).

100. According to Evans (1969) 38–9, Theophrastus supplies his Characters with 'marks of quality', which are 'the outward marks of a man, and not concerned with his inward nature in the strict sense of physiognomical interpretation.' Away from the *Characters*, Theophrastus is shown adopting a physiognomical approach, advising a blushing youth that 'virtue has just such a colour' (Antonius Melissa, *Loci communes* 2.71 = FHS&G 470; but see 32–3); equating the change in the colour of an octopus with the way a coward's complexion changes (Plutarch, *Natural explanations* 19 9–6B = FHS&G 365C); and joking about the nose of a friend of Cassander (Plutarch, *Quaestiones convivales* 633B = FHS&G 31; see 32). The eighteenth-century convergence of physiognomy with character-writing is traced by Smeed (1985) 292–4, culminating in the 'Physiognomical Sketches' illustrating the translation of the *Characters* by Frances Howell (1824). The sketches are conveniently reproduced by Anderson (1970). The tradition continues. On the day this note was written (23 Feb 2006), there appeared in *The Cambridge Student* under the heading 'Cambridge Characters' a description, complete with illustration, of 'The Theatre Reviewer'. In his behaviour at the theatre, he in part resembles Theophrastus' 'Repulsive Man'. According to the author, the inspiration for the series was not Theophrastus but the long-running 'Social Stereotypes' from the *Daily Telegraph Magazine*, text by Virginia Mather and drawings by Sue Macartney-Snape.

101. Any direct connexion with the *Nicomachean ethics* is briskly dismissed by Anderson (1970) xvi–ii, who places the *ethikoi* part of the title, as given by Diogenes Laertius (n. 10), on a level with the moralizing conclusions. He cites with approval Usher's argument (1993) 9 that Aristotle's ethical system could hardly embrace the *opsimathes* or *deisidaimon*. Jebb (1909) 13–16 disputes in detail supposed correspondences between the *Characters* and Aristotle's Great-Hearted Man. Smeed (1985) 6 notes the way in which Aristotle, in illustrating a philosophical or moral point, feels free to alternate between description of a character-type and the moral characteristic in the abstract: 'Thus the character sketch is, for all its eloquence, almost a luxury for him.'

102. For *megaloprepeia, mikroprepeia, salakoneia*, see n. 12. The thirteen pairs of vices listed in *Nicomachean ethics* are tabulated by Rusten (2002) 13–15, who notes the slightly different listing in *Eudemian ethics* (1120b38); the discrepancies are discussed by Woods (1992) 105–6. Fortenbaugh (1983a) argues for a close relationship between Theophrastus' work on ethics and the *Eudemian ethics*; accepted with reservations by Gotthelf (1983). Attribution of the fragment to Arrius is confirmed by Hahm (1980): 2938–43 for Stobaeus' technique as editor.

103. As Mann (1973) 192 points out with reference to Chaucer's pilgrims, 'Fools and rascals can be charming people.' The debate over positive characters has naturally focused on Joseph Hall's 'Characterisms of Vertues'. For Bennet and Hammond (1902) xli, they are 'homilies, and, as the virtues of a tedious preacher, provoke one to yawn. Virtue is not fitting material for this species of writing.' Hall seems himself to have sensed the disparity, but from the perspective of the pulpit. He writes in 'The proem' to his 'Characterisms of Vices': 'The fashions of some evils are, besides the odiousnesse, ridiculous; which to repeat is to seeme bitterly merry. I abhorre to make sport with wickednesse; and

forbid any laughter here but of disdaine.' The passage is quoted by Gordon (1912) 71, who closes (85–6) by identifying the mean implied by all character-writing as 'a burgess notion, condemned by its very principle to stare for life at the heroisms and excesses for which it can make no provision'.

104. Though they may delude themselves that they are victims of *hubris*: the 'Oligarchic Man's' (26.3) imagined sufferings at the hands of the *demos*, and (possibly) the 'Late Learner' (27.9) being beaten up by his rival in love; see Fisher (1992) 127. The non-criminal behaviour of the Characters is identified as such ('none of them is presented as irredeemably evil or reprehensible') by Habicht (1997) 122, and by Steinmetz (1970) 93–4, who suggests that their wrongdoing relates to the moral weakness of the 'average man'; though that concept is itself open to question. Closest to the approach taken in the text is the view expressed by Bennet and Hammond (1902) xxxii: the negative actions of the Characters were 'vices to the mind of the Greek, who measured his morality largely by the canon of good form. Any violation of good taste or breach of courtesy was morally vicious'.

105. The survival of Theophrastus through Arabic texts is examined by Gutas (1985) esp. 69–70.

106. The linguistic likelihood of speaker as *didaskalos* and listeners as *mathetai* is brought out by Diggle (2004) 234.

Others have revived the broad idea of *Characters*-as-entertainment. Green (1990) 69 specifically favours Jebb's reconstruction; for Lane Fox (1996) 141–2, 'The Characters were born from a new combination: philosophical classification and comic caricature.' Rusten (2002) 22–3 cites in addition to Pasquali, the 'complementary suggestions' of Gomperz (*Characters* as a preliminary collection of material for monographs on ethics) and Gaiser (material for lectures, 'where the giving of information, moral instruction, and entertainment intersect'). Those with experience of lecturing will confirm that audiences persist in remembering those parts of lectures intended as 'light relief'. One of my colleagues would break half-way through his lectures on Roman History to declaim Macaulay's 'How Horatius kept the Bridge'; another read extracts (in translation) from Soranus on *Gynaecology*. Twenty years later, it is salutary to discover that virtually all that attendees can recall of my own lectures on Sparta is the handing out of Spartan Chocolates (the ones with hard centres).

107. The quotations are presumably from Theophrastus' *Peri hupokriseos* or 'On delivery' (Diog. Laert. 5.48 = FHS&G 1.236). Its possible content and scope are discussed in Fortenbaugh (2005) 145–50, who includes exhaustive commentary on the two fragments (397–415), with cautious comments on their applicability to the *Characters* (408–9). Trenkner (1958) 149 n. 1 assimilates Theophrastus, reading out his character-sketches in a 'dramatic manner', to the *gelotopoioi* or comedians who 'half acted their stories as they told them' (but see below, n. 126). The merest hint of possible interaction between Theophrastus and his lecture-audience is provided by Jackson (1920) 193, teasing out from the text of Aristotle references to individual members of his audience.

108. Relevant in this respect is material from Steinmetz (1959): an attempt to present the *Characters* as an elaborate philosophical joke, expounding Peripatetic doctrine at the expense of the doctrines of other philosophers.

109. The status of Theophrastus' sayings in the *Gnomologium Vaticanum* and their possible Hellenistic origin is discussed by Fortenbaugh (2005) 47–8. The passages in the text, including textual difficulties, are analysed by Fortenbaugh (1984) 187–8, 254.

110. A further cross-bearing on the humour of the *Characters* is provided by another world: that of Rabelais, as conceived by Michael Bakhtin (1968). The contrast could hardly be greater: the 'grotesque' as opposed to classic canons (28–30); the laughter of the marketplace encompassing carnival, comic shows, parody and 'various genres of billingsgate' (4–5). This is humour emphatically from below, suspending rank and embracing those who laugh (10). Bakhtin expressly contrasts the people's laughter with that of the satirist who places himself above the object of his mockery (12). In fact, Bakhtin does allow some points of contact between the *Characters* and the comic world of Rabelais. In drawing a distinction between Rabelais and La Bruyère, he notes how the latter 'ignores the link between the *moralia* and the antique feasts, banquets, laughter which can still be traced in his predecessor Theophrastus' (110). But surely not the same kind of laughter? Theophrastus presumes his audience

to laugh at, not with, the Rabelaisian behaviour of the 'Disagreeable Man' at dinner (20.6), comparing his faeces with the broth on the table; or the unnamed character (19.10), spitting across the table and hitting the wine-waiter.

111. This, along with other parts of Plutarch's discussion, is presumed to have been taken from Theophrastus' lost monograph *Peri geloiou*; see Janko (1984) 210–11; Grant (1924) 34–7.

112. Sollenberger (1992) 3828 marshals the 'persuasive arguments for both views'. He reckons an average of sixty or so pupils per year to be 'not very remarkable', citing the remark attributed to Zeno (Plutarch, *Moralia* 545F = FHS&G 15), that Theophrastus had a larger but less harmonious chorus. On the other hand, Johnson's researches (1957) seem to suggest that the average sophist (admittedly not quite the same thing) 'was doing well to have half-a-dozen regular fee-paying pupils' (300). The nature and status of Aristotle's 'public lectures' at the Lyceum is discussed by Lynch (1972) 91–2; for the detailed terminology: Aulus Gellius, *Attic nights* 5.1–6; also in Düring (1957) 426–43. Fortenbaugh (2005) 150–1 cautiously identifies the two books entitled *deilinon* or 'Afternoon (discussions)' attributed tò Theophrastus (Diog. Laert. 5.47 = FHS&G 1.185) as collections of material for afternoon classes, following Aristotle's example. Theophrastus' letter to Phanias (see below, n. 115), with its reference to *paneguris* (public assembly) as opposed to *sunedrion* (select company), implies the existence of different types of audiences; not that Theophrastus expresses complete satisfaction with either sort.

113. 'Several sketches seem to assume the existence of a democratic government with functioning people's courts ... while others show the city in Cassander's hands': Habicht (1997) 123. The difficulty is side-stepped by Green (1990) 69–70 who, basing his conclusions on 8, 23, 26, presents the *Characters* as offering an impression of pro- and anti-collaborationist feeling in Athens under Macedonian rule. He contrasts with the vivacity of 'social life' enjoyed by individual Characters, 'the life of a recently defeated, junta-ruled city, with a Macedonian garrison quartered in the Piraeus,' adding, 'That provides the historian with a salutary corrective.'

114. Lane Fox (1996) 134 advises that, in respect of political change in late-fourth-century Athens, 'users of the *Characters* need to be chronologically alert'. My own approach to the *Characters* is framed so as to be less time-sensitive. In the updating of texts, specific references to contemporary individuals and events ('Boastful Man', 'Rumour-Monger') might more easily be altered than structural features relating to institutions. One of my lectures on Athenian Democracy has, over the past twenty years, preserved its basic configuration, while ending in successive denunciations of Thatcherite, Majorite, and currently Blairite autocracy.

115. On the interpretation of this difficult passage, see Sollenberger (1992) 3872–74, who opts (as in the text) for a complaint concerning the overly critical response of contemporary audiences (*hai helikiai*); rather than old age necessitating publication without the benefit of further revisions (as argued by Mejer (1998) 21). By way of illustration of his own explanation of how the text of the *Characters* evolved, Jebb (1909) cites the preface to Earle's *Microcosmography*. Here described is how Earle wrote his characters for private amusement (17 n. 1), 'to pass away the time in the country, and by the forcible request of his friends drawn from him: yet, passing severally from hand to hand, in written copies, grew at length to be a pretty number in a little volume: and among so many sundry dispersed transcripts, some very imperfect and surreptitious had like to have passed the press, if the author had not used speedy means of prevention.' (In fact, the passage is not by Earle himself, but is taken from the bookseller's notice, by Edward Blount.) Many of Earle's own phrases and sentences, absent from the first edition, are inserted in later editions. Although Jebb stresses that this is not intended as an analogy for the *Characters*, it does illuminate Lane Fox's observation (1996) 141 that we do not know what 'publication' of the *Characters* meant.

116. The notion that the *Characters* might have originated as a symposiastic game goes back to Edmonds (1929) 6–7 (cf. 72–3): 'But what capital after-dinner recitations they would make!' His specific suggestion (that *amelei*, as often used to introduce Characters' actions, answers an implied 'dinner-table' question) has since been dismissed; see Lane Fox (1996) 141 n. 146, who notes, 'Without this support the dinner-party theory is unfounded'. But we can only guess at the range of entertainments

thought appropriate at more intellectual gatherings. For a hint, there is the observation of Demetrius (*On style* 170): 'The prudent will use laughter at opportune times, as in feasts and at symposia and in rebukes against luxury and high living.'

117. The theory of *archon* as symposiarch is discussed by Sollenberger (1992) 3831.

118. The passage from Teles is translated by O'Neill (1977). Before taking his testimony on Theophrastus at face value, it should be noted that Teles elsewhere (Hense 17–18) has Socrates' jurors offering him the option of a fine, and Socrates himself tossing out the last drop of poison, exclaiming 'This for Alcibiades the fair'.

   For other students possibly switching away from Theophrastus (Metrodorus, Timagoras, Bion, Arcesilaus), see Glucker (1998) 301–3.

119. The *trichalkon*, worth one-sixteenth of a drachma, was approximately the size of a sequin; there is an actual-size illustration in Edmonds and Austen (1904) 14. The usual response to dropping a bronze as opposed to a silver coin may be inferred from respective numbers of Athenian coins found while excavating the Agora: some 14,000 bronze as opposed to 129 silver coins, of which a high proportion are deliberately discarded imitations; details in Kroll (1993) 1–2. Three *chalkoi* as an altogether trifling sum for a person of some wealth may be inferred from its being alleged by the 'Slanderer' (28.4) as the daily allowance that the husband under attack makes to his wife who brought him (at least) a one-talent dowry.

120. The passage is set in context with reference to the views of Aristotle and Dicaearchus by Fortenbaugh (1984) 182–4. For a hint of slave-ownership lower down the social scale: the passing mention of the 'slave of the piper Asteios' (8.4).

121. Lane Fox (1996) 131: 'My impression of his coarse types is that they are citizens of modest property, a run-of-the-mill hoplite's. The Rustic is certainly nothing more.' My own impression is marginally different, placing all the Characters on a more-or-less uniformly high level. I do not see why the *oiketai* with whom the *agroikos* discusses his important business need preclude ownership of slaves working his land. The hired men to whom he tells the affairs of the Assembly may be intended (as Lane Fox suggests) as slaves belonging to other people, but to tell citizens' business to metics hiring themselves out as day-labourers would be almost as pointed. Jones (1956) 139 n. 62 identified the *misthotai* of the *agroikos* with the *georgoi* listed eight times in *IG* II^2 10 (Rhodes and Osborne (2003) no. 4): a proposal to offer honours to non-citizens in the aftermath of the expulsion of the Thirty. Agricultural slaves are (to us) conspicuous by their absence from the *Characters*; even more so from the *oikos* as conceived by Aristotle in the first book of the *Politics*: supported by farming, but where *oiketes* with the sense of 'domestic slave' is almost invariably the term used. The location of slavery in the Aristotelian *oikos* is further explored in Millett (2007).

   Points of detail, all arising out of Lane Fox (130). The 'Boastful Man' is certainly not super-rich: the sums he names as *eranos* contributions and elsewhere are massively exaggerated (see 69–70), which is in line with his underlying character. But the fact that he lives in a rented house (23.9) need not have implications for his status. According to Lane Fox, 'In Attica renting implied dependence on another person, [and] would not be customary for a rich citizen.' But one Stratocles, wealthy enough to have his estate fought over in court (Isaeus 11.42–3), leased out two houses and presumably himself rented a third. Of course, a single counter-example proves nothing; but Theophrastus may intend to comment on the Character's veracity rather than his status: living in a rented house, there was nothing to prevent him moving if he wished. Again, citing Lane Fox: 'Specified sums of money are also compounded by the Characters to whom they apply.' As noted in the text, such is certainly the case with the 'Boastful Man's' handouts. But individual cases need to be taken on their merits: sums may be fantastical or merely exaggerated, according to context. So Diggle (2004) 495–6 argues for the three-*chalkoi* allowance and one-talent dowry from the 'Slanderer' (28.4) as both lying (just) on the boundaries of possibility. I would continue to make out a similar case (*pace* Lane Fox) for the 25% per day charged by the *aponenoemenos* in the guise of petty-usurer (6.9); see now Schaps (2004) 185 n. 49. We seem here to be involved with the 'two worlds of prices' within Athens (obols and drachmas; minas and talents), identified by Vickers and Gill (1994) 33–4: exemplified by Socrates' tour around the shops of the Agora, as reported by Plutarch (*Moralia* 470F); Teles (13 Hense) tells a similar story about Diogenes the Cynic.

122. Details in Smeed (1985) 38–9, who also picks out for discussion the main strands of 'The "Character" and society' (132–69). For Hall and Overbury in the King's service, see Aldington (1924) 10; note the additional character by Hall, 'A Description of A good and Faithfull Courtier', included by Kirk as an appendix (199–203) to his edition of *Heaven upon Earth* and *Characters of Vertues and Vices*. The catalogue of English imitators of the *Characters* compiled by Greenough (1947), with no claim to comprehensiveness, lists some 7000 separate subjects.

123. Given in full by Smeed (1985) 36–7, who also traces the incidence of wit in Overbury: 24–9, 39–46, 179–90. The burgeoning genre was surveyed from the early eighteenth century by Henry Gally in an extended 'Critical essay on characteristic-writings' which prefaced his translation of *The moral characters of Theophrastus* (1725). Earlier practitioners are taken to task for departing from the sharpness of the Theophrastan original, adorning their characters with 'quaint similes' which 'makes 'em appear like so many Pieces of mere Grotesque'.

124. Detail in Paylor's introduction to *The Overburian Characters* (vi–vii), who also identifies those characters that resemble Theophrastus in presenting a single fault.

125. Although those interviewed ostensibly speak for themselves, selections have frequently been reprinted under the title of *Mayhew's characters* (as edited by Peter Quennell). Smeed (1985) 169–78 has a valuable discussion of 'The poorer classes' appearing through time as characters; also earlier Viennese Sketches of poorer people (110–11). Representatives of 'lower class life' from Elizabethan pamphleteers are discussed by Paylor in his introduction to *The Overburian Characters* (xi–xiv).

126. Five fragments in all. *Peri komoidias*: (1) Athenaeus 6.261d-e = FHS&G 709. *Peri geloiou*: (2) Plutarch, *Quaestiones convivales* 633b = FHS&G 31; (3) *Gnomologium Vaticanum* no. 327 = FHS&G 453; (4) Athenaeus 8.347f-348a = FHS&G 710; (5) Plutarch, *Quaestiones convivales* 631D-E = FHS&G 711. Both titles and fragments receive exhaustive discussion in Fortenbaugh (2005) 138–45, 364–97. Of the five fragments, only no. 5 (cited above, 32) has any direct bearing on the *Characters*. What we can hope to know of Theophrastus' views on Comedy and laughter is reconstructed by Fortenbaugh (1981, 1995, 2000).

Diomedes, *The art of grammar* 3 (= FHS&G 708) contains a summary of three types of poetry. Although Tragedy is specifically attributed to Theophrastus, there is no warrant for associating him with the brief accounts of Epic and Comedy (given as 'apud Graecos'). In his discussion of the passage, Fortenbaugh (2005) 352–64 takes the absence of Aristotelian 'imitation of people worse than we are' from the summary of Comedy (*Poetics* 1449a32) as a hint that the author was responding specifically to New Comedy. But such a formulation cannot easily (if at all) accommodate the *Characters*. Janko (1984), in arguing for the attribution of the *Tractatus Coislinianus* to Aristotle, supplies cogent reasons for it not being by Theophrastus (48–52). The *Tractatus* (12) overlaps slightly with the *Characters* (1, 23) in listing as three 'characters of comedy', *bomolochika*, *alazonika*, and *eironika*.

Lane Fox (1996) 141 considers that the tone of the *Characters* more-or-less conforms to the Aristotelian mean of humour, as briefly discussed in the *Nicomachean ethics* (1127b32–28b4): *eutrapelia* or 'wittiness', with *bomolochia* and *agroikia* as its co-ordinates. *Agroikia* here has the sense of never saying anything funny and taking offence at those who do so; on its non-coincidence with Theophrastan *agroikia*, see Diggle (2004) 207–8. I do not find at all persuasive the attempt by Trenkner (1958) 150–4 to assimilate individual actions in the *Characters* to stock *geloia*: the skin of Aesop's crocodile marked by his ancestors' outdoor careers as physical trainers (Gibbs (2002) no. 189) as the inspiration for the appearance of the 'Offensive Man' (19.2); and many more. Similarly wide of the mark is her suggestion that 'The almost complete absence of erotic themes in Theophrastus may be due to Byzantine censorship at the time when the *Characters* were the school-book of morality' (152 n. 2). Apart from the 'Country Bumpkin's' secret liaison with a slave girl, a house allegedly full of *pornai*, at least three girl pipers, two *hetairai*, and an *eromene* are not a bad haul.

127. Ussher's identification of individuals, revived by Green (1990) 70–1, was anticipated by Jacob

Burckhardt (1998) 350–5: 'Apparently he [Theophrastus] followed up, over time, some individuals he had recognized as types; for his best chapters can hardly have been gradual random observation (351). From this he draws the 'overwhelming impression' that 'people in Athens were very much letting themselves go, chiefly in lying and deception, without caring for their good or bad name; there was an assumption of general barefaced impudence'.

128. The technique of building up a literary character may be compared with Francis Galton's 'composite photography': superimposing photographic images of a class or group (as in 'Jack Tar') in order to arrive at an image that resembled an individual, but somehow encompassed all its members. I owe the analogy to Nuttall (2003) 1–2. Lane Fox (1996) 141 rightly points out how 'Unlike modern caricatures or cartoons, the Characters are noticeably short of physical details or expressions'. He prefers to liken the *Characters* to a bundle of artist's sketches, complete with layers of varnish, needing the skill of the restorer (131–2).

129. Gombrich (1960) 279–303 considers further 'The Experiment of Caricature'. Sparkes (2004) traces the slow evolution of individual likeness in Greek art; adding point to the 'Toady's' exclamation (2.12) that his patron's portrait 'hits him off perfectly'. The drawings by Piet de Jong in Hood's *Faces of archaeology* (1998) beautifully demonstrate the fine dividing line in caricature between affection and its opposites. Dover (1974) 20–2 briefly addresses the problems of literary caricature, emphasizing the key question, who or what is being caricatured: another, a group of others, or ourselves?

130. This reading of the 'Chatterbox' differs from Jones (2004) 213–14, who sees the remarks as addressed 'across a multitude of persons', tentatively abstracting therefrom 'a rustic making a relatively rare visit to an unfamiliar environment'. Since (as he argues) no farmer would label as garrulous remarks on prices, rain and planting-plans, he here detects 'the essentially urban and urbane orientation of the sketch'. But as argued in the text, what is superfluous is the stringing together of comments which are individually unexceptionable.

131. Caution is called for in that the individual excesses of the 'Superstitious Man' continue to be taken at face value. For Humphreys (1993) 15, monthly visits to the Orphic mysteries by the man himself, children and wife or nurse demonstrate that 'The social life of the family as a united group took place almost entirely as a religious act'; contrast Lane Fox (1996) 153.

132. The point being that witnesses to repayment of interest could later testify that the debt existed. The 'Obtuse Man' (14.8) gets it straightforwardly wrong by having present witnesses of repayment to him of the principal, which it was in the interests of the borrower to record.

133. The tendency of Characters to be signed off 'par une *chute* imprévue, piquante, pittoresque' was noted by Navarre (1914) 426. Compare the 'Self-Centred Man' (15.11) who, having growled at his friends and fellow-citizens, closes by withholding credit from the gods; the 'Obsequious Man' (5.5), crushed beneath the weight of his host's sleeping children. Frequently, the last word is just that: some revealing comment direct from the Character himself, who leaves us with his words in our ears: 1, 7, 8, 2, 10, 11, 14, 17, 18, 20, 23, 24, 25. The idea of connected actions is opposed by Trenkner (1958) 147, who claims that any single episode 'would be enough to describe the type... they do not give a clearer or more profound or more varied picture in bulk than they do singly.' But Smeed (1985) 279–80 is surely right in tracing back to Theophrastus this method of softening what he terms the 'catalogue effect'.

134. 'You can see what an education it is to study this work' is Diggle's comment (2002) 58, having introduced into his discussion, 'just for the fun of it', the 'Conspicuous Consumer's' presumed cleaning of his teeth with mastich (*schinos*) from the island of Chios; concluding with 'This is not the kind of thing you learn by reading Euripides'. Nollard and Hug put in appearances in Diggle's commentary (2004) 95, 296.

135. It seems a pity that two of the testimonia offered by Lane Fox as occurring only in the *Characters* are excluded from Diggle's text: the Diazeugma ('Pier' or 'Mole') in the Piraeus (23.2) and Keramos ('Jug') as the popular term for Athens' prison (6.6). For reasons why, see n. 342. Hicks (1882) is a pioneering and still effective effort to tie in the *Characters* with the testimony of Athenian inscriptions (see n. 218). Law-court speeches offer an obvious control in reading the *Characters*; Lane Fox (1996)

155 comments on their 'wider overlap of values with earlier Attic oratory'. An overlap (rather than complete congruence) fulfills expectations: the Characters are from an imagined social level similar to perhaps a majority of litigants in preserved speeches. As argued below, both Theophrastus and law-court speakers are concerned with articulating from their different perspectives a system of values appropriate to democratic, egalitarian tradition.

The problem of historical generalization from fragments of evidence is nicely illustrated by Jebb (1909) who, by way of apologetic warning, concludes his preface by quoting from the *Oxford Spectator* an account of Oxford Commemoration given by an imagined historian writing in AD 4000. On the basis of a sentence from a private letter (ix): 'the whole University goes to Nuneham' is constructed the tradition of a ritual procession to Nuneham marking the final day of the Commemoration festival. Smeed's words against unsupported reading of characters-as-history (or sociology) may be reinforced by Thackeray's tongue-in-cheek suggestion (*Book of Snobs*, ch. 33, 35) that his account of 'Some Country Snobs' 'may be interesting to those foreign readers who ... want to know the customs of an English gentleman's family, and household'; which is presumably meant to be read on at least two levels.

136. It will not escape readers who know their *Characters* that Kitto confuses his 'Mean Man' with the victim of the 'Slanderer' who allegedly received a one-talent dowry. It seems likely that in his enthusiasm for the *Characters*, Kitto is here and elsewhere quoting from memory. For a more sophis-ticated mobilization of the testimony of the *Characters* against the notion of 'oriental seclusion' see D. Cohen (1989) esp. 8.

137. '[B]orn as a late Victorian' is presumably Kitto's own description, as recounted in the entertaining biographical entry on the back cover of early Penguin editions. The words imputed to Gladstone ('I do not care to hear a lady's name bandied about in general talk, whether for praise or dispraise') are designed to soften the statement on Athenian women attributed to Pericles (224): according to Kitto, not so much disdain as 'old-fashioned deference and courtesy'.

138. An opinion, in fact, shared by Parke (1977) 52: 'Theophrastus says in his *Characters* when describing that remarkable, but not unfamiliar, human type, the Late Learner ... the Late Learner is depicted as a rather pathetically eager extrovert.'

139. In his 'Rules of evidence' (1978), Keith Hopkins reflects on the problems and possibilities of writing ancient history. It should be emphasized that Kitto and Garland are by no means alone in their individual readings of the *Characters*. Rather, the detail and openness of their accounts invites investigation. Frequently those mining the *Characters* cite passages in footnotes without the context needed for readers to form their own judgments. So Harrison (1986) in his authoritative *The law of Athens* (1, 168 n. 6) offers the bare reference 'XXX.9, 15' as assuming the existence of 'slaves with a right to (1) their findings, (2) their earnings'. Nowhere does he disclose that the references are to the reprehensible behaviour of the 'Shabby Profiteer', or discuss in general terms the use of the *Characters* to write legal history. Maroi's study (1916–17) of private law in the *Characters* was not available to me.

One more example (a glance at the indexes of standard works on Athenian institutions will provide plenty more). Of the thirteen references to the *Characters* in Michell's classic study *Economics of ancient Greece* (1957), six are in some way questionable; either factually incorrect or drawing an unwarranted conclusion: (62 n. 1) the 'Man of Petty Ambition' (21.7) celebrating the sacrifice of an ox as evidence that 'Beef was seldom eaten as being too expensive, except where the meat was distributed after the sacrifices'; (124 n. 2) the 'Conspicuous Consumer' (5.8) as showing the export of salt from Attica to Byzantium (but 'salt' is one of many proposed conjectures in response to a textual crux; see Diggle (2004) 336–7); (172) the 'Country Bumpkin' (4.12) demonstrating that soles were fixed to uppers with nails (but he hammers in hobnails); (188) the 'Conspicuous Consumer' (5.6) gets shaved several times each month (the reference is to haircutting, with no indication of frequency, save *pleistakis*); (282) the 'Boastful Man' (23.4) has been given permission by Antipater to export duty-free timber to build his house (no mention of any house; correctly, 202); (343 n. 4) the 'Penny-Pincher' (10.10) as evidence that 'compound interest was charged by creditors' (no indication that this counted as extreme behaviour).

140. Jebb's letter is reprinted in Sandys' preface to the second edition of the *Characters* (x). In his own introduction (1), Jebb explains how the sketches 'treat of commonplace people and of everyday life', commenting on the 'frank homeliness which marked old Athenian life' as contained in the *Characters*. He identifies this homeliness in allusions to 'details of small households, to petty loans between neighbours, to minute economies in dress and the like', noting in passing, 'the simple life thus opened, and the candour which opens it'. An alternative reading might seek to replace this veiled primitivism with a different form of complexity.

141. Navarre (1914) 403–4 reports that Charpentier, supposedly welcoming La Bruyère into membership of the Académie française, delivered a speech in which he attacked the portraits created by La Bruyère as time-specific, against the timelessness of Theophrastus. Navarre agrees with the substance of the assessment, though not with the value-judgment, citing at length the 'Distrustful Man' as demonstrating how the *Characters* are situated in neither time nor space. For Edmonds and Austen (1904) xx, every one of the Characters is 'a fair sample of humanity, each like the other save in one respect, and all with their counterparts in modern life'. According to Anderson (1970) xx, 'he has caught perennial types in typical actions, a common denominator of urban man'. Bennet and Hammond (1902) x–xix summon up Thackeray in commenting at length on the essential sameness of character, ancient and modern, drawing a distinction between 'accidental types' (arising largely out of changes in offices and institutions) and the 'essential types' (intrinsic qualities in human-kind), such as have been drawn by Theophrastus.

   Among sporadic statements of discontinuity: Green (1990) 71 on the *Characters*' 'idiosyncratic no less than its perennial elements'; Gordon (1912) 60–3: Theophrastus' 'Arrogant Man' is not ours; Kitto (1951) 270 on the absence from the *Characters* of the 'Snob'; Dover (1974) 2: Theophrastan 'flattery' as 'alien to life as we know it'.

142. Cox (1998); Millett (1998, 1991). Even Athenian laundry practice (invariably sending clothes for cleaning outside the household) has been singled out as exemplified in the *Characters*: Becker (1845) 205 n. 15; Gordon (1912) 61; Michell (1957) 188.

143. Clustering set out in the text is according to Trenkner (1958) 147. Brief commentary by Navarre (1914) 407–8, arguing for the deliberate subtlety of Theophrastus' distinctions; as do Burckhardt (1998) 351 and Gordon (1912) 59–60.

144. Goldhill (1986) 57–78, esp. 75. One aspect of oral insecurity is highlighted by Lewis (1996) 75; cf. 77–96: 'The *logopoios* is an extreme example of the unofficial newsbringer, and of the problems he or she could cause.'

145. There are other candidates for significant shifts in meaning. Gordon (1912) 53 remarks how: '*authadeia*, which Aeschylus thought adequate to Promethean self-will, has sunk in Theophrastus to commonplace surliness.' The changing sense of *kairos* (and by implication *akairos*) from a normative to a more temporal meaning is documented by Wilson (1980) with Race (1981). For what can be recovered concerning Theophrastus' study *Peri kairon* (possibly 'critical moments'), see Podlecki (1985) 238–41.

146. Needham demonstrates how the implications of polythetic classification, familiar in branches of the natural sciences, may at first seem problematically imprecise, but possibly correspond more closely to the realities of social categories (358): 'Polythetic classes are likely to accommodate better than monothetic the variegation of social phenomena: they have … a high content of information, and they carry less risk of an arbitrary exclusion of significant features.' Irony/*eironeia* might seem to present an extreme case. Rosenmeyer (1996) in his 'necessarily selective' list of 'Ironies in serious drama' (510–15), accounts for almost one hundred varieties grouped under four broad headings. For Ariston's *eiron* (different again), see n. 240.

147. More difficult to explain are occasions where the *Characters* unexpectedly escapes mention; for example, by Grote in his *History* (1846–56): see n. 62. Perhaps Mahaffy has the reason (1887) xxxv–xxxvi; Grote, 'a radical and a democrat', turned 'with indignation from the later politics of the petty states of Greece'. This cannot, however, account for the absence of the *Characters* from the

appropriate volumes of the new edition of the *Cambridge ancient history* (vols. 6 and 7 pt. 1); perhaps uncertainty over date has caused it to slip down the awkward crack between classical and Hellenistic.

148. 'apparently non-politicized' in light of the innovatory reading of Menander by Susan Lape (2004); discussed below, 45.

Gagarin (2000) 354–64 deploys the *Characters* as a point of reference to identify possible change in the climate of law under Demetrius. While accepting that legal institutions remained largely untouched, he contrasts the high profile of litigation for the Characters (affecting fourteen of them) with its restricted appearance in plays of Menander. Dating the *Characters* to c.319 (therefore reflecting life in the 320s) and Menander's first production to c.320, he argues for a decrease in the use of formal legal procedures, especially by the rich. This he ties in with declining public competition, including increased irrelevance for the élite of success or failure in the courts. 'And thus, the peculiar Athenian symbiosis of broad-based political power and aristocratic competition for individual honor came to an end.' He sees wealthy citizens turning instead to private business, 'which flourished in a strong economy' (362). The argument is carefully stated but needs to be substantiated at several points. The dating of the content of the *Characters* to the 320s is not secure; omission by Menander need not indicate non-existence (pederasty is a case in point; also absent from the *Characters*); élite competition after honour arguably found new outlets rather than ending; and what is the evidence for the strength of the economy?

149. See the summary statement (more moderate than most) on 'The time of crises' in Austin and Vidal-Naquet (1977), 131–55; Theophrastus' *agroikos* puts in an appearance on 372–5 (below, 48).

150. Rostovtzeff (certainly), Ehrenberg (probably) and Mossé (possibly) intend 'bourgeois' in a positive sense; but the concept can cut both ways: for Anderson (1970) xix, the Characters exhibit 'petty failings of petty bourgeois types'.

151. The debate to which the 'Talker' refers may be the prosecution by Aristophon of the commanders Iphicrates, Menestheus and Timotheus during the Social War (356–5). His additional allusion to a contest at Sparta in the time of Lysander may refer to the public debate in 400 between Agesilaus and Leotychidas over succession to the throne. For details and possible alternatives, see Diggle (2004) 271–3, with Weil (1890).

152. The confusing succession of régimes down to 262 (at least nine of them) complete with four outside interventions, four blockades and three uprisings is memorably summarized by Ferguson (1911a) 95. Evidence for continuity in democratic forms is recorded by Habicht (1997), who highlights the stability of Athenian institutional frameworks (2), concluding that 'Nothing justifies the occasional claim that political participation declined in the Hellenistic age' (4). In terms of effective democracy, some qualification is needed (as in part supplied by Habicht himself, 90–1). Oliver (2003) points to the large number of Assembly-decrees from the overtly oligarchic régime overseen by Antipater (322–19) serving to 'lay to rest any misconceptions that remain about public decrees acting as a *direct* index of democratic activity' (40–1). Other indicators of ongoing democracy exist. For the régime succeeding Demetrius of Phalerum in 307–1, evidence assembled by Habicht includes not only intense activity by the Assembly (71), but also erection of statues to Harmodius and Aristogiton (68) and reconstruction of the Long Walls (70). The Kallias decree (as in the text) contrasts the 'oligarchy' before 287 'when democracy was overthrown' with 'the democracy of all the Athenians' (ll. 80–3). But who constituted 'all the Athenians'? No longer the disenfranchised Athenians and their descendants induced by Antipater to emigrate to Thrace (Plutarch, *Phocion* 27–8); 12,000 of them, according to Green (2003) 1–2; far fewer on Baynham's reckoning: (2003) 23–6. An additional unknown is the presumed absence of public pay and its impact on levels of participation. But overall, the cumulative evidence supports Lape's argument for the continuing strength of democratic ideology.

153. Major (1977) has presented the case for Menander as a 'known sympathizer with Macedonian imperialism' (45). His argument may be questioned at several points; notably, his linking of Menander with Theophrastus. He makes the connexion through 'Theophrastus' definition of comedy as "a story of private affairs involving no danger"' (56–7), suggesting that Menander 'wrote plays congruent with

ENDNOTES

Theophrastus' conception of comedy by setting his dramas in a specifically domestic sphere' (59). In fact, it is by no means certain that the definition as cited by Diomedes is from Theophrastus (see n. 126). In any case, the content of the *Characters* (not mentioned by Major) is sufficient to establish a strong political element in Theophrastus' own humorous writing. While I accept Major's distancing of Theophrastus from the active Athenian political scene (58–9), it is hardly realistic to reconstruct the general character of Theophrastus' political writings from the few surviving citations. Philodemus' criticism of Theophrastus for placing political before domestic matters (*P. Herc.* 1424 col. vii = FHS&G 659), noted by Major himself (57), should not be disregarded (59).

154. There is independent support for a persisting democratic mentality in early Hellenistic Athens from the careful reading of the *Characters* by Leppin (2002) 48–56.

155. Podlecki concludes (243) that Theophrastus continued the tradition of politico-historical inquiry beginning with Aristotle, suggesting that duplication of titles between the two might indicate collaboration (234–5): cataloguers were uncertain to whom to attribute individual works. Similar suggestions have been made about Theophrastus' philosophical writings.

156. The English edition of *Charicles* represents, according to the translator's preface (ix–x), a slimmed-down and bowdlerized version of the German original. Jebb (2005) x–xi singled out Becker's *Charicles* as symptomatic of a dead-end approach to Greek antiquity, as if 'peopled by beings who existed solely in the interests of unborn archaeologists. Dinners, kottabos, marriages, funerals and striking emergencies of the wardrobe succeed each other with a disregard of probability as placid and complete as if the instructive lives of the personages had been prearranged by a Board of Studies.' And his alternative: 'The facts of ancient life are dead unless the imagination is exercised in seizing the social tone which is suggested by their relation to each other.' This enlightened approach to the reading of the Orators ties in with Jebb's earlier intentions in editing and translating Theophrastus, as noted by Easterling and Edwards (2005) XI–XII.

157. For modern as worse: Mahaffy (1874) 484–9: 'Modern Europe is travelling in the opposite direction [to the ancient Greeks], and yearly attaining a condition less favourable for a diffused intensity of life.' Asserting the 'Modernness of the Athenian': Tucker (1911) 311–15. Having briskly summed-up the sub-genre of 'social life', Hobsbawm's conclusion is uncompromising (1971) 72: 'It requires no comment'. But in light of continuing popularity, its implicit perspectives do deserve comment, as teased out for Mahaffy (1874) and Ehrenberg (1951) by Harriet Moynihan (1997).

158. I am aware how this differs from the technique of the 'thick description' exemplified by Clifford Geertz (1973) in his deservedly influential essay, 'Notes on the Balinese cock fight'; similarly adapted by Keith Hopkins (1983) in his account of gladiator shows (1 n. 1). Also relevant to reading the *Characters* as history are Hopkins' reflections on writing history from fiction (1993) esp. 206–12.

159. Arguably, too close, in that the reading depends on finely drawn distinctions between Theophrastus' 'Oligarch', the Xenophontic *Constitution of the Athenians*, and oligarchy in Plato and Aristotle.

160. Patronage: Millett (1989) 30–3; usury: (1991) 179–99; exchange: (1990) 182–94.

161. The notion of a more open phalanx with individuals up to six feet apart is convincingly asserted by Hans van Wees (2000a) 126–34, (2004) 184–7. Hoplite warfare as a defining feature of life as a citizen in the classical polis: Hanson (1989) esp. 219–12, (2000) 219–22. Its invocation in the *Characters* is interestingly late.

162. Konstan (1995) 100 also distinguishes two senses of *agroikia*: 'But the image of the rustic cuts both ways, carrying connotations of sturdy independence, straightforwardness, hard work and honesty alongside those of taciturn or uncouth sociability.' The division may be reflected in the ancient grammarians' distinction by different accentuation (not apparent in actual manuscripts) between *agroikos* as boor and as countryman; see Pollux, 9.12 with Konstantakos (2005) 2 n. 4.

Hanson (1995) shares Jones's reading of the *agroikos* from the *Characters* (5): 'Twenty-four centuries ago, Theophrastus, the urban philosopher, portrayed this "other" Greek as an oaf and a clod'; so giving a distorted perspective on 'the typical Greek farmer'. But Hanson seems to assimilate others of the *Characters* to the same category: (156) the 'Chatterbox' (3.3, with my n. 130); (140) the 'Penny-

Pincher' (10.11, 13) is a 'stingy farmer'. I do not follow the argument that his entertaining of fellow-demesmen is 'a tactic that indicates real tension'.

163. It is unfortunate that Rosivach (2000), in an otherwise helpful analysis, seems to assume that Athenian farmers were more-or-less insulated from the economic life of the city. Exchange relations apart, were the city-walls perpetually the 'formidable social and cultural divide' argued for by Jones (6–9)? Alternative approaches elsewhere reassess the role of apparent physical barriers in encouraging, under the right circumstances, 'zones of interaction'; mountain-ranges: Horden and Purcell (2000) 130–1; frontiers: Whittaker (1994) 98–131. There are hints from Aristophanes of a distinct if downbeat cultural milieu, gathered round the city-gates.

164. Ancient Athens as a Sjobergian pre-industrial city? That calls for a study in its own right. A start has been made by Jennifer Kosak (2000), exploring ideas from the fifth century linking cities with disease. Certainly, the Characters seem preoccupied with their health and that of those around them, including their slaves (17.6). The 'Offensive Man' (19) is a walking repertory of unpleasant afflictions. Other Characters and their associates vomit (3.3), have a fever (12.3), are kept off school through illness (30.14), or through pretended illness (22.6); illness might be feigned to avoid a meeting (1.4). Apart from wounding in battle (25.5), dangers to health include falling from a horse (27.10), catching a chill at a dinner-party (2.10), and washing in cold water in winter (28.5). Possible treatments involve purging (20.5), abstention from wine on doctor's orders (13.9), and making a dedication at the Asklepieion (21.10).

165. Robin Lane Fox confirms to me that D. H. Macindoe (his Housemaster at Eton and Classical Tutor) was certainly familiar with the Characters.

166. Without wishing to press the analogy, Cricket dialogue, obviously addressed to public-school and club-cricketers, in part parallels the restricted audience envisaged for the Characters. The notion of norm-reversal has, of course, been loosely applied to the Characters: 'Theophrastus conveys a sense of the norms of behavior by showing how his characters deviate from them in serious or trivial ways.': Habicht (1997) 123; most systematically by Leppin (2002); cf. Schnayder (1962) 21; Bingen (1980) 28.

167. By analogy with Stephen Clark's brilliant construction of Aristotle's Man (1975). Bingen's label (1980) 29 is 'pseudo-Théophrast'.

168. Here and elsewhere, in an effort to avoid the danger of descriptive caricature, I make extensive use of direct quotation from The corrupting sea. For a sample of the dangers, there is the summary by J. and E. Fentress (2001) in their review of The corrupting sea of 'the primitivist approach of Moses Finley, which lumped all of economic history in the classical world into a minimalist view of a largely self-sufficient society, in which trade is an epiphenomenon practiced by or for the elite few'. What can they have been reading?

169. For Theophrastus as a possible pupil of Plato (Diog. Laert. 3.46), see Sollenberger (1992) 3806–7; detailed discussion of his likely experiences in Assos: Gaiser (1985); for his possible invitation to Aristotle to travel to Mytilene (Diog. Laert. 5.9): Lynch (1972) 70–2. Maxwell-Stuart (1996) ingeniously constructs on the basis of geographical references in the scientific works a plausible itinerary for Theophrastus on his journey to and from Macedonia.

170. On the mobility of philosophers in general: McKechnie (1989) 150–2, a work which now looks ahead of its time. Theophrastus is listed by Plutarch among philosophers enjoying the benefits of exile, voluntary or otherwise (On exile 605A-B = FHS&G 25), and by Cicero (Tusc. disput. 5.107 = FHS&G 24). According to Aelian (Varia historia 4.20 = FHS&G 513), Theophrastus praised Democritus of Abdera for his extensive travelling, accumulating knowledge rather than material goods. For 'machinery, institutions, which promote assimilation and acculturation' of outsiders, see Horden and Purcell (2000) 378.

171. 'Theophrastan' in that his authorship is not secure; text and translation conveniently in Hort (1916). Apart from general advice concerning weather conditions, observations are made with specific reference to Parnes and Phyle (§§43, 47), Hymettus (§§4, 20, 22), Euboea (§22), Aegina (§25), Athos (§34), and Pontus (§41). Fraser (1995) 170 n. 11 describes the work as 'full of vivid observation of

weather signs, still easily recognized in Greece today, and ... an excellent vade-mecum for the traveller'. On the other hand, he offers persuasive arguments (180–1) against Capelle's theory of a long-term visit to Africa by Theophrastus: 'Theophrast in Ägypten' (1956); 'Theophrast in Kyrene?' (1958).

172. Detail of Theophrastus' sources for the mangrove swamps (the explorers Nearchus and Androsthenes) is set out by Fraser (1995) 176, who tells what is known of the wide range of oral and written sources on which he might have drawn. The Alexander connexion (all from *Inquiry into plants*): Zeus Ammon: (4.3.5; 5.3.7); Alexander forbidding his troops from eating diarrhoea-inducing mangoes (4.4.5); Gedrosia (4.4.13); Alexander and his army returning from India crowned with ivy growing on Mt. Meros (4.4.1); Harpalus unsuccessfully trying to grow ivy in the Gardens of Babylon (4.4.1); Greeks with Alexander naming a tree as a fig (4.4.4); Macedonians bursting through consuming 'strong' wheat (4.4.5); tree as food for naked Indian sages (4.4.5); Alexander's men keeping their horses under control so as not to eat a poisonous shrub (5.4.12).

173. Collected references to localities: Einarson and Link (1976) xxiii. Fraser (1995) 169–70 points out how the accounts of planting, pruning, and harvesting in *On the causes of plants* 'are clearly based on personal knowledge', which he relates to Theophrastus' ownership of an estate in Stageira. Capelle (1954) imaginatively recreates the flora of Theophrastus' garden in the Lyceum. But direct acquaintance with basic agricultural processes should not be extended, as by Schnayder (1962) 30–3, 36, to incorporate a unique interest in working people. As pointed out by Gottschalk (1964) 69, Theophrastus' concern lay with the practices of artisans rather than the artisans themselves. Theophrastus presumably followed Aristotle's advice (as expressed in *Nicomachean ethics* 1143b12) to search out information from people like hunters and fishermen with practical experience of the natural world.

174. Particular trees are similarly identified in Antandaros (2.2.6), at the mouth of the cave on Mt. Ida (3.3.4), in the gymnasium at Rhegium (4.5.6), and in the agora at Megara (5.2.4). Precision is here surely intended as an endorsement of omniscience; like Lord Haw-Haw supposedly boasting of his knowledge that the town-hall clock at Croydon was ten minutes slow.

175. Anderson (1970) xix emphasizes what he sees as the isolation of the Characters from the wider Greek world: 'The dominant impression is one of individuals moving within their miniature, highly egocentric worlds.' There is a strong consensus in favour of the *Characters* as focused deliberately onto Athens: Lane Fox (1996) 129 notes that: 'No Character does or mentions anything which has to be referred to a city other than Athens', and amply demonstrates (133) Theophrastus' 'remarkably sharp eye for Attic detail'. In general terms, the character-genre is an urban phenomenon: Smeed (1985) 102–4, 111–13.

176. The quotation within the quotation is from Braudel (1972–3) 388. It is unclear whether the daily peram-bulation of the 'Superstitious Man' (16) takes him out into the countryside. His sprinkling with water on the seashore (§13) occurs in an apparent interpolation; but Diggle's restoration in the text of his visit to *three* springs (§2) would certainly take him outside the city-walls. Other Characters, sharing the 'Chatterbox's' preoccupation with the weather, might be thought to have a stake in the countryside: the 'Ungrateful Grumbler' (17.4) complaining because Zeus did not send rain sooner.

177. The text is problematic, but not hopelessly so; Diggle's detailed reconstruction (2004) 487–91 is followed here.

178. The tapestry depicting Persians may be presumed to be an import from Persia. The detailed reading of the Maltese dog's epitaph is open to question; see Diggle (2004) 411–12.

179. The lame conclusion to the 'Oligarchic Man' (26.6) has him address his views 'to *xenoi* and to citizens of similar disposition and political persuasion'.

180. *Polis* in the *Characters* is commonly ambiguous: is it just the *astu* or *astu* plus *chora* within which the 'Oligarchic Man' (26) cannot co-exist alongside the *ochlos* (§3), and which sycophants make so intolerable (§4)? The sense in 23.4 (*pace* Diggle) cannot be 'city' as the 'Boastful Man' has earlier been placed in the Piraeus. Elsewhere (5.8), the 'Conspicuous Consumer' aims to publicize his purchases over the whole polis; more pointed if embracing the entire territory? Likewise the allegedly

polis-wide talk reported by the 'Rumour-Monger' (8.7), and the polis-wide admiration the 'Toady' claims for his patron (2.2).

181. In his denigration of Sosidemus (§2) he is answering an initial inquiry; in his denunciation of the household of uncontrollable women (§3) gossip is already underway ('what's being said isn't idle talk'); he seems to respond to a question, but the text is irremediably corrupt. Both sums of money (*one* talent; three coppers *per day*) incorporate more-than-plausible restorations. Posideon was indeed the bleak mid-winter: from December to January.

182. The essential bibliography on 'honour and shame' is given in the 'Bibliographical Essay to Chapter XII' from Horden and Purcell (2000) 637–41. Particularly helpful have proved Davis (1977), Gilmore (1987), Herzfeld (1980), Peristiany (1965a), Peristiany and Pitt-Rivers (1992), and Williams (1993). Stewart (1994) attempts with mixed success to answer the question what honour actually is; the approximate answer being the right to respect (21). A suitable case for polythetic treatment?.

183. It is difficult to summarize Williams' subtle arguments which depend in large part on locating guilt with respect to shame; see the helpful review by Fisher (1995). Williams' discussion overlaps with the valuable introduction to Cairns' study of *aidos* (1993) 1–47. They agree in rejecting the straightforward distinction between shame and guilt cultures. Both see shame not as depending on others' attitudes but as reflecting internalized values. Williams develops this idea, identifying shame as crucial in establishing the individual's identity, reconciling standards set by self and by the wider community. In the endnote 'Mechanisms of shame and guilt' (219–23), Williams presents shame as offering more scope for moral autonomy ('character') than guilt. The former involves an internalized figure as watcher or witness, commenting on the individual's failure; the latter involves an internalized victim or enforcer, punishing the fault.

184. To Millett (1984) 'Hesiod and his world' should now be added Edwards' careful study *Hesiod's Ascra* (2004). Amongst other works cited by Horden and Purcell on ancient non-aristocratic honour and shame, Cairns (1993) viii explicitly declines to discuss Aristophanes, Greek historians and Attic Orators.

185. Again, I make use of direct quotation to minimize distortion in what is necessarily a highly selective résumé; compare the synopsis, from a different perspective, by Horden and Purcell (489–92). Like them (489), I adopt the 'ethnographic present' in describing a community which has apparently all but disappeared. Campbell (262 n. 1) in his treatment 'The Values of Prestige' (263–320) notes 'obvious parallels with Homeric society', and acknowledges benefits gained from works by Bowra, Snell, Finley and Adkins. But Homeric approaches do not seem to underpin his analysis, so that comparison with the later Greek world of the *Characters* is not compromised.

186. The phrase 'limited good' is not used by Campbell; for its explicit application to Mediterranean honour, see Brandes (1987) 121–2. But the idea is vividly present in the Sarakatsan story that God, after creating all other countries, made Greece out of the stones and rocks left in his sack. In terms of practicalities, good grazing is scarce so that its allocation by the village president to one Sarakatsan family means another does less well (204).

187. If the *ostal* of medieval Montaillou, south of Carcassonne, seems too Mediterranean (Le Roy Ladurie (1978) 25–42), there are the family groupings from rural Shropshire at the turn of the seventeenth century, detailed pew-by-pew from the village church by Richard Gough in his remarkable *History of Myddle* (1981).

188. Tribe, phratry and deme represent a minimum of associations comprising the *koinonia* of the polis. For their relationships with each other and to central authority (including selected 'voluntary' associations), see the detailed analysis by Jones (1999).

189. *Philotimos* crops up among the Sarakatsani with a different meaning: being so concerned with one's own nobility of conduct as to take into account how one's actions affect the honour of others (294–5). For a different perspective on *philotimia* ('high-souled generosity'): Peristiany (1965a) 178–87.

190. 'clansmen (*tous phrateras*)' are Diggle's inclusion in the list of admirers (2004) 460–2, so avoiding an anomalous pair of items in asyndeton by adding a noun 'which regularly appears in partnership with the other two'.

191. The potential conflict between honour and legal redress is analysed with regard to the modern Mediterranean by Pitt-Rivers (1965) 30: 'For to go to law for redress is to confess publicly that you have been wronged and that the demonstration of your vulnerability places your honour in jeopardy, a jeopardy from which the "satisfaction" of legal compensation at the hands of a secular authority hardly redeems it.' The litigant in Demosthenes' speech *Against Conon* (54), bringing a charge of assault, faced a similar dilemma. He knows (or claims to) that his opponent will argue how the whole affair was merely an altercation arising out of some *hetaira* or other; how boys will be boys (§14). He therefore seeks to raise his accusation onto a higher plain of seriousness by presenting the case as if one of *hubris*: Millett (1998) 203–6, 227–8; Fisher (1992) 50–1. Halliwell (1991) 288 draws a neat contrast between the playful and essentially innocuous skylarking claimed by the defendant, and calculated mockery involving *hubris* asserted by the prosecution. The Theophrastan vignette is considered from a stylistic point of view by Diggle (2004) 22–3.

192. Horden and Purcell (2000) 505 illustrate 'obsession with apparent trivia' by quoting Davis' account from 1970 of fieldwork in the hill-town of Pisticci on the instep of Italy. 'Provocations to ethical appraisal' include the amount of food bought and consumed, how often clothes and bedding were washed and their condition, how often clothes were changed, and whether girls took the shortest routes to their destinations. 'All these things are quickly noted and, and conclusions drawn about the conduct of the family' (72–3). The level of observation (even actual observations) corresponds to behaviour encountered in the *Characters*.

193. So Horden and Purcell (2000) 506–7: 'The common feature of almost all reports of Mediterranean honour is ... a focus on the sexuality of women, as fundamental to their own honour or shame, and also the point at which the honour of the family or patriline is most vulnerable and most in need of protection.' The theme is explored by Gilmore (1987) 3–5: honour's 'basic currency and measurement is the "shame" of women, by which Mediterraneanists mean female sexual chastity'. 'Of vigilance and virgins' is the title of a key paper by Schneider (1971), locating women as a crucial element in the family patrimony.

194. A Sarakatsan husband is expected to be the protector of his wife: Campbell (1964) 150, but without unjust oppression (153). Compare the contrasting behaviour imputed to unsatisfactory heads of household by Theophrastus' 'Slanderer' (above, 182).

195. It will be appreciated that here and in much that follows the account of interpersonal relations is at odds with the presentation of Athenian economy and society by Cohen (2000) in *The Athenian nation* (esp. 104–29), which he constructs as a 'society of relative anonymity' (105). This is not the place to engage in detail with his arguments. In brief, I do not accept his attempt to dislodge the current orthodoxy (which is not merely the view of 'a few specialists': 105 n. 4) that *key elements* in the Athenian polis did function as equivalent to 'face-to-face' societies. A case in point: the evidence for social-interaction in shops and workshops around the Agora as presented and analysed by Lewis (1995). The relative mobility of population for which Cohen argues need not be a barrier to ongoing integration of relationships. Here are two counter-cases: Gough's *Myddle* (1981) combined plenty of mobility with what was evidently a closely knit community (see n. 187); my own Cambridge College might seem to approach the Laslettian ideal of a face-to-face society, yet at least one third of its total population changes each year.

196. Behaviour of the 'Slanderer' and his like in the Assembly adds to the range of informal ways in which 'ordinary citizens' might hope to influence proceedings; others are collected and analysed by Tacon (2001).

197. Smeed (1985) 288–9 astutely compares the 'high-minded' satisfaction derived from character collections as historically and sociologically illuminating, with 'the more vulgar type of curiosity which also motivates us: "characters" provide a sort of high-class gossip about typical specimens of our fellow-men'. It is to this potential for gossip across the ages that he in part ascribes the enduring popularity of the 'Character'.

198. Parker (2006) 311 points out that the terminology (*meris*) of 17.2 typically refers to a cut of sacrificial

meat, 'and the point is also ... to involve friends in the sacrifice'. The slandering of those in power by the 'Morally Degraded Man' (6.2) is very likely an interpolation.

199. Although the text is not entirely certain, the general sense seems clear. For possible negative undertones of *euphues* ('too clever by half') and *philetairos* ('loyal to a faction'), see Diggle (2004) 502.

200. The passage is quoted as part of their conclusion by Horden and Purcell (2000) 502, who discuss in their opening chapter the construction of 'Mediterraneanism' as an ideology comparable to 'orientalism'. That many classicists might seem in some ways to prefer the traditional conception of the Mediterranean to the supposed modernity of northern Europe complicates but does not disarm Herzfeld's objection. Nor (presumably) does Cohen's attempt (2000) to recreate classical Athens as something approaching the modern conception of a nation-state.

201. Since what follows is intended primarily as a study of what the *Characters* as a text can tell the historian, I rarely cite additional, supporting evidence for the economy and society of later fourth-century Athens.

202. FHS&G here translate *aidos* as 'respect'. Parallel passages are cited by Fortenbaugh (1984) 187.

203. They were, in fact, abolished by Demetrius of Phalerum: Wilson (2000) 270–6; for the complaint of the 'Oligarchic Man' as stereotypical: 184–7. I can find no evidence to support the statement by Gottschalk (n. 82) that Theophrastus himself advocated abolition of liturgies. The basic mechanism of reciprocity at the heart of the liturgy system and some of its practical implications are discussed in Millett (2000), supplemented by Johnstone (1999) 93–108.

204. The passage is rightly interpreted by Diggle (2004) 438–41, correcting my reading (1991) 157, where the five talents handed out to needy citizens are wrongly conflated with the ten talents in *eranos* loans.

205. For Cicero (attuned to the Roman games) as misunderstanding the nature of the expenditure advocated by Theophrastus, see Fortenbaugh (1984) 246–7. The 'Illiberal Man's' wooden strip is exposed as a 'contemptibly mean monument' by Wilson (2000) 243–4.

206. *Light of the soul B, Anthology* ch. 7, *De alacritate* = FHS&G 506. The behaviour of the 'Man of Petty Ambition' is discussed by Diggle (2004) 23–5 to demonstrate how style of speech can contribute to characterization.

207. Why exactly the *agroikos* objects to the coin is unclear. The text as transmitted (*lian men lupron*) makes no sense; Diels' emendation of *lian molubron* ('too leaden') makes some sort of sense: the coin is discoloured and so looks like lead. But it stretches credibility that an Athenian countryman should be so unfamiliar with silver coinage as not to appreciate its tendency to tarnish. Better would be some word for 'light' in the sense of 'underweight', but no plausible suggestion has been made. How would the *mikrophilotimos* acquire his newly minted coin? This obsession would cost him. He – more likely his slave – is to be imagined taking coinage already in circulation to the mint in the Agora, having returned to him an equal weight (not number) of coin, and paying a mint-charge into the bargain.

208. The comic effect is drawn out by Diggle (2004) 409. Aristophanes has Lysistrata (555–64) comment sarcastically on those who do their marketing in the Agora dressed in armour and carrying weapons. I can find no reference to the *mikrophilotimos* passage in either Bugh (1988) or Spence (1993). In addition to being the sole reference to wearing of spurs by Athenian *hippeis* (Lane Fox (1996) 143), it surely has something to tell about perceptions of the Athenian cavalry. According to Spence (202; cf. 210), 'The Athenians ... basically perceived their cavalry and cavalry class as a group of wealthy aristocratic youths', which conceivably adds to the incongruity of the presumably middle-aged *mikrophilotimos* parading through the Agora.

209. The potential of etiquette as a socio-cultural indicator is further explored below, 114.

210. For Burckhardt's concept of 'agonal man' and its seventh-century origins, see Ehrenberg (1973) 20–7. Others have commented with reference to the *Characters* on the apparent openness of Athenian society, with consequent traps for the unwary or imperfectly behaved: Giglioni (1980) 85, 95. Lane Fox (1996) 145–6 notes ways in which the Characters are repeatedly placed in settings (arbitrations, *eranoi*, *epidoseis*) which show up the demands made on good citizens.

211. This brief summary does not reflect the richness of the chapter. Before moving on to introduce individual contributions to the volume (26–9), Goldhill focuses attention on four notions which help to explain the

instructive power for the Athenians of performance culture: spectacle, audience, construction of self, self-consciousness (8–10). He also identifies as among key authors Bakhtin, Austin, Foucault (10–18), and indicates elements of Athenian democracy overlapped by performance culture (20–6).

212. In fact, the 'show of the streets' does put in a brief appearance in 'Programme notes' (18), through the multi-faceted representation of London and Paris as part of 'Street theatre's social drama'. The discussion is prefaced by a quotation from Thorstein Veblen (leisure as a 'performance'), to whom we will return in chapter 11.

213. 'Pop's bun in the oven' is Diggle's proposal: *popanourgia* for *panourgion*. What embarrassing thing the 'Disagreeable Man' goes on to say to his mother is barely recoverable, even in outline; perhaps something along the lines that childbirth brings both pleasure and pain, and how it is not easy to find a person who does not experience both. But Diggle (2004) 399–400 has no confidence in any of the suggested restorations. The person (*ton pheronta*) to whom the 'Ungrateful Grumbler' (17.2) complains about being diddled out of his soup and wine may be intended as a slave: so identified by Edmonds and Austen (1904) index, *s.v.* 'Slaves'.

214. *Andrapodon* or 'man-footed', the (to us) dehumanizing word used by the narrator to describe the 'Ungrateful Grumbler's' purchase, is found only here in the *Characters*. Words elsewhere for slaves: *pais* (17 times), *paidarion* (2), *paidion* (1), *akolouthos* (4), *oiketes* (4), *titthe* (2), *paidagogos* (2), *therapaina* (1), *mageiros* (1), *oinochoos* (1), *sitopoios* (1).

215. The fragment may be from Theophrastus' lost work in two books *Peri timorias* or 'On retribution': Diog. Laert. 5.45 = FHS&G 1.160; see Fortenbaugh (1984) 258–9. The passage is set in context by Harris (2001) 320–1, who appositely cites Socrates from the *Republic* (548E-549A), indicating harshness towards slaves as characteristic of an imperfectly educated man, who lacks a suitable sense of his own superiority. Harris does not quite bring out the heightened sense of revenge implicit in Theophrastus' advice; apparent in Latin paraphrases of Theophrastus from later collections of sayings (FHS&G 527A-B). The motive behind delaying punishment was, however, correctly understood by Dick Bultitude, the often-beaten schoolboy magically transformed into the appearance of his father, Paul, in F. Anstey's excellent novel *Vice versâ* ((1882) ch. 14). The ponderous headmaster Dr Grimstone (wrongly believing he addresses the father) pronounces: '"An ancient philosopher, my dear sir, was accustomed to postpone the correction of his slaves until the first glow of his indignation had passed away. He found that he could – " "Lay it on with more science," suggested Dick, while Paul writhed where he stood.' But the whole book needs to be read.

216. By contrast, the 'Obsequious Man' is never servile. *Areskeia* is defined by Aristotle (*Nicomachean ethics* 1127a7–10) as excessive sociability; the *kolax* is *areskos* in the hopes of gain. The object of the 'Toady's' attentions is almost entirely colourless. It is arguably inappropriate to label him 'patron' as we learn nothing of his response to all the flattery, save that he seems to tolerate it. He is evidently fashion-conscious, shopping for Iphicratids (lightweight footwear), and wealthy, having a nicely built house (*eu erchitektonesthai*) and a naturalistic portrait (§12). According to Davies (1978) 165, who gives a technical sense to *architektoneo*, for the later fourth century this was 'trendy twice over'. Lane Fox (1996) 145 in part demurs: although in the 320s realistic portraits were at the forefront of fashion (see n. 129), an architect-designed house has no classical parallel. However, approximately a century later, Ariston could implicitly criticize the 'Know-it-all' (col. 18) for *not* employing the services of an *architekton* for building both house and boat.

217. Problems with the text, interpretation of the fragment as a whole and its relationship with other works attributed to Theophrastus (*De nuptiis*; Book 1 of the pseudo-Aristotelian *Oeconomica*) are discussed by Fortenbaugh (1984) 254–7. Book 1 of the *Oeconomica* is explicitly attributed to Theophrastus by Philodemus (*Peri kaklon kai ton antikeimenon areton* cols. 7.37–12.2). Possible overlap with Theophrastus' writings (including the *Characters*) is assessed by Zoepffel (2006) 199–204, who concludes that attribution to Theophrastus is possible but ultimately unclear.

218. Lane Fox (1996) 149–50 gives detail of the norm of 'severe simplicity, this Attic good taste' (Hicks's phrase) shown by inscriptions on the tombstones of Attic women (see n. 135).

219. According to Jebb, irony was here intended in that 'Greek wives were seldom busy'. In support of my suggestion (Diggle (2004) 370 n. 84) that Jebb was 'misled by the behaviour of women in upper-middle-class families in his Cambridge', there is the testimony of his great-niece, Gwen Raverat (1952) esp. 96: 'I have defined Ladies as people who did not do things themselves.'

220. Strange, in that even given the fluidity of slave terminology, the antithesis of *doulos* and *therapon* might seem to suggest those working outside and inside the house. Perhaps the words might be reversed, or the negatives struck out. FHS&G offers respectively 'household slaves' and 'male attendants', for which, on the basis of the *Characters* (where *douloi* and *therapon* do not occur), *oiketai* or *paides*, and *akolouthoi* might be expected (see n. 214). Agreement between Theophrastus' observations on women in the *oikos* and Peripatetic thinking in general is endorsed by Fortenbaugh (1984) 198–200.

221. The rationale of children's reciprocal obligation towards their parents in later life is discussed (along with a conspectus of texts) in Millett (1991) 132–4.

222. Halliwell (1991) 287 points out from this snippet how tolerance of mockery could be regarded as aberrant behaviour. Compare the 'Dissembler' (1.2), who perversely seems to forgive those who speak abusively about him.

223. See Diggle (2004) 516–17 for the identification of the expenditure during Anthesterion to which the 'Shabby Profiteer' takes exception as the ancient equivalent of school trips.

224. The *eromene* of the 'Tactless Man' is surely to be understood as a *hetaira*, but who are the *gunaikes*, in whose presence the Late-Learner (27.15) feels moved to practice dance-steps, humming his own accompaniment?

225. The analogy of the house-as-stage may be taken further, with furniture functioning as theatrical properties (the couches debugged by the 'Illiberal Man'; the kitchenware, couches and chests shifted by the 'Penny-Pincher'). References are collected by Edmonds and Austen (1904) 155–6 *s.v.* 'Furniture, implements, and utensils', adding a little to our sense of the likely contents of an upper-class Athenian house.

226. The homogeneity of Athenian housing (at least in terms of prevailing ideology) is set out by Millett (1998) 206–11, where the house of the 'Conspicuous Consumer' is incorrectly attributed to the 'Man of Petty Ambition' (210–11). Nevett (1999) esp. 161–2 effectively brings to bear the evidence of archaeology on the trend attested in fourth-century literature to larger, more differentiated housing. Although her analysis is consciously weighted towards reinterpreting the material remains, the testimony of the *Characters* may have something to add to the debate.

227. The stylistic device of the so-called 'identification riddle' (when is an 'x' a 'y'?) as here deployed by Theophrastus is discussed in detail by Diggle (2002) 65–6.

228. Cicero plainly has in mind the style of hospitality practiced by Rome's élite: 'Furthermore for those who wish to enjoy great power in an honourable manner, it is also extremely useful to have strong resources and influence among foreign peoples thanks to guest-friends (*per hospites*)'. However, he goes on to cite by way of illustration, how 'Theophrastus indeed writes that at Athens Cimon was hospitable even to the people of his own district, the Laciads. For he so arranged [matters] and ordered his stewards, that everything should be put at the disposal of any Laciad who might visit his villa.' Cicero is naturally attracted to the closest approximation from classical Athens to aristocratic patronage over perceived inferiors (Millett (1989) 23–5), which he seems to locate at the humbler end of hospitality. Implications of Theophrastus on Cimon for the concept of *megaloprepeia* are discussed by Fortenbaugh (1984) 247–8.

229. Still more vigorous is the assault made by the 'Late Learner' (27.9) on the door of his reluctant *hetaira*, with the Character himself likened, in Herwerden's conjecture, to a *krios* or '(battering)-ram'; see Diggle (2004) 482–3. Ariston's 'Hostile Man' supplies from a century later additional detail of the etiquette of making and returning visits (col. 17): 'If he has been invited out, he doesn't return the invitation. When he knocks at another's door and is asked, "Who is it?" he doesn't answer until the man comes outside. If a friend pays him a visit while he's ill, he won't say how he is feeling, and when he himself visits someone, he won't even ask such a question.'

230. Who are these people to whom he delegates hospitality? According to Diggle: 'employees'; Ussher: 'servants'; Anderson: 'staff'; Jebb and Rusten: 'subordinates'; Navarre: 'inférieurs'. Steinmetz (1962) 276, 282 translates as 'einem seiner Leute', supplying references (Xen. *Cyrop.* 1.5.3, 3.3.6, 8.8.5; Hdt. 7.108; Thuc. 1.110.2) where the phrase is used with respect to vertical relationships in Persian contexts. He suggests that the expression represents a particularly developed sense of dependence and domination, which therefore reflects the view of the *huperephanos* himself. Plainly, the dependents cannot be slaves, but employment of hired labour in this capacity would be unprecedented and inconceivable, even for a *huperephanos*. Just possibly they are to be imagined as freedmen or, more likely, the broad equivalent of the *kolax*.

231. In an otherwise subtle piece, Geddes underplays scope for individualistic adaptation of broadly indistinguishable garments (see further 101). The ubiquity of the *himation* is attested by its frequent appearance in Aristophanes: Stone (1981) 155–60, who concludes that 'Many passages testify to the high esteem in which an Athenian held his *himation*; poor-looking *himations* (*Birds* 1416; *Eccl.* 409–10) and fancy ones (*Frogs* 1061; *Plutus* 940) are both referred to twice' (160).

232. To the earlier warning about the unreliability of Teles (n. 118) should be here added alternative testimony to Theophrastus' asceticism: by implication, the last man in Athens to be spotted wearing linen (above, 88); his saying that 'We ought to accustom ourselves to live on a little, in order that we may do nothing shameful for the sake of money' (*Florilegium Monacense* 202 = FHS&G 510); his urging, according to Vitruvius (6 Introduction 2 = FHS&G 491), that men should be educated rather than rely on money.

233. In what are almost certainly interpolations (Diggle (2004) 288–90, 312–13), the 'Rumour-Monger' and his kind (8.11) lose their cloaks while holding forth at the baths; the 'Penny-Pincher' and his like (10.14) are described as wearing cloaks that are too short, having shaved heads, going barefoot in the middle of the day and 'insisting to the fullers that their cloaks should have plenty of earth, so that they don't get dirty too soon'. The motif of an inelegantly worn *himation* is chosen by Theophrastus Such as likely to have set him apart in Sappho's Mytilene from 'the accomplished fair ones who were so precise in adjusting their own drapery about their delicate ankles' (ch. 2, 16).

234. Which is why §§7–10, describing pointlessly disruptive behaviour, have been persuasively identified as belonging to an otherwise lost Character; see Diggle (2004) 386.

235. 'infested with lice' is Diggle's compelling suggestion: *phtheirodeis* for *theirodeis* ('beastlike').

236. Bremmer (1991) 18–19 provides supporting material and compares the 'Arrogant Man' in the street with Aristotle's Great-Hearted Man: deep-voiced and slow-walking (1125a12–16).

237. Textual problems with this brief text (requiring two emendations) and its implications for Theophrastus' ethical and rhetorical theory are discussed by Fortenbaugh (1984) 251–4. On the implications of direct speech for portrayal of the Characters, see further 116–7.

238. Burke is explicitly concerned with 'The Art of Conversation in Early Modern Europe' (89–122), but includes a backward glance to 'Classical and Medieval Traditions' (96–8), encompassing Plato's Socrates, Plutarch, Dio Chrysostom and Cicero.

239. The relationships of this anecdote to the Character of the *lalos* (7), and between *lalia* and *adoleschia* (2) are discussed by Fortenbaugh (1984) 176–8. Compare *Florilegium: best and first lessons* no. 64 (= FHS&G 451): 'When Theophrastus was asked, "Which of the things in life is good or bad?" he said, "The tongue".' But the saying is also attributed to Anacharsis, Thales and Aesop (see n. 68). The importance of knowing when not to speak is intriguingly pursued by Burke in his 'Notes for a social history of silence' (1993) 123–4.

240. Different in tone (far more self-deprecating) is the lengthy conversation of Ariston's *eiron* (cols. 22–3). His concluding comment gives the flavour: 'He is the sort who says to whoever he happens to be talking to, "Friends, you must explain to me my ignorance and other blunders, and not let me make a fool of myself"; or "Please tell me about so-and-so's happy state, so that I may have the pleasure of being like him, if I can." Why go on?'

241. Ariston's *authades* is similarly unco-operative in his conversation (col. 17): 'If someone asks him what

he intends to do, he says "That's for me to know." If someone criticizes, he smirks, "Look who's talking!" If he is called to a meeting for a man who seeks advice, he refuses to say what he thinks unless the man is definitely going to follow it...'

242. The Deigma was the part of the Piraeus where samples of goods were displayed to prospective purchasers. The term (well attested elsewhere) was restored by Casaubon, replacing the 'diazeugma' of the MSS, a word that was otherwise unknown until its discovery in a papyrus of the first century AD (*P. Lond.* 131.205), with the apparent meaning of a connecting structure. Diggle (2004) 432–3, who notes two further, overlooked but inconclusive appearances of the term, accepts Casaubon's conjecture as referring to a 'natural meeting-place for foreigners, ship-owners, and gossips'. It would be agreeable if the supposedly colloquial 'Keramos' or 'Jug' could be retained in place of *desmoterion* for the *aponenoemenos*' home-from-home (Molesworth's 'Back in Jug Agane'); but *keramon* is the reading solely of the so-called 'Munich Epitome', which Diggle (42–3) does not accept as an independent witness.

243. The social function of barbershops and shops in general in Athens is explored by Sian Lewis (1995). She identifies shops as intermediate in terms of public display between houses and the Agora (435): 'The symposium is a public occasion within the private sphere, while the shop is a private meeting in the public sphere.' The interplay of houses, shops and workshops around the Agora is assessed by Tsakirgis (2005).

244. Following Diggle's interpretation (2004) 299–30. Ariston's *authades* also puts in an appearance at the baths (cols. 16–17): 'He is the sort (Ariston says), who demands hot or cold water in the bath without first asking his fellow-bather whether it is all right. ... When someone rubs him with oil, he doesn't do the same in return' (though this could be at the gymnasium). The 'Rumour-Monger' (8.11) is presented in an interpolated passage as getting a crowd round him at the baths and losing his cloak.

245. 'Loiterers in gymnasia are usually suspected of looking for boys to pick up': Diggle (2004) 236, with supporting texts. But pederasty is not a part of this Character's obsession with ostentatious display, which includes high-profile time-wasting: *diatribein* in the gymnasia, *prosphoitan* of the bankers' tables.

246. The text that follows on directly from the sober dancing of the *kordax* resists all attempts at emendation (Diggle (2004) 253–4), but seems somehow to refer to a mask worn (or not worn) in a comic chorus. The location is possibly, though not necessarily, the theatre: Aristoph., *Clouds* 540, with Pickard-Cambridge (1966) 167–9. Audiences on a more modest scale are manipulated by the 'Conspicuous Consumer' (5.10), delaying his entrance to the miniature arena attached to his house until the spectators are already seated and able to identify him to each other as the owner.

247. It is unfortunate that a lacuna leaves us ignorant of the behaviour of the 'Late Learner' (27.12) at the meeting of his fellow-*dekadistai*: combining together to sacrifice and feast on the tenth day of each month.

248. The text as translated is problematic (§4): *to plethos kai amnemon* combines restorations by Schneider and Diggle (2004) 471–3.

249. Textual corruption conceals what was presumably the 'Oligarchic Man's' explanation of how Theseus' synoecism led to the appearance of latter-day demagogues: see Diggle (2004) 473–6. In fact, his juxtaposing of synoecism with democracy exactly matches Xenophon's crypto-oligarchic account from the *Hellenica* of the fate of Mantinea in 385 (5.2.1–7). The Spartans, annoyed by its unco-operative democracy, captured the place and imposed a 'dioecism' (synoecism in reverse), with the population being 'split up into four separate villages, just as they used to be in ancient times'. These villages were henceforth ruled by landowning aristocrats, and that was the end of the 'troublesome demagogues'.

250. Stylistic aspects of the passage are discussed by Diggle (2004), who concludes (23): 'This is the kind of picture Dickens loves to draw, where farce and exaggeration teeter on the borders of the credible'.

251. Although *hoi periestekotes* is regularly used of bystanders in the courts, the passage may refer to an oath being sworn in some other public place: Diggle (2004) 331–2. The 'Morally Degraded Man' (6.2) swearing an oath off pat does so in an interpolation. The notion of law courts in Athens as delivering 'justice in the community' (in contrast to English courtrooms cut off from the outside world) is expressed by Millett (2005) 40–6.

252. As Athenian jurors were not supposed to discuss or agree beforehand on their verdict, Gagarin (2000) 360 n. 33 envisages the 'Talker' as distracting his fellow-jurors when they come forward to cast their votes. But a more likely assumption is that the 'Talker's' obsession causes him to ignore rules of court procedure. The 'Friend of Villains' (29.6) similarly overrides the law in attempting to rig the voting of the juries on which he sits.

253. For usurers in Athens, see Millett (1991) 179–88, with Schaps (2004) 185–6; for the rate of interest, above n. 121.

254. As detailed by von Reden (2003) 107 and Millett (1998) 211–28, concluding with the notion (n. 46) that 'Other places have their Agoras. ... The Cambridge equivalent is the Tea Room in the University Library'. For seventeenth-century London should be added the aisle in St. Paul's Cathedral or 'Paul's Walk', the subject of a 'character' by Earle (41), beginning '[It] is the land's epitome, or you may call it the lesser isle of Great Britain'.

255. The 'Illiberal Man' (22.10) hires from the 'women's market' a slave-girl to attend on his wife. Both Diggle (2004) 194 and Lane Fox (1996) 143–4 conclude on the basis of this passage, with Pollux (10.18), that the 'women's market' was the location in the Agora where female slaves were bought or hired. Presumably certain among them were effectively *pornai*, available for hire for sexual purposes. It was not therefore a place where a respectable citizen would wish to be seen; compare the embarrassment of the philosopher Arcesilaus at being spotted in the part of the Agora known as 'Kerkopes', allegedly specializing in stolen goods (Diog. Laert. 9.7.). This would help answer Diggle's question (he marks the passage as an interpolation), how the 'Toady's' 'breathless activities in the women's market serve the man he is flattering' (193); though problems of style and language remain.

256. Other Characters are less directly involved in the business of the Agora. The 'Chatterbox' (3.3) has seen (or perhaps heard) that wheat is on sale there at a bargain price.

257. Ideally, Theophrastus' insistence in his *Laws* that market-magistrates (*agoranomoi*) should attend not only to truthfulness on the parts of buyers and sellers but also to 'orderly conduct in the Agora' would have nipped in the bud the behaviour of at least the 'Shameless Man' (Harpocration on *kata ten agoran apseudein* = FHS&G 651).

258. Fortenbaugh (1984) 250 favours a less personal reading: the capacity of the *politeia* to honour or punish; but reciprocity remains central. The fragment is presumably from one of five or six lost works, the titles of which seem to confirm Theophrastus' interest in what we would call reciprocity: *Peri timorias* or 'On retribution' (Diog. Laert. 5.46 = FHS&G 1.160, cf. 436.22); *Peri philias* or 'On friendship' (Diog. Laert. 5.45 = FHS&G 1.165, cf. 436.23a-b; see below, n. 259); *Peri philotimias* or 'On ambition' (Diog. Laert. 5.46 = FHS&G 1.166); *Peri charitos* or 'On gratitude' (Diog. Laert. 5.48 = FHS&G 1.240, cf. 436.24; *Peri kolakeias* or 'On flattery' (Diog. Laert. 5.547 = FHS&G 1.206, cf. 436.25); *Homiletikos* or 'Concerning social interaction' (Diog. Laert. 5.47 = FHS&G 1.219, cf. 436.32). Concern over the detailed process of reciprocity as between gods, humans and animals is also evident in Theophrastus' reflections on sacrifice, paraphrased by Porphyry, *On abstinence from eating animals* (2.15.7.2–25.7 = FHS&G 584A.52–260). The forger of Aristotle's *Letter to Philip* (4.1–5 = FHS&G 518) sought to lend verisimilitude to his fabrication by having the author praise 'my associate Theophrastus' for his sound views on reciprocity. The theme of reciprocal obligation plays no significant part in character-building by Hall, Overbury or Earle.

259. I am aware that the view given in the text of the primacy of reciprocity in *philia*, essentially following Millett (1991) 109–26, has been questioned: notably by Konstan (1997), Schofield (1998), and Foxhall (1998a). Although in light of these criticisms I would certainly wish to modify my position concerning the affective element in *philia*, I do not believe that the underlying role of reciprocity has been challenged. I hope to examine the question further in a forthcoming paper. Millett (2005) 26–8 tries to demonstrate the centrality of reciprocal relations in maintaining communities of family and polis through their attempted subversion by Strepsiades in Aristophanes' *Clouds*.

260. The phrase *koina ta philon* is proverbial. For parallel expressions and for the novelty of Theophrastus' addition of friends of friends, see Fortenbaugh (1984) 290–1.

261. This Character could benefit by lessons from Diogenes the Cynic (Diog. Laert. 6.62): 'When someone asked that he might have back his cloak, "If it was a gift," he replied, "I possess it; if it was a loan, I am using it".' Diogenes' relentless challenging of etiquette as opposed to the transgressions of the Characters would repay further study.

262. Entirely acceptable is reversing the process of gift and sale: the 'Toady' (2.6) buys apples and pears which he then gives (with a kiss) to the children of his host.

263. Often quoted because commonsensical or controversial? The latter is certainly the case with Theophrastus' opinion regarding friendship and shame, as cited by Aulus Gellius (*Attic nights* 1.3, 8–14, 21–9 = FHS&G 534): 'A small … and slight disgrace or bad repute is to be endured, if by this a great advantage can be gained for a friend. For the trifling loss involved in diminished honour is paid back and compensated by another greater and more important honour involved in assisting a friend, and that minimal stain as it were hole in one's reputation is repaired by the bulwark of advantages obtained for a friend' (§23). Fortenbaugh (1990) argues for continuity from Plato to Aristotle and Theophrastus: the good man is a better judge of right behaviour than potentially inappropriate laws. But Theophrastus' statement is taken by Konstan (1997) 132–3 not only as supplementing Aristotle's writing on *philia*, but just possibly responding to changed circumstances in Athens after Alexander: 'Perhaps the imposition of a regime backed by Macedonian military power set the climate for concern about the ethical limits of personal allegiances.' The practice of admitting to friendship only those judged to be worthy need not cut across implied criticism of those Characters refusing to take the initiative in forming a relationship.

264. Diggle (2004) 448 sees the 'Arrogant Man' (24.6) as refusing the first approach in the sense of declining a greeting: 'The one who makes the first approach or greeting implicitly acknowledges the superior status of the other, or, at any rate, strives to be polite' (with latter-day protocols of greeting illustrated *via* the late George Psychoundakis' *The Cretan runner* 130–1).

265. The Character of the 'Ungrateful Grumbler' is enrolled by Fortenbaugh (1985) 215–224 in an attempt to distinguish Theophrastus' thinking on the features of 'faultfinding' (*mempsis*) as opposed to anger and rage (FHS&G 438). He tentatively concludes that marking off the faultfinder from the angry man (apart from the relative triviality of the circumstances) are the inevitability with which the former states his complaint and the possible absence of desire to inflict harm. Also relevant is Theophrastus' brief disquisition on 'envious men' (*phthoneroi*) as being especially unfortunate in feeling pained not only by their own mishaps, but also by the successes of others (Stobaeus, *Anthology* 3.38.43 = FHS&G 443); not a fault of the 'Ungrateful Grumbler'.

266. Detail on the *eranos* concept and its practical workings in Millett (1991) 153–9. I see no reason (*pace* Cohen (1992) 207–15) to alter my view that *eranos* loans did not bear interest. Schaps (2004) 187–9 esp. n. 61 inclines towards friendship as a frequent feature.

267. Cited by Walter Burley, *On the life and character of philosophers* (68.8 = FHS&G 546). 'Modern studies of reciprocity could well take this text as their epigraph', comments Lane Fox (1996) 146 on the ingratitude of the 'Ungrateful Grumbler'. Precisely how the 'Dissembler' (1.5) responds *pros tous daneizomenous kai eranizontas* is lost in a lacuna, but, in light of what follows, where he says he has nothing to sell, something along the lines 'he says he has no money' seems highly probable. The juxtaposing of *daneizein* and *eranizein* of itself implies two different types of transaction; though Cohen would disagree: (1992) 207 n. 112.

268. 'Asking for them back' is a popular restoration for the obvious lacuna; opposed by Diggle (1996) 217 on the ground that 'to demand back a borrowed object in the middle of the night is uncharacteristically troublesome behaviour'. But the point about the *agroikos* is that, in his ignorance, he fails to recognize it as such. Broadly comparable is Strepsiades in the opening scene from *Clouds*, lying awake before dawn, insisting on waking up his son to share his cunning plan for dodging his debts. Similarly impervious to the etiquette of lending and borrowing is the 'Tactless Man' (12.11), turning up to ask for interest on a loan when people are sacrificing and out of pocket.

269. For money as 'good to think with' in Athens, there are the forty or so references in the index to Edmonds and Austen (1904) *s.v.* 'Money'. It seems strange that Melville Jones (1993) in his helpful collection

of texts about Greek coinage, finds no place for the *Characters*. Some implications of 'Coinage and democracy at Athens' are considered by Trevett (2001); to which might be added several striking money-metaphors (in addition to *charakter*-character). The possible psychological impact of the appearance of money in earlier Greece is intriguingly explored by Seaford (2004). The material role of money in fourth-century Attica has recently been addressed by Shipton (1997, 2000, 2001). In so far as her conclusions can be substantiated, I do not consider that they significantly affect Finley's (or indeed my own) broad ideas on Athenian economy and society. I intend to reconsider the problem in light of recent research in a forthcoming paper.

270. Langdon (1994), in a closely argued defence of sales of state property by the *poletai* as true auctions, notes how we regard auction sales, 'in which there is an equal opportunity for all to participate, as inherent to democracies' (264). In which case, why should auctioneering be included, alongside gambling and acting as a hired cook, in the list of shameful occupations attributed to the 'Morally Degraded Man' (6.5)? Of course, the role of the auctioneer could be seen as parasitical, charging a fee merely for extracting the highest possible price from the buyer. But whose democracy does Langdon have in mind? In the context of private sale in fourth-century Athens, the auctioneer removed from the exchange process any personal engagement between buyer and seller, involving a range of buyers (in the case of non-real property, possibly including non-citizens) in potentially disruptive competition. But other explanations are possible. Rauh (1989) provides detailed testimony for 'Auctioneers and the Roman economy'; his line of enquiry is summed up by the problematically ambivalent status of the *praeco* Quintus Granius (the subject of Cicero's anecdote in the *Brutus*; see n. 3). Juvenal (3.31) echoes Theophrastus in associating auctioneers with 'fullers, sewer-cleaners and corpse-haulers'. Rauh associates their generally low reputation with their role as middlemen, combined with a disagreeable public profile (460): 'the ancient equivalent of today's used-car salesman, and as such their profession could only be described as *sordidus*'.

271. For Theophrastus' apparent familiarity with buyer's repartee, there is the saying attributed to him by Athenaeus (347f-48a = FHS&G 710) that 'No rotten fish is large'. The passage as a whole, problematic in its detail, is discussed at length by Fortenbaugh (2005) 377–84.

272. Compare Ariston's *authades* (col. 17), who in ending a letter does not add *to chairein* or *errosthai*. How does the behaviour of Theophrastus' 'Arrogant Man', handing the calculator to his slave, match up with the 'Obtuse Man' (14.2), 'who does a calculation with his counters and after computing the total asks the person sitting next to him "What does it come to?"' Merely an illustration of his own incompetence, or is he naively handing the abacus to the person with whom he is involved in an exchange transaction?

273. Citations that follow are from the reprint of the original edition of 1899; an excerpted version is available in the Penguin series 'Great Ideas' under the title *Conspicuous consumption: unproductive consumption of goods is honourable* (2005).

274. He adds (xiii) that Veblen drops his readers 'through the looking-glass into the fantastic world of social reality'; not far off Theophrastus with the *Characters*. The bibliography on Veblen must be massive; I have not attempted even to contemplate it. For the briefest of listings, see Davis (1968) 307–8. Dorfman's intellectual biography (1935), written shortly after Veblen's death, seems fundamental. Something of the controversy provoked by his writings on the right, left and liberal centre can be sampled in Tilman (1992). There is a lively, pointed discussion of the man and work by Heilbroner (1961) 181–213, and a summary assessment of his economic writings in Roll (1978) 439–54.

275. Veblen was by all accounts well read in contemporary anthropology (Boas, Tylor, Frazer, Morgan), from which he drew support for his evolutionary approach: a target for his later opponents; see Tilman (1992) 43–4, 57–8, 273–4.

276. Which is not to say that Veblen, any more than Mauss, was unaware of appropriate Greek material: Lane Fox (2004) 211 n. 104.

277. Concepts of consumption of non-necessary goods in the Archaic Greek world are assessed and refined by Foxhall (1998b).

278. Hornblower's 'Sticks, stones, and Spartans' (2000) is a fascinating exploration of *bakterion-* and *skeptron-*wielding Greeks; in the case of the Spartans (61), arguably, 'for intimidation and as an arrogant assertion that one belongs to a superior order of creation'. But the overall behaviour of the 'Conspicuous Consumer' makes it unlikely that he is to be envisaged as assuming along with his stick any serious Spartan ideology. Wilson is close to the mark in describing him as 'almost an ancient dandy' (2000) 72.

279. It is further irony that the *Characters*, where hardly any of the thirty-one protagonists do any work (the *agroikos* in his ignorance comes closest), should be one of the key sources for Harris in his compilation of occupations known from classical Athens: (2002) 88–99. The multi-tasking of the 'Morally Degraded Man' offers at least the possibility that individuals might double- or even treble-up with more than one named job. Webster (1956) 128 unrealistically thinks it plausible that one person might do all these things on the grounds that they overlapped and were part-time. I find it hard to classify this Character as a 'businessman', as does Cohen: (2000) 189–90.

280. Thackeray in the *Book of Snobs* (ch. 33, 136) tells how the Pontos, his family of Country Snobs, 'keep a boy called Thomas or Tummus. Tummus works in the garden or about the pigstye and stable; Thomas wears a page's costume of eruptive buttons, as thus:–' (followed by Thackeray's illustration). On the apparent absence of productive slaves from Aristotle's imagined *oikos* from the *Politics*, see n. 121.

281. At the close of his preface, Veblen wrote that 'the few quotations that have been introduced, chiefly by way of illustration, are also such as will commonly be recognized with sufficient facility without the guidance of citation.' Fair enough for 'ferae natura' (261), 'ignava ratio' (288), even 'otium cum dignitate' and 'the maxim "fruges consumere nati"' (391; cf. 95). But what about (in addition to *Carmen saeculare*): 'nota notae est nota rei ipsius' (41); 'Summum crede nefas animam praeferre pudori, / Et propter vitam vivendi perdere causas' (43)? The former is apparently a medieval paraphrase of Aristotle (*Categories* 5.3b4, and elsewhere): 'Whatever is said of the predicate will hold also of the subject'; the latter is from Juvenal (8.83–4). Other classical allusions are relatively unproblematic: 'the Diogenes-like consumer' (157); the 'Maecenas function' of the well-to-do (381–2); save that Veblen compares the contemporary view on the admission of women to higher learning ('derogatory to the dignity of the learned craft') with the ancient attitude towards [non-] participation of women in the Eleusinian Mysteries (376). Cocking a complicated snook at the classically half-educated reader?

Veblen's strictly classical learning seems to have been patchy and his attitude towards the Classics complex. His early and possibly inadequate classical education is documented by Dorfman (1935) 9, 18; but it was sufficient to publish while an undergraduate at Carleton College in Minnesota 'in complicated Latin a poem entitled "Carmen", written in praise of the god Bacchus' (33). While he was reading for his doctorate in philosophy and economics at Yale in the early 1880s, his two most important teachers, Noah Porter and William Graham Sumner, were engaged in a bitter dispute over the place of Classics in the curriculum: denounced by Sumner in terms prefiguring those of *The leisured class* (43–4). In the years of unemployment that followed, Veblen returned to the study of Latin and Greek, with idea that he might become a philologist. When his Greek proved inadequate, he turned instead to the Icelandic Sagas (67), an interest that continued through his life (492–5). In 1910 he made an unsuccessful application for funding to support an 'Inquiry into Baltic and Cretan antiquities' along comparative lines (297–300). Shortly after, in a celebrated course of lectures delivered at Missouri on 'Economic Factors in Civilization', Veblen traced the collapse of Minoan civilization (not entirely peaceable as shown by the bull and axe in its religion), and diagnosed the Trojan War as arising out of competition for customs dues (321). In his lectures he might quote from memory 'stanza after stanza from a medieval Latin hymn' (317). Tilman (1992, 9–10) cites a bookseller's anecdote (trying to sell Veblen a copy of his own book), which features Veblen ordering an obscure volume of Latin hymns.

282. Theophrastus' farewell to his pupils as reported by Diogenes (5.40–1 = FHS&G 1.52–60) is less direct in its references to the shortness of life. Detailed comparison is drawn by Mejer (1998), who concludes that 'both seem to be based on a more-or-less identical view of Theophrastus' (17).

283. Detailed discussion by Mejer (1998) 11–12, and Sollenberger (1992) 3874–6. Theophrastus' immersion in the philosophical life and (relative) disassociation from affairs of rulers (*basileis*) is attested by Philodemus (*P. Herc.* 240 fr. 16.3–10 = FHS&G 27).

284. As borne out by the variety of texts, archaeological and topographical material included in the fourth-century essays in *Kosmos*: Cartledge, Millett and von Reden (1998).

285. In what follows I adopt with modifications the translation in the Loeb edition by Rackham (1934).

286. 'Greatness of Heart' rather than the more usual 'Greatness of Soul' or 'Magnanimity' on the grounds that (246–7) *megalopsuchia* 'is more than a mental attitude, and involves some aspect of motivation that is not rational in itself'. The more accurate alternative to what Pakaluk describes as a 'place-holder' would be a variety of phrases: 'aiming to do something truly great with one's life' or 'consistently acting on admirable ideals'. For detail of previous, negative views of the Great-Hearted Man (including Hardie's 'prig with the conceit and bad manners of a prig'), see 242–3. Pakaluk (2005) sets in context his thinking on the Great-Hearted Man (esp. 151–80). For Plato's Socrates as possible part-model for *megalopsuchia*: Pakaluk (2004a).

287. Pakaluk responds to an observation by Hardie (quoted on 243): 'a description with many graphic strokes, of the minor attributes and demeanour of the great man ... [concluding], in the manner of Theophrastus, with his deep voice and unhurried movements.' Pakaluk's objections are based on broad differences in nature (putative virtue as opposed to foibles and vices), presence and absence of motive (abundant as opposed to bare use of *gar*: 'for', 'because'), organization of elements in place of randomly arranged actions, absence and presence of reported speech, concern with the deliberate and rational as opposed to the absurd and irrational, a common thread to behaviour contrasted with single traits described in diverse ways. Jebb (1909) 10–16 deployed a selection of similar arguments in his opposition to Petersen's much earlier association of the *Characters* with the *Nicomachean ethics*. The theory of a direct connexion with the *Ethics* has been restated in detail by Steinmetz (1959) 216–19; see n. 58.

288. The material is here ordered according to Rackham (1934), with 1123b26–9 following on immediately from 1123b15.

289. The detail of Aristotle's Vain Man certainly overlaps with Theophrastus' 'Man of Petty Ambition': '...foolish persons, who are deficient in self-knowledge and expose their defect: they undertake honourable responsibilities of which they are not worthy and then are found out. They are ostentatious in dress, manner and so on. They want people to know how well off they are, and talk about it, imagining that this will make them respected' (1125a27–33). Here are the other apparent overlaps between what the *Characters* do and what the Great-Hearted Man does not. The 'Dissembler': 'He must be open both in love and hate, since concealment shows timidity; and care more for truth than what people think; and speak and act openly, since as he despises other men he is outspoken and frank, except when speaking with ironical self-deprecation, as he does to common people' (1124b26–1125a1). The 'Flatterer' (and the flattered): 'He will be incapable of living at the will of another, unless a friend, since to do so is slavish, and hence flatterers are always servile, and humble people flatterers (*hoi tapeinoi kolakes*). He is not prone to admiration, since nothing is great to him' (1125a1–3). The 'Self-Centred Man': 'He does not bear a grudge, for it is not the mark of greatness of heart to recall things against people, especially the wrongs they have done you, but rather to overlook them' (1125a.3–5). The 'Slanderer': 'He is no gossip (*anthropologos*), for he will not talk either about himself or about another, as he wants neither to receive compliments nor to hear other people run down (nor is he lavish of praise either); and so he is not given to speaking evil himself, even of his enemies, except when he deliberately intends to give offence' (1125a5–9). The 'Ungrateful Grumbler': 'In troubles that cannot be avoided or trifling mishaps he will never cry out or ask for help, since to do so would imply that he took them to heart' (1125a9–10). The 'Coward': 'For instance, one cannot imagine the Great-Hearted running at full speed when retreating in battle, nor acting dishonestly; since what motive for base conduct has a man to whom nothing is great?' (1123b30–33).

290. 'by chance persons' for *para ton tuchonton*; in preference over Rackham's rendering 'by common people'.

291. The parallel is admittedly not perfect: the 'Shameless Man' is described as deliberately withholding repayment of his first loan.
    Here I briefly part company with Pakaluk, who sees the Great-Hearted Man returning more than an equal amount as being likely to extend into the future the relationship between giver and receiver (271): 'If you give what justice requires, the exchange comes to an end with that. To give more in return, however, is a pleasant and unexpected surprise (that is surely suggested by "come off well", *eu peponthos*); the other fellow thinks to himself something like "I really ought to be giving something to this guy more often, because, when I do, I come off the gainer"; and then he is likely to reply with another initiative later on.' Interpretation is admittedly problematic, depending on imputing motivations to both the Great-Hearted Man and his imagined creditor, who is presumed not to be similarly Great-Hearted. Alternatively, 'Balanced Reciprocity' (exchange according to justice) would not preclude further exchange: 'I can trust this man; he always gives back exactly what is owing; I'll deal with him again.' On the other hand, repeatedly receiving more than one's due might create apprehension: 'I'm always getting deeper into this man's debt; that means I'm no longer a free agent.' A reference point for returning more than originally given (not 'interest' as in Rackham's version) is supplied by Hesiod in the *Works and days* (349–51), who also advises to give back 'better if you can; so that if you are in need afterwards, you may find him sure'. It does indeed seem unlikely that such a pragmatic and calculating approach would be appropriate to the Great-Hearted Man. Alternatively, he wishes to reinforce his superior status as a giver rather than a receiver. Aristotle goes on to observe parenthetically (1124b14) how 'the recipient of a benefit is the inferior of his benefactor, whereas they desire to be the superior.'

292. Different from the 'Dissembler', who merely pretends not to care about those who do him down. Different again is the 'Conspicuous Consumer', who wants luxury items only as illustrating his status to others; whereas the Great-Hearted Man 'likes to own beautiful and useless things, rather than useful things that bring in a return, since the former shows his independence more' (1125a10–12).

293. The phrase is adapted from Michael Herzfeld's (1985) 16: the Cretans he studied were less concerned with 'being a good man' than 'being good at being a man'.

294. The approach taken to the *Politics* in the text is prompted by Jean Roberts' treatment of 'Justice and the polis' (2000). It remains unclear to me whether the recommended behaviour implied in the *Characters* is intended more to assist individuals or to move democracy towards justice (385).

295. It seems likely that Casti, the librettist, distinguished between *Characters* as appropriate reading for the serious-minded woman, and Plato for her male equivalent. The *Characters* also put in a musical appearance as being, by Eliot Carter's own admission, part of the inspiration for his *Variations for Orchestra*.

296. Echoing (and translating) Casaubon's phrase: La Bruyère (1962) 6; Steinmetz (1970) 96. Others respond to the *Characters'* 'special charm': Habicht (1997) 123; cf. Rostovtzeff (1941) 1.163–4. According to Navarre (1921) 36, 'une des oeuvres les plus agréables et les plus spirituelles que nous ait léguées l'antiquité grecque'. Experience makes it difficult to disagree with Smeed (1985) 169, for whom the reading of 'characters' (not just by Theophrastus) constitutes 'a voyage of discovery through the society of past ages'. He continues: 'It is doubtful whether anybody, in whatever discipline, could study these little works without either learning something fresh or being prompted to ask new questions or reassess previously held certainties.' For Roman expressions of admiration for Theophrastus' writings, see Diggle (2002) 56–7. It would be agreeable if Cicero's saying preserved by Plutarch (*Cicero* 24.5–6 = FHS&G 53) that he called Theophrastus his 'private indulgence' (*truphen idian*) might be thought to include the *Characters* (never explicitly mentioned in Cicero's surviving writings). Wilamowitz's dismissal of Theophrastus as 'ein Pedant', exercising professorial wit based on tired material, is effectively challenged by Lane Fox (1996) 157.

297. The critique, though it appears in the MS immediately after Character 15, is headed 'The end of the *Characters* of Theophrastus', prompting Navarre (1914), who translates the passage in full, to conclude that it was originally placed so as to sum up the whole work (391).

298. Mubassir, *Choicest maxims and best sayings*, 'Sayings by a number of philosophers', no. 120 = FHS&G

545. The saying continues with an illustration: the sandalwood tree offers shade to snakes, which in turn protect the tree from being felled.

299. Mahaffy also identifies 'the *Land Question* [his italics] as coming forward and forming one branch of the socialistic movements of the third century B.C.' But it is in his *Social life in Greece* (1874) that he really gets into his stride, offering the opinion (88–9) that the present-day Irish were not fitted to the rule of law as given and enforced by the English: 'I believe even a harsh despotism would be more successful, and perhaps in the end more humane.' See further in the index, under 'Irish, the, compared with the Greeks'. Oscar Wilde, in an anonymous review, criticized his former teacher for having treated the Greek world as 'Tipperary writ large'; see Stanford and McDowell (1971) 81, who label Mahaffy as 'the Alcibiades of Irish politics' (xiii), and (with possible irony) identify his conversational humour with Theophrastus' *Characters* (78). James Diggle suggests to me that Mahaffy's antipathy to the *Characters* may in part be explained by its championship by Jebb, for whom no scholarly love was lost: Stanford and McDowell (1971) 159–65.

300. The latest datable events in the botanical works (nothing later than 300) are listed by Einarson and Link (1976) viii–ix, who note that, for purposes of dating, *Inquiry* but not *Causes* makes occasional use of the Athenian calendar (xlvi.).

301. There is independent support for an ongoing democratic ethos in early Hellenistic Athens from Leppin (2002).

302. See Horden and Purcell (2000) 499; Brandes (1987) 124–7. I have tentatively argued elsewhere (1993) 34–44 that key aspects of interpersonal relations in the city of Athens may have had their origin in rural communities.

303. Stephen Mennell's *Norbert Elias* (1992) is the essential guide: encompassing a brief intellectual biography of Elias (1–26), a 'reorganized contents page' for *The civilizing process* (32–4), an account of its complex and fascinating publishing history reaching back to Prague in 1937 (18–19), and a masterly summary of its contents (34–111).

304. *The civilizing process* is subjected to a sympathetic though searching critique by Bryson (1998), 10–18, who adds commentary on allied lines of enquiry developed by Freud, Foucault and Bourdieu. Bryson emphasizes the historical significance of manners beyond mere 'form' (1–3), as embodied in the proverbial force of 'manners maketh man'. She further points to the enduring device of generating humour by the failure of foreigners to comprehend standards and codes of conduct; not far removed from the predicament of the Characters.

305. Theophrastus, when reproved by his wife for not letting his useless son approach, even though he was 'from him', is said to have spat and said: 'And indeed this too is mine, but it's not useful' (*Codex Vaticanus Graecus* 742 f.66v 1.9–12 = FHS&G 22). But the anecdote is attributed to other philosophers and Theophrastus was unmarried. The motif of the wittily spitting philosopher recurs in Diogenes' life of Diogenes the Cynic (6.32). Repeatedly warned by his host not to expectorate in his fine house, he eventually spat in his face; 'unable', as he said, 'to find a meaner receptacle'. In fact, the obsessively transgressive behaviour of Diogenes provides a counterpart for the Characters: deliberately challenging norms so as to demonstrate their artificiality (see n. 261).

306. Although Elias' concern is almost entirely with early-modern Europe, he acknowledges that 'the process has no beginning' (52–4). In 'Walking, standing and sitting in ancient Greek culture' (1991) 28–9, Bremmer links back Erasmus' instructions on walking in *De civilitate* to Stoic precepts.

307. Leppin (2002, 51–2) refers intriguingly to Elias' work and then seems to step back, on the grounds that there was operating in Athens none of the court-culture that plays such a large part in *The civilizing process*. Agreed. But Elias' conception of the court as (398) 'a kind of stock exchange; as in every "good society", an estimate of the "value" of each individual is continuously being formed' does not seem so far removed from the *koinonia* of the polis. Elias' emphasis on the use of force by individuals in warrior society and its increasing monopolization by the state (365–79) has a broad parallel in the shifting balance within Greek society between competitive and co-operative virtues (as in part acknowledged by Leppin, 54).

308. For a brief statement of the 'strong' and 'weak' views of discourses as respectively affecting or reflecting the 'real world', see Lane Fox (1996) 128.

309. The point is well made by Henry with reference to Eliot: Rignall (2000) *s.v. Impressions of Theophrastus Such*: 'Theophrastus exposes the myths of history, the teleological narratives that retrospectively order the scattered and conflicting accounts of historical events. *Impressions* demands that readers impose coherence on the disordered information Theophrastus supplies about himself. The work suggests that the identity of individual subjects, like that of nations, is constructed through a process of selection and exclusion that resembles the process of making art.'

310. The suggestion was tentatively made by W. Pötscher in his edition of *Peri eusebeias* (122); cited by Mari (2003) 86–7.

311. 'An Aristotelian is not a natural candidate for democratic sympathies,' notes Lane Fox (1996) 133, who summarizes what is known of Theophrastus' para-political activities and associations (133–4). With his reputation for hostility as a young man to tyranny in Eresus (Plut 1097B, 1126F = FHS&G 133A, 133B) and possible association *via* his will with Olympiodorus, hero of the democratic restoration in 286 (n. 24), Lane Fox tentatively concludes (133) that the Characters 'are not sketches from the oligarchic fringe'. For alternative but unverifiable views, see Leppin (2002) 50 n. 34.

312. See earlier comments on style of presentation: 16. There is an early and sometimes perceptive attempt to isolate the excellence of the *Characters* by Gally in the 'Critical essay on characteristic-writings' which prefaces his translation from 1725.

313. The direct speech of the Characters (also frequent in surviving fragments from Ariston) has been identified as reproducing everyday language: Diggle (2004) 202 for 'The ring of popular speech'. For a list of possible colloquialisms and thoughts on the non-literary richness of language in the *Characters*, see Navarre (1914) 433–9. The use of speech as an essential element in delineation of character is discussed briefly by Smeed (1985) 280–1.

314. It would have appealed to Keith Hopkins' wry sense of humour (and his attitude to evidence) that it has so far proved impossible to identify the written source of this quotation.

APPENDIX 1

NAMING THE CHARACTERS

Titles are taken from the following editions and translations: Healey (1616), Jebb (1909), Edmonds (1929), Bennet and Hammond (1902), Anderson (1970), Vellacott (1973), Rusten and Cunningham (2002), Diggle (2004), La Bruyère (1687), Navarre (1921). Where, as occasionally happens, translators offer several renderings, only one or two are given. There are additional sets of translated titles by Aldington (1924), Klose (1970), Leppin (2002), and Loicq-Berger (2002).

	1 *eiron* 'Dissembler'	2 *kolax* 'Flatterer'	3 *adolesches* 'Chatterbox'
Healey	caviling	flattery	garrulitie
Jebb	ironical	flatterer	garrulous
Edmonds	dissembling	flattery	garrulity
Bennet & Ham.	dissembler	flatterer	garrulous man
Anderson	insincere man	flatterer	garrulous man
Vellacott	ironical man	toady or flatterer	chatterer
Rusten	dissembling	flattery	idle chatter
Diggle	dissembler	toady	chatterbox
La Bruyère	la dissimulation	la flatterie	l'impertinent
Navarre	le dissimulé	le flatteur	le bavard

	4 *agroikos* 'Country Bumpkin'	**5** *areskos* 'Obsequious Man' + 'Conspicuous Consumer'	**6** *aponenoemenos* 'Morally Degraded Man'
Healey	rusticity or clownishness	fair speech or smoothness	senselessness or desperate boldness
Jebb	boor	complaisant	reckless
Edmonds	boorishness	self-seeking affability	wilful disrep utableness
Bennet & Ham.	boor	affable man	the rough
Anderson	boor	complaisant man	man without moral feeling
Vellacott	boor	anxiety to please	outcast or demoralized man
Rusten	boorishness	obsequiousness	shamelessness
Diggle	country bumpkin	obsequious man	man who has lost all sense
La Bruyère	la rusticité	le complaisant	l'image d'un coquin
Navarre	le rustre	le complaisant	le cynique

	7 *lalos* 'Talker'	**8** *logopoios* 'Rumour-Monger'	**9** *anaischuntos* 'Shameless Man'
Healey	loquacity or overspeaking	news-forging or rumour spreading	impudency
Jebb	loquacious	newsmaker	shameless
Edmonds	loquacity	newsmaking	unconsciableness
Bennet & Ham.	bore	news-monger	shameless man
Anderson	talkative man	fabricator	shameless or greedy man
Vellacott	talker	rumour-monger	shameless man
Rusten	garrulity	rumour-mongering	sponging
Diggle	talker	rumour-monger	shameless man
La Bruyère	le grand parleur	le débit des nouvelles	l'effronterie causée par l'avarice
Navarre	le loquace	le nouveliste	l'homme sans scrupules

	10 *mikrologos* 'Penny-Pincher'	11 *bdeluros* 'Repulsive Man'	12 *akairos* 'Tactless Man'
Healey	base avarice or parsimony	obscenity or ribaldry	unseasonableness
Jebb	penurious	gross	unseasonable
Edmonds	penuriousness	buffoonery	tactlessness
Bennet & Ham.	mean man	impudent man	tactless man
Anderson	pennypincher	offensive man	hapless man
Vellacott	skinflint or stingy man	abominable man	unseasonable man
Rusten	pennypinching	obnoxiousness	bad timing
Diggle	penny-pincher	repulsive man	tactless man
La Bruyère	l'épargne sordide	l'impudent	le contre-temps
Navarre	le mesquin	l'incongru	l'intempestif

	13 *periergos* 'Overzealous Man'	14 *anaisthetos* 'Obtuse Man'	15 *authades* 'Self-Centred Man'
Healey	impertinent diligence or over officiousness	blockishness or stupidity	stubbornness or fierceness
Jebb	officious	stupid	surly
Edmonds	officiousness	stupidity	surliness
Bennet & Ham.	over-zealous man	stupid man	surly man
Anderson	officious man	absent-minded man	unsociable man
Vellacott	overdoing it	fecklessness	hostile man
Rusten	overzealousness	absent-mindedness	grouchiness
Diggle	overzealous man	obtuse man	self-centred man
La Bruyère	l'air empressé	la stupidité	la brutalité
Navarre	l'empressé	le stupide	le brutal

	16 *deisdaimon* 'Superstitious Man'	17 *mempsimoiros* 'Ungrateful Grumbler'	18 *apistos* 'Distrustful Man'
Healey	superstition	causeless complaining	diffidence or distrust
Jebb	superstitious	grumbler	distrustful
Edmonds	superstitiousness	querulousness	distrustfulness
Bennet & Ham.	superstitious man	thankless man	suspicious man
Anderson	superstitious man	faultfinder	suspicious man
Vellacott	superstitious man	chip on shoulder or with a grievance	distrustful man
Rusten	superstition	griping	mistrust
Diggle	superstitious man	ungrateful grumbler	distrustful man
La Bruyère	la superstition	l'ésprit chagrin	la défiance
Navarre	le superstitieux	l'homme chagrin	le défiant

	19 *duscheres* 'Offensive Man'	20 *aedes* 'Disagreeable Man'	21 *mikrophilotimos* 'Man of Petty Ambition'
Healey	nastiness	unpleasantness or tediousnesss	base and frivolous affectation of praise
Jebb	offensive	unpleasant	petty ambition
Edmonds	nastiness	ill-breeding	petty-pride
Bennet & Ham.	gross man	disagreeable man	man of petty ambition
Anderson	repulsive man	unpleasant man	the exquisite
Vellacott	offensiveness	tiresome man	petty ambition
Rusten	squalor	bad taste	petty ambition
Diggle	offensive man	disagreeable man	man of petty ambition
La Bruyère	un villain homme	un homme incommode	la sotte vanité
Navarre	le répugnant	un fâcheux	le vaniteux

	22 *aneleutheros* 'Illiberal Man'	**23** *alazon* 'Boastful Man'	**24** *huperephanos* 'Arrogant Man'
Healey	illiberality or servility	ostentation	pride
Jebb	mean	boastful	arrogant
Edmonds	parsimony	pretentiousness	arrogance
Anderson	stingy man	show-off	arrogant man
Bennet & Ham.	penurious man	braggart	pompous man
Vellacott	meanness	boaster	arrogance
Rusten	lack of generosity	fraudulence	arrogance
Diggle	illiberal man	boastful man	arrogant man
La Bruyère	l'avarice	l'ostentation	l'orguiel
Navarre	le parcimonieux	le vantard	l'orgeilleux

	25 *deilos* 'Coward'	**26** *oligarchos* 'Oligarchic Man'	**27** *opsimathes* 'Late Learner'
Healey	timidity or fearfulness	oligarchy	late-learning
Jebb	coward	oligarch	late-learner
Edmond	cowardice	oligarchy	late-learning
Anderson	coward	oligarchical man	later learner
Bennet & Ham.	coward	oligarch	late learner
Vellacott	cowardice	authoritarian	late learning
Rusten	cowardice	authoritarianism	rejuvenation
Diggle	coward	oligarchic man	late learner
La Bruyère	la peur	les grands d'une république	une tardive instruction
Navarre	le poltron	l'oligarque	le tard instruit

	28 *kakologos* 'Slanderer'	**29** *philoponeros* 'Friend of Villains'	**30** *aischrokerdes* 'Shabby Profiteer'
Healey	detraction or backbiting	——————	——————
Jebb	evil-speaker	patron of rascals	avaricious
Edmond	backbiting	friendship with rascals	meanness
Anderson	slanderer	vicious man	avaricious man
Bennet & Ham.	backbiter	lover of bad company	basely covetous man
Vellacott	slanderer	love of evil	avaricious man
Rusten	slander	patronage of scoundrels	chiseling
Diggle	slanderer	friend of villains	shabby profiteer
La Bruyère	la médisance	——————	——————
Navarre	le médisant	l'ami de la canaille	le profiteur éhonté

APPENDIX 2

CHARACTERS IN *PUNCH* MAGAZINE

Non-explicit imitations of the *Characters* appeared in *Punch* from the earliest issues. Vol. 2 from 1842 (62–74) included on the theme of 'Punch's Valentines' illustrations with verse-captions of 'The Drawing-Room Captain', 'The Speculative Mama', 'The Lawyer', 'The Pet Parson', 'The Accomplished Young Lady', 'The Literary Gentleman', 'The Footman', 'The Medical Student', 'The Man About Town', 'The Milliner' and 'The Politician'.

Here is the only attributed set of imitations known to me:

From *Punch, or the London Charivari* 20 March, 1901 (216)

THEOPHRASTUS UP TO DATE

"Literary Characters."

THE NEW PUBLISHER

New publishing may be defined as the puffing of unknown authors for the sake of gain.

The New Publisher is one who will do his own reviewing, and fill many columns of the papers with eulogies of his own publications. Warming to the work, he will hire sandwich-men to parade the streets proclaiming their aspirations or their sin. Great is his belief in anonymity, and having propounded the riddle he is well pleased to keep silent and reap the harvest from a puzzled world. He is very apt to bring discredit to his profession.

THE NEW JOURNALIST

New Journalism is the framing of fictitious sayings and doings at the pleasure of him who makes journals.

The New Journalist is a person who will condemn a prisoner before he has been tried, or ruin a man's reputation to sell a single issue of his paper. When a sensational trial is in the courts, he will be quick to scent out any savoury gossip and horrible revelation. It is quite in his manner, too, to publish the evidence of a witness who has not yet appeared in the box. Hearing that a degree of frost has been registered during the night, he hastens to write a par. on "Blizzards at Brixton," adding that Wandsworth and Wimbledon are in winter's icy grasp. He is also called Yellow.

THE NEW WAR CORRESPONDENT

New War Correspondence is a distressing indifference to style and subject, where popularity is concerned.

The New War Correspondent is one who, though he has seen little of war, and who knows little of politics, will cheerfully go to the front, and write home criticism of the General's tactics and of the Government. There is no need for him to leave his quarters in order to give a graphic account of the latest battle. He is apt to refer to a scouting reconnaissance as an advance in force, adding that on this day he messed with the — Regiment who had looted a barrel of whisky. If half-a-dozen Boers are dislodged from a kopje, he will describe it as a great victory, though he will point out that, but for the blundering of the General engaged, the loss of five British Officers might have been avoided. He is quite likely to write a novel, in which he will discourse much of "Glass-eye," "Pom-pom" and "Ard-work." He is very apt to use this kind of phrase, "The lioness of Britain whelps heroes still." He is a "quill-driving lump of skin."

APPENDIX 3

CLASSICAL ALLUSION IN THACKERAY'S *BOOK OF SNOBS*

'I belong to nine [*sic*] clubs. The Union Jack, the Sash and Marlingspike – Military Clubs. The True Blue, the No Surrender, the Buff and Blue, the Guy Fawkes, and the Cato Street – Political Clubs. The Brummell and the Regent – Dandy Clubs. The Acropolis, the Palladium, the Areopagus, the Pnyx, the Pentelicus, the Ilyssus, and the Poluphloisboio Thalasses – Literary Clubs. I never could make out how the latter set of Clubs got their names; *I* don't know Greek for one, and I wonder how many other members of these institutions do' (ch. 45, 189).

Whatever the case with Mr Snob, Thackeray of course did know Greek: Charterhouse was followed in 1829 by the recently instated Classical Tripos at Cambridge: Taylor (1999) 32–66. He chose to read for an Honours degree and early letters from Cambridge tell of his resolution to study hard: Peters (1987) 24–6; the outcome was a second, though he never took a full degree. There is no need to take at face value, as critics have tended, Thackeray's doubting remarks made elsewhere in *Punch* about the discipline of Classics, based on alleged experiences in the schoolroom: (1895) ch. 3, 'Punch in the East'; (1906) 80. The *Book of Snobs* has classical references on every other page; far more than *Theophrastus Such*, but they are part of the common patrimony of classical education rather than learning, and so familiar to at least a substantial minority of *Punch's* middle-class readership. A case in point, referred to in the text (14), is 'a quotation from Horace, which I hope you have never heard...' ('Prefatory Remarks', 5). Surely ironic, in that the verses translated are from the first book of the *Odes* (4.13–14): the equivalent of a 'set-text' for those then learning even elementary Latin. The implication of hoping that readers have 'never heard' the quotation is therefore the hope that they have never had to learn Latin.

R. D. McMaster in *Thackeray's cultural frame of reference* (1991) 25–43 has a valuable study of classical allusion and its manipulation in Thackeray's later novel *The Newcomes* (1853–5). He identifies the numerous Latin quotations as being, for the most part, well-known ones, taken from 'works conned in school by generations of grammar-school boys' (25), with Horace far to the fore. McMaster concludes that allusion in *The Newcomes* operates on different levels, serving to signal a character's status, adding depth of time to repeated actions; and above all, by both reverently presenting and also parodying classical learning, reassuring readers of their membership of an educated in-group. With the earlier *Book of Snobs* (1846–7), fewer classical demands are made on the reader and the sense of subversion seems stronger. Here are the details. A list seems unavoidable.

Untranslated Latin is far thinner on the ground than in *The Newcomes*: 'ingens patebat tellus' ('Prefatory Remarks' 5); 'lapis offensionis' (ch. 12, 52); 'locum tenens' (ch. 25, 99); 'sub iisdem trabibus' (ch. 26, 106); 'cui bono' (ch. 38, 158); 'sic vos non vobis' (ch. 19, 78). With one possible exception (see below) Latin quotations are neither lengthy nor essential to the sense of the passages where they occur.

Straightforward classical allusions are frequent but largely unproblematic. In addition to those listed in the text (14–15) are: 'By Moonlight, in the Colosseum' ('Prefatory Remarks', 4), a deliberate commonplace: cf. 'under the shadowy arches of the Colosseum' (ch. 27, 113); 'Publicoaler' used to affright a snobbish Colonel (Prefatory Remarks' 6); 'the Honourable Poly Anthus', playing on botanical Latin (ch. 1, 7), 'Croesus' regularly as the name for any wealthy individual (ch. 5, 24, 25; ch. 40, 169; ch. 41, 173; ch. 42, 175); 'she, as solemn as Minerva – she, as chaste as Diana' (ch. 6, 30); 'In the time of Boadicea' (ch. 7, 32); 'a shovel-hatted fuzz-wigged Silenus', describing typical caricatures of Sidney Smith (ch. 11, 50); 'The Goths have got into Rome', on the railway reaching Cambridge (ch. 13, 56); 'Apollo or Antinous' as better-looking than Mr Punch (ch. 16, 67); 'the popular *bellua*', quoting the *Quarterly Review* on the unstoppable demand for political reform (ch. 20, 84–5); the popular novelist Mrs Gore appears as 'Mrs. Cruor' (ch. 17, 72); 'Libertas' as the name of a literary critic (ch. 17, 72); a writer on the aristocracy who calls himself Hampden Junior 'is as much like John Hampden as Mr. Punch is like the Apollo Belvedere' (ch. 21, 87); 'the gladiator of five-and-twenty-campaigns', describing a veteran private soldier (ch. 22, 91); a 'solemn old toothless patrician' is cultivated by a tufthunter (ch. 36, 105); 'the jays with peacock's feathers' are Snobs, and never so numerous 'since the days of Aesop' (ch. 26, 110); 'this charming Arcadian spot', as being free from Snobs (ch. 31, 127); 'and are there any Snobs in this Elysium?' (ch. 32, 134); 'there is the parson, Doctor Chrysostom' (ch. 34, 142); 'mouldy Doric temples with black chimney-pots, in the finest classic taste', being gate-lodges to Castle Carabas (ch. 35, 145); 'a huge Ionic portico, approached by a vast, lonely, ghastly staircase', being Castle Carabas itself (ch. 35, 146); 'Snobium Gatherum', parodying the dog-Latin 'omnium gatherum' (ch. 39, 161); 'every man who has been jostling in the world for three or four lustres' (ch. 40, 166); 'the herculean plushed one went back to open the carriage door' (ch. 42, 175); 'Bacchus is the divinity to whom Waggle devotes his especial worship' (ch. 48, 203); 'severe Doric', describing the pretentious dining room at the 'Sarcophagus Club' (ch. 50, 211), where the library contains 'Dugdale's *Monasticon*', described by the ignorant clubman to his guests as 'a most valuable, and I believe, entertaining book'. On closer inspection it turns out to be one of a series of fakes, concealing a cleaner's cupboard (213).

The vignette, drawn by Thackeray, which opens chapter 23 'On Radical Snobs' (93), showing Hector in his helmet, frightening Astyanax in the arms of Andromache, has no discernible bearing on what follows, and might stand as emblematic for the general run of classical references in the *Book of Snobs*: the reader who ignores or is ignorant of them will suffer only a slight though cumulative loss.

This minimalist approach is accompanied by the more-or-less gentle subversion of classical learning. We have already met (14–15) Crump, the President of St. Boniface College, 'a rich specimen of a University Snob', who, having begun as a 'Charity-boy', now reckons himself (ch. 14, 59) 'the greatest Greek scholar of the greatest College of the greatest University of the greatest Empire in the world'. While poking fun at Crump's pedantic scholarship, Mr Snob does not begrudge him his preferment; rather his assumption that all others are capable of identical self-improvement. At the other extreme on the scale of classical learning is the Governess, Miss Wirt, who teaches every subject under the sun, including 'Latin and the rudiments of Greek if desired', along with the 'Ancient and Modern history, no young woman can be without'. Mr Snob ungallantly tricks her into revealing her ignorance (ch. 33, 135–6). Classical education is also deployed as a foil for obvious intellectual and moral inadequacy. A young nobleman cannot spell, but 'may yet be a very fine classical scholar for what I know: having had his education at Eton…'(ch. 36, 149). A young wastrel is characterized as a vandal and an inebriate, but attends Merchant Tailors' School, 'where he is getting sound a classical education' (ch. 49, 207).

In only one extended passage from the *Book of Snobs* does classical allusion have a structural role; but even here, it is not indispensable. Mr Snob writes concerning Literary Snobs to one Mr Smith 'a celebrated penny-a-liner' (ch. 17). He turns to admire the success of 'Ben de Minories' (Benjamin Disraeli), who 'must know more of politics than any man, for he has been (or offered to be) everything' (74–5). How would it have been for Peel, speculates Mr Snob, had he appreciated his value? 'I turn from the harrowing theme, and depict to myself the disgust of the Romans when Coriolanus encamped before the Porta del Populo, and the mortification of Francis the First when he saw the Constable Bourbon opposite him at Pavia. "Raro antecedentem, etc., deseruit pede Poena claudo".' Here is the longest Latin quotation in the work (Horace, *Odes* 3.31–2), which the author immediately undercuts by adding (in parentheses), 'as a certain poet remarks'. Why does Mr Snob replace the single word 'scelestum' with 'etc.'? Does he not wish to say openly (not even in Latin) that he considers Peel a criminal? But all readers who had learnt their Horace could supply the missing word. He continues: 'and I declare nothing more terrible than Peel, at the catastrophe of a sinister career – Peel writhing in torture, with the Nemesis de Minories down upon him!' There might seem plenty in this paragraph to puzzle those without much formal classical education. But the problem for non-classicists is potentially resolved with the next sentence: 'I know nothing in Lemprière's Dictionary itself, more terrific than that picture of Godlike vengeance.' Here as elsewhere (ch. 44, 185; see 14), the classically-challenged but inquisitive reader is obliquely offered the solution to his or her problems.

With its attack on Peel, this is one of the most 'political' passages in the *Book of*

Snobs. Is it coincidental that it contains the longest piece of Latin? There is a hint of an answer in the chapter published three weeks later (ch. 20), 'On Conservative or Country-Party Snobs'. Here Mr Snob offers even Peel forgiveness, addressing him directly: 'We take him in our arms and say, "Bobby, my boy, let bygones be bygones; it is never too late to repent. Come and join us, and don't make Latin quotations, or vent claptraps about your own virtue or consistency; or steal anybody's clothes any more"...'(83). Was Peel more prone than his contemporaries to break into Latin in his speeches? He was certainly an accomplished classical scholar. The formal reading list in Classics for his first year at Oxford is formidable enough; and, as is well known, he secured a double first (possibly the top firsts) in Classics and Mathematics: Gash (1961) 56–9. At the time of his death, his library contained the standard classics and, 'to judge from his references in debate ... Peel's favourites were Cicero and Horace': Gash (1972) 691–2.

All this is in line with the introduction of classical themes into *Punch* for the first fifty years or so of its history. Such Latin and Greek is included as might be recalled by those receiving a standard classical education, with other classical allusions largely self-explanatory. Baffled readers are regularly provided with an escape route. Mentioning Lemprière is a favourite *Punch* device, simultaneously pointing the reader towards elementary classical knowledge, while comforting him or her that this might be the source of the author's own learning. Alternatively, classical allusion might be parodied or otherwise subverted. The passage with which this Appendix began offers a good illustration. 'Poluphloisboio Thalasses' would instantly be recognized by any reader with a smattering of Homeric Greek: one of the most familiar formulas in Homer, but here undercut for the benefit of the Greekless reader by Mr. Snob's '*I* don't know Greek for one...'.

Like many other Greek and Latin tags, *poluphloisboio thalasses* has its own life in the pages of *Punch* (at least four appearances down to the Great War) and was apparently a favourite with Thackeray. It twice appears in his spoof novel 'George de Barnwell', parodying Bulwer Lytton, which appeared in 1847 as first in the series 'Punch's Prize Novelists': Thackeray (1906) 467–77. The poor but scholarly youth, George de Barnwell, serves as shopkeeper to his uncle. He is interrupted in his Homeric studies by a customer, an attractive but unprincipled girl, destined to be his downfall. Thackeray's illustration (468) shows George reading from a folio volume across which is written (in Greek script) *poluphloisboio*. Set apart from the text, the reader is free to appreciate or ignore it. George is moved by his reading to quote another Homeric tag ('*ton d'apameibomenos prosephe*'), which is parodied by the girl ('A pretty grocer's boy you are ... with your applepiebomenos and your French and lingo...'). In the final scene (just four pages later), George, having fallen into bad company, lies in prison, awaiting execution. He meets his fate philosophically, likening the true 'Spirit of Man' to 'Him who wanders by the *thina poluphloisboio thalasses*, and shrinks awe-struck before that Azure Mystery'. A letter survives by Thackeray to a friend ((1906) xxvii–iii), in which he introduces George de Barnwell ('He will quote Plato, speak in big phrases'), and expresses concern lest Bulwer Lytton should feel betrayed 'after having had my legs *sub iisdem trabibus*'.

The reader will recognize Horace's phrase from the near-contemporary *Book of Snobs*. Apparently another of Thackeray's current classical favourites.

It is my intention to produce a detailed study of the uses of classical themes in *Punch* across its hundred-and-fifty-year history.

BIBLIOGRAPHY

Aldington, R. (1924) (ed.) *A book of 'Characters' from Theophrastus; Joseph Hall, Sir Thomas Overbury, Nicholas Breton, John Earle, Thomas Fuller, and other English authors; Jean de La Bruyère, Vauvenargues, and other French authors*, London.

Algra, K. (1992) '"Place" in context: on Theophrastus fr. 21 and 22 Wimmer', in W. W. Fortenbaugh, D. Gutas (eds.) *Theophrastus: his psychological, doxographical, and scientific writings*, Rutgers University Studies in Classical Humanities, vol. 5, New Brunswick, NJ, 141–65.

Algra, K., Barnes, J., Mansfeld, J., Schofield, M. (2005) (eds.) *The Cambridge history of Hellenistic philosophy*, Cambridge.

Altick, R. D. (1997) *Punch: the lively youth of a British institution 1841–1851*, Columbus, OH.

Anderson, W. (1970) (trans.) *Theophrastus: the character sketches*, Kent State, OH.

Anstey, F. (1882) *Vice versâ, or a lesson to fathers*, London.

Austin, J. L. (1962) *How to do things with words*, Cambridge.

Austin, M. M., Vidal-Naquet, P. (1977) *Economic and social history of ancient Greece: an introduction*, London (originally published as *Économies et sociétés en Grèce ancienne*, Paris, 1972).

Bakhtin, M. (1968) *Rabelais and his world*, trans. H. Iswolsky, Cambridge, MS.

Balme, D. M. (1962) 'Development of biology in Aristotle and Theophrastus: theory of spontaneous generation', *Phronesis* 7, 91–104.

Barnes, J. (1985) 'Theophrastus and hypothetical syllogistic', in Fortenbaugh (1985b), 125–42.
    (2005) 'Logic: the Peripatetics', in Algra *et al.* (2005), 77–83.

Baynham, E. (2003) 'Antipater and Athens', in Palagia and Tracy (2003), 23–9.

Becker, W. A. (1845) *Charicles, or illustrations of the private life of the ancient Greeks*, translated by F. Metcalf, London (originally published in German, 1840).

Bennet, C. E., Hammond, W. A. (1902) (trans.) *The Characters of Theophrastus*, New York.

Bennet, J. (1962) *George Eliot: her mind and art*, Cambridge.

Bingen, J. (1980) 'Les *Caractères* de Théophrast, témoignage authentique et déconcernant', *Grec et latin en 1980*, Études et documents dédiés à Edmond Liénard, ed. G. Viré, Univ. de Bruxelles Fac. de Phil. & Lettres Sect. de Philol. Class., 27–39.

Blackman, D. J. (1997) 'Archaeology in Greece 1996–7', *Archaeological Reports for 1996–1997*.
    (2002) 'Archaeology in Greece 2001–2002', *Archaeological Reports for 2001–2002*.

Bobrick, E. A. (1991) (ed.) *Theophrastus' Characters*, Bryn Mawr Commentaries, Bryn Mawr, PA.

Bolkestein, H. (1929) *Theophrastos' Charakter der Deisidaimonia als religiongeschichtliche Urkunde*, Giessen.

Boyce, B. (1947) *The Theophrastan character in England to 1642*, with the assistance of notes by C. N. Greenough, Harvard, MA (reprinted London, 1967).

Brandes, S. (1987) 'Reflections on honor and shame in the Mediterranean', in Gilmore (1987), 121–34.

Braudel, F. (1972–3) *The Mediterranean and the Mediterranean world in the age of Philip II*, London, (first published in French, 1949).

Bremmer, J. (1991) 'Walking, standing, and sitting in ancient Greek culture', in J. Bremmer, H. Roodenburg (eds.) *A cultural history of gesture, from antiquity to the present day*, Cambridge, 15–35.

Bryson, A. (1998) *From courtesy to civility: changing codes of conduct in early modern England*, Oxford.

Budgell, E. (1713) (trans.) *The Moral Characters of Theophrastus; translated from the Greek*, London.

Bugh, G. R. (1988) *The horsemen of Athens*, Princeton, NJ.

Burckhardt, J. (1998) *The Greeks and Greek civilization*, ed. O. Murray, trans. S. Stern, London.

Burke, P. (1993) *The art of conversation*, Cambridge.

Cairns, D. L. (1993) *AIDOS: the psychology and ethics of honour and shame in ancient Greek literature*, Oxford.

Campbell, J. K. (1964) *Honour, family and patronage: a study of institutions and moral values in a Greek mountain community*, Oxford.

Canetti, E. (1979) *Earwitness: fifty characters*, trans. J. Neugroschel, London (originally published in German as *Der Ohrenzeuge: fünfzig Charaktere*, Munich, 1974).

Capelle, W. (1954) 'Der Garten des Theophrast' in *Festschrift für Friedrich Zucker*, Berlin, 46–82.

 (1956) 'Theophrast in Ägypten', *Wiener Studien* 69, 173–86.

 (1958) 'Theophrast in Kyrene?', *RhM* 100, 169–89.

 (1959) 'Farbenbezeichungen bei Theophrast', *RhM* 101, 1–41.

Cartledge, P., Millett, P., von Reden, S. (1998) (eds.) *Kosmos: essays in order, conflict and community in classical Athens*, Cambridge.

Cazelles, J. (1922) 'La Bruyère Hélleniste', *REG* 35, 180–97.

Chroust, A.-H. (1972) 'Did Aristotle own a school in Athens between 335/34 and 323 B.C.?', *RhM* 115, 310–18.

Clark, S. R. L. (1975) *Aristotle's Man*, Oxford.

Clausen, W. (1946) 'The beginnings of English character-writing in the early seventeenth century', *Philological Quarterly* 25, 32–45.

Cohen, E. E. (1992) *Athenian economy and society: a banking perspective*, Princeton, NJ.

 (2000) *The Athenian nation*, Princeton, NJ.

Cohen, D. (1989) 'Seclusion, separation, and the status of women in classical Athens', *G&R* 36, 3–15.

Cox, A. C. (1998) *Household interests, property, marriage strategies, and family dynamics in ancient Athens*, Princeton, NJ.

Davies, J. K. (1978) *Democracy and classical Greece*, 2nd edn., London, 1978.

Davis, A. K. (1968) 'Thorstein Veblen', in *International Encyclopedia of the Social Sciences*, 18 vols., London, vol. 16, 303–8.

Davis, J. (1970) 'Honour and politics in Pisticci', *Proceedings of the Royal Anthropological Institute for 1969*, 69–81.

 (1977) *People of the Mediterranean: an essay in comparative social anthropology*, London.

Diels, H. (1909) (ed.) *Theophrasti Characteres*, Oxford Classical Texts, Oxford.

Diggle, J. (2002) 'The *Characters* of Theophrastos', *Praktika tes Akademias Athenon* 77, 56–68.

 (2004) (ed.) Theophrastus, *Characters*, Cambridge Classical Texts and Commentaries 43, Cambridge.

Dorandi, T. (1998) 'Qualche aspetto della vita di Teofrasto e il Liceo dopo Aristotele', in van Ophuijsen and van Raalte (1998), 29–38.

 (2005) 'Organization and structure of the philosophical schools', in Algra *et al.* (2005), 55–64.

Dorfman, J. (1935) *Thorstein Veblen and his America*, London.

Dover, K. J. (1974) *Greek popular morality in the time of Plato and Aristotle*, Oxford.

Düring, I. (1957) *Aristotle in the ancient biographical tradition*, Göteborg.

Earle, J. (1899) *Microcosmography, or A piece of the world discovered in essays and characters* (includes a translation of Theophrastus' *Characters* by J. Healey), ed. W. H. D. Rouse, London.

Easterling, P. E. (2005) '"The speaking page": reading Sophocles with Jebb', in C. Stray (ed.) *The owl of Minerva: the Cambridge praelections of 1906*, PCPS supplementary vol. 28, Cambridge, 25–46.

Easterling, P. E., Edwards, M. J. (2005) (eds.) 'New Introduction' to R. C. Jebb (ed.) *Selections from the Attic Orators*, Exeter.

Edgeworth, M. (1988) *The absentee*, ed. W. J. McCormack, K. Walker, The World's Classics, Oxford.

Edmonds, J. M. (1929) (ed.) *The* Characters *of Theophrastus*, Loeb edn., London.

Edmonds, J. M., Austen, G. E. V. (1904) (eds.) *The* Characters *of Theophrastus*, London.

Edwards, A. T. (2004) *Hesiod's Ascra*, Berkeley, CA.

Ehrenberg, V. (1951) *The people of Aristophanes: a sociology of Attic comedy*, 2nd edn., Cambridge.

 (1973) *From Solon to Socrates: Greek history and civilization between the sixth and fifth centuries B.C.*, 2nd edn., London.

Einarson, B., Link, G. E. (1976–1990) (eds.) Theophrastus, *De causis plantarum*, Loeb edn., 3 vols., Cambridge MS.

Elias, N. (2000) *The civilizing process: sociogenetic and psychogenetic investigations*, ed. E. Dunning, J. Goudsblom, S. Mennell, trans. E. Jephcott, revised edn., Oxford (first published in German, 1939).

Eliot, G. (1994) *Impressions of Theophrastus Such*, N. Henry (ed.), Iowa.

(1995) *The* [sic] *impressions of Theophrastus Such*, ed. D. J. Enright, London.

(1954–1978) *The George Eliot letters*, ed. G. S. Haight, 9 vols., London.

Enright, D. J. (1995) (ed.) 'Introduction' to Eliot (1995), xix–xxviii.

Evans, E. C. (1969) *Physiognomics in the ancient world*, Transactions of the American Philosophical Society, vol. 59.

Fairweather, J. (1974) 'Fiction in the biographies of ancient writers', *Ancient Society* 5, 231–75.

Ferguson, W. S. (1911a) *Hellenistic Athens: an historical essay*, London (reprinted Chicago, 1974).

(1911b) 'The laws of Demetrius of Phalerum and their guardians', *Klio* 11, 265–76.

Fentress, J., Fentress, E., (2001) 'The hole in the doughnut', review of Horden, Purcell (2000), *Past & Present* 173, 203–19.

Fisher, N. R. E. (1992) *Hybris: a study in the values of honour and shame in ancient Greece*, Warminster.

(1995) Review of Williams (1993), *CR*, 71–3.

Forbes, C. A. (1945) 'Expanded uses of the Greek gymnasium', *CP* 40, 32–42.

Fornara, C. W. (1983) (ed.) *Archaic times to the end of the Peloponnesian War: translated documents of Greece and Rome*, vol. 1, 2nd edn., Cambridge.

Fortenbaugh, W. W. (1975) 'Die Charaktere Theophrasts: Verhaltensregelmassigkeit und aristotelische Laster', *RhM* 118, 62–82 (reprinted and translated as 'The *Characters* of Theophrastus, behavioural regularities and Aristotelian vices', in Fortenbaugh (2003) 109–30).

(1978) 'The thirty-first character sketch', *Classical World* 71, 333–9 (reprinted in Fortenbaugh (2003) 319–26).

(1981) 'Theophrast über den komischen Charakter', *RhM* 124, 245–60 (reprinted and translated as 'Theophrastus and comic character', in Fortenbaugh (2003) 295–306).

(1983a) 'Arius, Theophrastus, and the *Eudemian ethics*', in (id.) (1983b), 203–23 (reprinted in Fortenbaugh (2003) 109–30).

(1983b) (ed.) *On Stoic and Peripatetic ethics: the work of Arius Didymus*, Rutgers University Studies in Classical Humanities, vol. 1, New Brunswick, NJ.

(1984) (ed.) *Quellen zur Ethik Theophrasts*, Amsterdam.

(1985a) 'Theophrastus on emotion', in (id.) (1985b), 209–30.

(1985b) (ed.) *Theophrastus of Eresus: on his life and work*, Rutgers Studies in Classical Humanities, vol. 2, New Brunswick, NJ (reprinted in Fortenbaugh (2003) 71–91).

(1990) 'Teofrast, fr. 534 FHS&G', *Filozofska Istrazivanja* 37, 1039–49 (reprinted and translated as 'Theophrastus, Fr. 534 FHS&G: on assisting a friend contrary to the law' in Fortenbaugh (2003) 150–61).

(1994) 'Theophrastus, the *Characters* and rhetoric', in W. W. Fortenbaugh, D. C. Mirhady (eds.) *Peripatetic rhetoric after Aristotle*, New Brunswick, NJ, 15–35 (reprinted in Fortenbaugh (2003) 224–23).

(1995) 'Theophrastus, Source no. 709 FHS&G' in J. Abenes, S. Slings and I. Sluiter (eds.), *Greek literary theory after Aristotle*, Amsterdam, 1–16 (reprinted in Fortenbaugh (2003) 307–16).

(1998) 'Theophrastean titles and book numbers: some reflections on titles relating to rhetoric and poetics' in W. Burkert (ed.), *Fragmentsammlungen Philosophischer texte der Antike*, Göttingen, 182–200 (reprinted in Fortenbaugh (2003) 195–212).

(2000) 'Une analyse du rire chez Aristote et Théophraste' in M-L. Desclos (ed.) *Le rire des Grecs: anthropologie du rire en Grèce ancienne*, Grenoble, 333–54 (reprinted and translated as 'An Aristotelian and Theophrastean analysis of laughter' in Fortenbaugh (2003) 91–106).

(2003) *Theophrastean studies*, Philosophie der Antike 17, Stuttgart.

(2005) (ed.) *Theophrastus of Eresus: sources on rhetoric and poetics* (texts 666–713), commentary vol. 8, Leiden.

Fortenbaugh, W. W., Schütrumpf, E. (2000) (eds.) *Demetrius of Phalerum: text, translation and discussion*, Rutgers Studies in Classical Humanities, vol. 9, New Brunswick, NJ.

Foxhall, L. (1998a) 'The politics of affection: emotional attachments in Athenian society', in Cartledge, Millett, von Reden (1998), 52–67.

(1998b) 'Cargoes of the heart's desire: the character of trade in the archaic Mediterranean world', in N. Fisher, H. van Wees (eds.) *Archaic Greece: new approaches and new evidence*, London, 295–310.

Fraser, P. M. (1995) 'The world of Theophrastus', in S. Hornblower (ed.) *Greek historiography*, Oxford, 167–91.

Furley, D. J. (1953) 'The purpose of Theophrastus' *Characters*', *SO* 30, 56–60.

Gaiser, K. (1985) *Theophrast in Assos: zur Entwicklung der Naturwissenschaft zwischen Akademie und Peripatos*, Heidelberg.

Gagarin, M. (2000) 'The legislation of Demetrius of Phalerum and the transformation of Athenian law', in Fortenbaugh and Schütrumpf (2000), 347–65.

Gally, H. (1952) 'A critical essay on characteristic-writings' from his translation of *The* Moral Characters *of Theophrastus* (1725), introduction by A. H. Chorney, The Augustan Reprint Society, Los Angeles, CA.

Garland, R. (1990) *The Greek way of life*, London.

Gash, N. (1961) *Mr. Secretary Peel: the life of Sir Robert Peel to 1830*, London.

(1972) *Sir Robert Peel: the life of Sir Robert Peel after 1830*, London.

Geddes, A. G. (1987) 'Rags and riches: the costume of Athenian men in the fifth century', *CQ* 37, 307–31.

Gehrke, H.-J. (1978) 'Das Verhältnis von Politik und Philosophie im Wirken des Demetrios von Phaleron', *Chiron* 8, 149–93.

Geertz, C. (1973) 'Deep play: notes on the Balinese cockfight', in (id.) (ed.) *Interpretations of culture*, New York, 412–54.

Gibbs, L. (2002) (ed.) Aesop, *Fables*, The World's Classics, Oxford.

Giglioni, G. B. (1980) 'Immagini di una società: analisi storica dei "Caratteri" di Teofrasto', *Athenaeum* 58, 73–102.

Gill, C. (1990) 'The character-personality distinction', in Pelling (1990), 1–31.

Gilmore, D. (1987) (ed.) *Honour and shame and the unity of the Mediterranean*, Washington, DC.

Glucker, J. (1998) 'Theophrastus, the Academy, and the Athenian philosophical atmosphere', in van Ophuijsen and van Raalte (1998), 299–316.

Goldhill, S. D. (1986) *Reading Greek tragedy*, Cambridge.

(1999) 'Performance notes', in Goldhill and Osborne (1999), 1–32.

Goldhill, S. D., Osborne, R. (1999) (eds.) *Performance culture and Athenian democracy*, Cambridge.

Gombrich, E. H. (1960) *Art and illusion: a study in the psychology of pictorial representation*, Oxford.

Gombrich, E. H., Kris, E. (1940) *Caricature*, Harmondsworth.

Gordon, G. S. (1912) 'Theophrastus and his imitators', in (id.) (ed.) *English literature and the Classics*, Oxford, 49–86.

Gottschalk, H. B. (1964) 'The *De coloribus* and its author', *Hermes* 92, 59–85.

(1998) 'Theophrastus and the Peripatos', in van Ophuisen and van Raalte (1998), 281–98.

(2000) 'Demetrius of Phalerum: a politician among philosophers or a philosopher among politicians?', in Fortenbaugh and Schütrumpf (2000), 367–80.

Gough, Richard, (1981) *The history of Myddle*, ed. D. Hey, Harmondsworth.

Gotthelf, A. (1983) 'Comments on Professor Fortenbaugh's paper with special attention to *pathos*', in Fortenbaugh (1983b), 224–36.

Grant, M. A. (1924) *The ancient rhetorical theories of the laughable: the Greek rhetoricians and Cicero*, University of Wisconsin Studies in Language and Literature 21, Madison, WI.

Grayeff, F. (1974) *Aristotle and his school: an inquiry into the history of the Peripatos*, London.

Green, P. (1990) *Alexander to Actium: the historical evolution of the Hellenistic age*, Berkeley, CA.

(2003) 'Occupation and co-existence: the impact of Macedon on Athens, 323–307', in Palagia and Tracy (2003), 1–7.

Greenough, C. N. (1947) *A bibliography of the Theophrastan character in English with several portrait characters*, prepared for publication by J. M. French, Westport, CT.

Grote, G. (1846–56) *A history of Greece*, 8 vols., London (cited from the edition of 1888, 10 vols, London).

Gutas, D. (1985) 'The life, works, and sayings of Theophrastus in the Arabic tradition', in Fortenbaugh (1985b), 63–102.

Habicht, C. (1997) *Athens from Alexander to Antony*, trans. D. L. Schneider, Cambridge, MA (originally published in German, 1995).

Hahm, D. E. (1980) 'The ethical doxography of Arius Didymus', *ANRW* pt. 2 vol. 36.4, 2935–3055.

Haight, G. S. (1968) *George Eliot: a biography*, Oxford.

Hall, Joseph (1948) *Heaven upon Earth* and *Characters of Vertues and Vices*, ed. R. Kirk, Rutgers Studies in English 6, New Brunswick, NJ.

Halliwell, S. (1990) 'Traditional Greek conception of character', in Pelling (1990), 32–59.

(1991) 'The uses of laughter in Greek culture', *CQ* 41, 276–96.

Hanson, V. D. (1989) *The western way of war: infantry battle in classical Greece*, London.

(1995) *The other Greeks: the family farm and the agrarian roots of western civilization*, New York.

(2000) 'Hoplite battle as ancient Greek warfare: when, where, and why?', in van Wees (2000b), 201–32.

Harris, E. M. (1992) 'Women and lending in Athenian society: a *horos* re-examined', *Phoenix* 46, 309–21.

(2002) 'Workshop, marketplace and household', in P. A. Cartledge, E. E. Cohen, L. Foxhall (eds.) *Money, labour and land: approaches to the economies of ancient Greece*, London, 66–99.

Harris, W. V. (2001) *Restraining rage: the ideology of anger control in classical antiquity*, Cambridge, MA.

(2005) (ed.) *Rethinking the Mediterranean*, Oxford.

Harrison, A. R. W. (1986) *The law of Athens*, vol. 1: *the family and property*, Oxford.

Healey, J. (trans.) (1616) *Theophrastus, his* Morall Characters *or descriptions of manners*, London (reprinted as and cited from an appendix to Earle (1899).

Heilbroner, R. L. (1961) *The worldly philosophers: the lives, times and ideas of the great economic thinkers*, New York.

Henry, N. (1994). 'Introduction' to Eliot (1994), vii–xxxvii.

(1997) 'George Eliot, George Henry Lewes, and comparative anatomy', in J. Rignall (ed.) *George Eliot and Europe*, Aldershot, 44–63.

(2001) 'George Eliot and politics', in G. Levine (ed.) *The Cambridge companion to George Eliot*, Cambridge, 138–58.

(2002) *George Eliot and the British Empire*, Cambridge.

Herzfeld, M. (1980) 'Honour and shame: problems in the comparative analysis of moral systems', *Man* 15, 339–51.

(1985) *The poetics of manhood: contest and identity in a Cretan mountain village*, Princeton, NJ.

(1987a) *Anthropology through the looking glass: critical ethography on the margins of Europe*, Cambridge.

(1987b) 'As in your own house: hospitality, ethnography and the stereotype of Mediterranean society', in Gilmore (1987), 75–89.

Hibbett, H (1959) *The Floating World in Japanese fiction*, London.

Hicks, E. L. (1882) 'On the *Characters* of Theophrastus', *JHS* 3, 128–43.

Hinz, V. (2005) Review of Diggle (2004), *Exemplaria Classica* 9, 227–39.

Hobsbawm, E. (1971) 'From social history to the history of society', *Daedalus* 100, 20–45 (reprinted in, and cited from, E. Hobsbawm, *On history*, London, 1997, 71–93).

Hood, R. (1998) *Faces of archaeology in Greece: caricatures by Piet de Jong*, Oxford.

Hopkins, K. H. (1978) 'Rules of evidence', *JRS* 98, 178–86.

(1983) 'Murderous games', in (id.) *Death and renewal*, Sociological Studies in Roman History, vol. 2, Cambridge, 1–30.

(1993) 'Novel evidence for Roman slavery', *Past and Present* 138, 3–27 (reprinted in, and cited from, R. Osborne (2004) (ed.), *Studies in ancient Greek and Roman society*, Cambridge, 206–25).

Hornblower, S. (2000) 'Sticks, stones, and Spartans: the sociology of Spartan violence', in van Wees (2000b), 57–83.

Horden, P., Purcell, N. (2000) *The corrupting sea: a study of Mediterranean history*, Oxford.

(2005) 'Four years of corruption: a response to critics', in W. V. Harris (ed.) *Rethinking the Mediterranean*, Oxford, 348–75.

Hort, Sir Arthur (1916) (ed.) Theophrastus, *Enquiry into plants*, 2 vols., Loeb edn., Cambridge, MA.

Howell, F. (1824) *The* Characters *of Theophrastus, illustrated by physiognomical sketches*, London.

Humphreys, S. C. (1993) *The family, women and death*, 2nd edn., Ann Arbor, MI.

Hunter, V. J. (1973) *Thucydides: the artful reporter*, Toronto.

(1994) *Policing Athens: social control in the Attic lawsuits, 420–320 B.C.*, Princeton, NJ.

Jackson, H. (1920) 'Aristotle's lecture room and lectures', *The Journal of Philology* 25, 191–200.

Jameson, M. H. (1999) 'The spectacular and the obscure in Athenian religion', in Goldhill and Osborne (1999), 321–40.

Janko, R. (1984) *Aristotle on comedy: towards a reconstruction of* Poetics II, London.

Jebb, R. C. (1907) *Life and letters of Sir Richard Claverhouse Jebb*, Cambridge.

(1909) (ed.) *The* Characters *of Theophrastus*, new edn., ed. J. E. Sandys, London.

(2005) (ed.) *Selections from the Attic Orators*, new introduction and bibliography by P. E. Easterling, M. J. Edwards, Exeter (first published, London, 1888).

Jenkyns, R. (1980) *The Victorians and ancient Greece*, Oxford.

Johnson, R. (1957) 'A note on the number of Isocrates' pupils', *AJPh* 78, 297–300.

Johnstone, S. (1999) *Disputes and democracy: the consequences of litigation in classical Athens*, Austin, TX.

Jones, A. H. M. (1956) *Athenian democracy*, Oxford.

Jones, N. F. (1999) *The associations of classical Athens: the response to democracy*, Oxford.

(2004) *Rural Athens under the democracy*, Pennsylvania, PA.

Kapsalis, G. D. (1982) *Die Typik der Situationen in den Characteren Theophrasts und ihre Rezeption in der neugriechischen Literatur*, Bochum.

Kitto, H. D. F. (1951) *The Greeks*, Harmondsworth.

Klose, D. (1970) (ed.) Theophrast, *Charaktere*, with 'Nachtrag' by P. Steinmetz, Stuttgart.

Konstan, D. (1995) *Greek comedy and ideology*, Oxford.

(1997) *Friendship in the classical world*, Cambridge.

Konstantakos, I. M. (2005) 'Aspects of the figure of the *agroikos* in ancient comedy', *RhM* 148, 1–26.

Körte, A. (1929) '*Charakter*', *Hermes* 64, 69–86.

Kosak, J. C. (2000) '*Polis nosousa*: Greek ideas about the city and disease in the fifth century BC', in V. M. Hope, E. Marshall (eds.) *Death and disease in the ancient city*, London.

Kroll, J. H. (1993) *The Greek coins*, with contributions by A. S. Walker, *The Athenian Agora* vol. 26, Princeton, NJ.

La Bruyère, J. de (1962) *Les* Caractères *de Théophraste traduits du grec avec les caractères ou les moeurs de ce siècle*, ed. R. Garapon, Paris.

Lane Fox, R. J. (1994) 'Aeschines and Athenian democracy', in Osborne and Hornblower (1994), 135–56.

(1996) 'Theophrastus' *Characters* and the historian', *PCPS* 42, 127–70.

(2004) 'Sex, gender and the other in Xenophon's *Anabasis*', in (id.) (ed.) *The long march: Xenophon and the Ten Thousand*, Yale, NH.

Langdon, M (1994) 'Public auction in Athens', in Osborne and Hornblower (1994), 253–65.

Lape, S. (2004) *Reproducing Athens: Menander's comedy, democratic culture, and the Hellenistic city*, Princeton, NJ.

Leppin, H. (2002) 'Theophrasts "Charaktere" und die Burgermentalität in Athen im Ubergang zum Hellenismus', *Klio* 84, 37–56.

Le Roy Ladurie, E. (1978) *Montaillou, Cathars and Catholics in a French village 1294–1324*, B. Bray (trans.), London (first published in French, 1975).

Lewis, S. (1995) 'Barbers' shops and perfume shops: symposia without wine', in A. Powell (ed.) *The Greek world*, London, 432–41.

(1996) *News and society in the Greek polis*, London.

Loicq-Berger, M.-P. (2002) 'Athènes au quotidien à l'époque de Théophraste', *Folia Electronica Classica* 4 http://bcs.fltr.ucl.ac.be/FE/04/theocomm.html

Lynch, J. P. (1972) *Aristotle's school: a study of Greek educational thought*, Berkeley, CA.

McCabe, R. A. (1995) 'Refining Theophrastus: ethical concerns and moral paragons in the English character book', *Hermathena* 52, 33–50.

McClure, L. (1993) 'On knowing Greek: George Eliot and the classical tradition', *Classical and Modern Literature* 13, 139–56.

McDonagh, J. (1997) *George Eliot*, Plymouth.

McKechnie, P. (1989) *Outsiders in the Greek cities in the fourth century BC*, London.

McMaster, R. D. (1991) *Thackeray's cultural frame of reference: allusion in* The Newcomes, Montreal.

McSweeney, K. (1991) *George Eliot: a literary life*, Basingstoke.

Mahaffy, J. P. (1874) *Social life in Greece from Homer to Menander*, 7th edn, London.

(1887) *Greek life and thought from the age of Alexander to the Roman conquest*, London.

Major, W. E. (1977) 'Menander in a Macedonian world', *GRBS* 38, 41–73.

Mann, J. *Chaucer and the medieval Estates satire*, Cambridge, 1973.

Marasco, G. (1984) *Democare di Leuconoe: politica e cultura in Atene fra IV e III sec. A.C.*, Florence.

Marcovich, M. (1974) 'Theophrastus, *Characters*: the new papyrus', *Ziva Antika* 24, 132.

(1976) 'The genuine text of Theophrastus' thirty-first character: Papyrus Lychnopolitana: editio princeps', *Ziva Antika* 26, 51–2.

Maroi, F. (1916–17) 'Sul diritto privato greco nei *Caratteri* di Teofrasto', *Rendiconti della Reale Accademia dei Lincei* 5.25, 1227–54.

Mari, M. (2003) 'Macedonians and anti-Macedonians in early Hellenistic Athens: reflections on *asebeia*', in Palagia and Tracy (2003), 82–92.

Matelli, E. (1989) 'Libro e testo nella tradizione de *Caratteri* di Teofrasto', *Scrittura e Civiltà* 13, 329–86.

Maxwell-Stuart, P. G. (1996) 'Theophrastus the traveller', *PdP* 289, 241–67.

Mayhew, H. (n.d.) *Mayhew's Characters*, with an essay on the English character by P. Quennell, London.

Meadows, A., Shipton, K. (2001) (eds.) *Money and its uses in the ancient Greek world*, Oxford.

Mejer, J. (1998) 'A life in fragments: the *Vita Theophrasti*', in van Ophuijsen and van Raalte (1998), 1–28.

Melville Jones, J. R. (1993) (ed.) *Testimonia numaria: Greek and Latin texts concerning ancient Greek coinage*, vol. 1, *Texts and translations*, London.

Mennell, S. (1992) *Norbert Elias: an introduction*, Oxford.

Michell, H. (1957) *The economics of ancient Greece*, 2nd edn., Cambridge.

Mignucci, M. (1998) 'Theophrastus' logic', in van Ophuisen and van Raalte (1998), 39–66.

Milbradt, J. (1974) 'Der Charakter: zu den Menschenbild der Zeit der Poliskrise und seiner Aufnahme durch die römische Komödie', in E. C. Welskopf (ed.) *Hellenische Poleis: Krise, Wandlung, Wirkung*, 3 vols., Berlin, vol. 3, 1413–49.

Miller, N. (1987) (ed.) Menander, *Plays and fragments*, Penguin Classics, Harmondsworth.

Millett, P. C. (1984) 'Hesiod and his world', *PCPS* 30, 84–115.

(1989) 'Patronage and its avoidance in classical Athens', in A. W. Wallace-Hadrill (ed.) *Patronage in ancient society*, London, 15–48.

(1990) 'Sale, credit and exchange in Athenian law and society', in P. Cartledge, P. Millett, S. Todd (eds.) *Nomos: essays in Athenian law, politics and society*, Cambridge, 167–94.

(1991) *Lending and borrowing in ancient Athens*, Cambridge.

(1998) 'Encounters in the Agora', in Cartledge, Millett, von Reden (1998), 203–28.

(2000) 'The rhetoric of reciprocity', in C. Gill, N. Postlethwaite, R. Seaford, (eds.) *Reciprocity in ancient Greece*, Oxford, 227–54.

(2005) 'The trial of Socrates revisited', *European Review of History* 12, 23–62.

(2007) 'Aristotle and slavery in Athens', *G&R* 54, 178–209.

Momigliano, A. (1965) review of C. Hignett, *Xerxes' invasion of Greece* in *EHR* 80, 370.

Mossé, C. (1973) *Athens in decline 404–86 B.C.*, London.

Moynihan, H. (1997) *Everyday-life history: practice and progress*, unpublished dissertation, Classical Faculty, Cambridge.

Müller-Schwefe, G. (1972) 'Joseph Hall's *Characters of Vertues and Vices*; notes towards a revaluation', *Texas Studies in Literature and Language* 19, 235–51.

Navarre, O. (1914) 'Théophraste et La Bruyère', *REG* 27, 384–440.

(1921) (ed.) Caractères *de Théophraste*, Budé edn., Paris.

(1924) (ed.) Caractères *de Théophraste*, Paris.

Needham, R. (1975) 'Polythetic classification: convergence and consequences', *Man* 10, 349–69.

Nevett, L. C. (1999) *House and society in the ancient Greek world*, Cambridge.

Nuttall, A. D. (2003) *Dead from the waist down: scholars and scholarship in literature and the popular imagination*, New Haven, CT.

Oliver, G. J. (2003) 'Oligarchy at Athens after the Lamian War: epigraphic evidence for the *Boule* and the *Ekklesia*', in Palagia and Tracy (2003), 40–51.

O'Neill, E. N. (1977) (ed.) *Teles (the Cynic teacher)*, Missoula, MT.

Osborne, R., Hornblower, S. (eds.) (1994) *Ritual, finance, politics: Athenian democratic accounts presented to David Lewis*, Oxford.

O'Sullivan, L. (2002) 'The law of Sophocles and the beginnings of permanent philosophical schools in Athens', *RhM* 145, 251–62.

Overbury, T. J. (1936) *The Overburian Characters, to which is added a Wife*, ed. W. J. Paylor, Oxford.

Owen, G. E. L. (1983) 'Philosophical invective', *Oxford Studies in Ancient Philosophy* 1, 1–26.

Pakaluk, M. (2004a) 'Socratic magnanimity in the *Phaedo*', *Ancient Philosophy* 24, 101–117.

(2004b) 'The meaning of Aristotelian magnanimity' *Oxford Studies in Ancient Philosophy* 26, 241–75.

(2005) *Aristotle's Nicomachean ethics: an introduction*, Cambridge.

Palagia, O., Tracy, S. V. (2003) (eds.) *The Macedonians in Athens, 322–229 BC*, Oxford.

Parke, H. W. (1977) *Festivals of the Athenians*, London.

Parker, R. (2006) 'The learned commentator of Theophrastus', review of Diggle (2004), *CR* 56, 308–11.

Patterson, C. (2000) 'The hospitality of Athenian justice: the metic in court', in V. Hunter, J. Edmondson (eds.) *Law and social status in classical Athens*, Oxford, 93–112.

Pattison, M. (1870) review of first edn. of Jebb (1909), *The Academy* 15 November, 52–4.

Pelling, C. (1990) (ed.) *Characterization and individuality in Greek literature*, Oxford.

Peristiany, J. G. (1965a) 'Honour and shame in a Cypriot highland village', in (id.) (1965b), 171–90.

(1965b) (ed.) *Honour and shame: the values of Mediterranean society*, London.

Peristiany, J. G., Pitt-Rivers, J. (1992) (eds.) *Honour and grace in anthropology*, Cambridge.

Peters, C. (1987) *Thackeray's universe: shifting worlds of imagination and reality*, London.

Phillips, K. C. (1978) *The language of Thackeray*, London.

Philological Society of Leipzig (1897) (M. Bechert, C. Cichorius, A. Giesecke, R. Holland, J. Illberg, O. Immisch, R. Meister, W. Ruge), *Theophrasts Charaktere*, Leipzig.

Pickard-Cambridge, A. (1966) *Dithyramb, tragedy and comedy*, 2nd edn., revised by T. B. L. Webster, Oxford.

Pitt-Rivers, J. (1965) 'Honour and social status', in Peristiany (1965b), 19–78.

Podlecki, A. J. (1985) 'Theophrastus on history and politics', in Fortenbaugh (1985b), 231–49.

(1998) *Perikles and his circle*, 1998.

Race, W. H. (1981) 'The word *kairos* in Greek drama', *TAPA* 111, 197–213.

Rackham, H. (1934) (ed.) Aristotle, *The Nicomachean ethics*, Loeb edn., revised edn., Cambridge, MA.

Rauh, N. K. (1989) 'Auctioneers and the Roman economy', *Historia* 38, 451–71.

Raverat, G. (1952) *Period piece: a Cambridge childhood*, London.

Rendall, V. (1947) 'George Eliot and the Classics', *Notes and Queries* 13 December, 544–6, 564–5.

Regenbogen, O. (1937) 'Eine Polemik Theophrasts gegen Aristoteles', *Hermes* 72, 469–77.

(1940) 'Theophrastos von Eresos', in Pauly-Wissowa, *Real-Encyclopädie der classischen Altertumswissenschaft*, Stuttgart, Suppl. vol. VII cols. 1354–1562 (separately reprinted, Waldsee, 1950).

Rhodes, P. J., Osborne, R. (2003) (eds.) *Greek historical inscriptions 404–323 BC*, Oxford.

Ribbeck, O. (1876) 'Ueber den Begriff des *eiron*', *RhM* 25, 381–400.

(1882) *Alazon; ein Betrag zur antiken Ethologie und zur Kenntniss des griechisch-römischen Komödie*, Leipzig.

(1884) 'Kolax: eine ethologische Studie', *Abhandlungen der königlich sächsischen Gesellschaft der Wissenschaft* 21, 1–114.

(1888) 'Agroikos: eine ethologische Studie', *Abhandlungen der königlich sächsischen Gesellschaft der Wissenschaft* 23, 1–68.

Rignall, J. (2000) (ed.) *Oxford reader's companion to George Eliot*, Oxford.

Roberts, J. (2000) 'Justice in the polis', in C. J. Rowe, M. Schofield (eds.) *The Cambridge history of ancient political thought*, Cambridge, 344–65.

Roll, E. (1978) *A history of economic thought*, 4th edn., London.

Rosenmeyer, T. G. (1996) 'Ironies in serious drama', in M. S. Silk (ed.) *Tragedy and the tragic: Greek theatre and beyond*, Oxford, 497–519.

Rosivach, V. J. (2000) 'Some aspects of the fourth-century Athenian market in grain', *Chiron* 30, 31–64.

Rostovtzeff, M. (1941) *Economic and social history of the Hellenistic world*, 3 vols. Oxford; cited from the corrected reprint, Oxford, 1953.

Rupp, D. W. (2002) *Peripatoi: Athenian walks*, Athens.

Rusten, J. (2002) (ed.) Theophrastus, *Characters*, with I. C. Cunningham (ed.) Herodas, *Mimes:* Sophron, *and other mime fragments*, 3rd edn., Cambridge, MA.

Saller, R. (1980) 'Anecdotes as historical evidence for the principate', *G&R* 27, 69–83.

Schaps, D. M. (2004) *The invention of coinage and the monetization of ancient Greece*, Ann Arbor, MI.

Schmitt, C. B. (1971) 'Theophrastus in the Middle Ages', *Viator* 2 , 251–70.

Schnayder, J. (1962) 'Soziologisches in den Werken des Theophrasts', *Eos* 52, 17–38.

Schneider, J. (1971) 'Of vigilance and virgins', *Ethnology* 10, 1–24.

Schofield, M. (1998) 'Political friendship and the ideology of reciprocity', in Cartledge, Millett, von Reden (1998), 37–51.

Seaford, R. (2004) *Money and the early Greek mind: Homer, philosophy, tragedy*, Cambridge.

Sedley, D. (2003) *Plato's Cratylus*, Cambridge.

Sharples, R. W. (1998) 'Theophrastus as philosopher and Aristotelian', in van Ophuisen and van Raalte (1998), 267–80.

Shear, T. L. (1978) *Kallias of Sphettos and the revolt of Athens in 286 BC*, Hesperia Supplement 17, Princeton, NJ.

Shipton, K. (1997) 'The private banks in fourth-century Athens: a reappraisal', *CQ* 49, 396–422.

(2001) 'Money and the élite in classical Athens', in Meadows and Shipton (2001), 129–44.

(2000) *Leasing and lending: the cash economy in fourth-century BC Athens*, Bulletin of the Institute of Classical Studies Supplement 74, London.

Sjoberg, G. (1960) *The preindustrial city: past and present*, New York.

Smeed, J. W. (1985) *The Theophrastan 'character': the history of a literary genre*, Oxford.

Smith, D. N. (1918) (ed.) *Characters from the histories and memoirs of the seventeenth century*, Oxford.

Sollenberger, M. G. (1985) 'Diogenes Laertius 5.36–57: the *Vita Theophrasti*', in Fortenbaugh (1985b), 1–62.

(1987) 'A note on the lives of Theophrastus and Strato in Diogenes Laertius 5.57–8', *CP* 82, 228–30.

(1992) 'The lives of the Peripatetics: an analysis of the contents and structure of Diogenes Laertius' *Vitae philosophorum* book 5', *ANRW* vol. 36 pt. 6, ed. W. Haase, Berlin, 3794–879.

Sorabji, R. (1988) 'Theophrastus on place', in W. W. Fortenbaugh, R. W. Sharples (eds.) *Theophrastan studies on natural science, physics and metaphysics, ethics, religion and rhetoric*, Rutgers University Studies in Classical Humanities, vol. 3, New Brunswick, NJ, 139–66.

— (1998) 'Is Theophrastus a significant philosopher?', in van Ophuijsen and van Raalte (1998), 203–22.

Sparkes, B. (2004) 'So few people look like themselves', in S. Keay, S. Moser (eds.) *Greek art in view: essays in honour of Brian Sparkes*, Oxford, 1–23.

Spence, I. G. (1993) *The cavalry of classical Greece: a social and military history with particular reference to Athens*, Oxford.

Spina, L. (1981) 'Un oligarca nella crisi della città', *Quaderni di storia* 13, 271–9.

Stanford, W. B., McDowell, R. B. (1971) *Mahaffy: a biography of an Anglo-Irishman*, London.

Stange, G. R. (1980) 'The voices of the essayist', *Nineteenth-Century Fiction* 35, 312–30.

Stark, R. (1960) 'Zu Theophrasts "Charakteren"', *RhM* 103, 193–200.

Stein, M, (1992) *Definition und Schilderung in Theophrasts Charakteren*, Stuttgart.

Steinmetz, P. (1959) 'Der Zweck der Charaktere Theophrasts', *Annales Universitatis Saraviensis* (Philosophie) 8, 209–46.

— (1960a) 'Menander und Theophrast: Folgerungen aus dem Dyskolos', *RhM* 103, 185–91.

— (1960b) Theophrast, *Charaktere*, vol. 1, *Textgeschichte und Text*, Munich.

— (1962) Theophrast, *Charaktere*, vol. 2, *Kommentar und Übersetzung*, Munich.

— (1970) 'Nachtrag' to D. Klose (ed.) Theophrast, *Charaktere*, Stuttgart.

Stephen, Sir Leslie (1902) *George Eliot*, London.

Stewart, F. H. (1994) *Honor*, Chicago, IL.

Stray, C. (forthcoming) 'A cultured commentator: Sophocles' Jebb'.

Stone, L. M. (1981) *Costume in Aristophanic comedy*, New York.

Szegedy-Maszak, A. (1981) (ed.) *The "Nomoi" of Theophrastus*, New York.

Tacon, J. (2001) 'Ecclesiastic *thorubos* and Athenian democracy', *G&R* 47, 173–91.

Taylor, D. J. (1999) *Thackeray*, London.

Taylor, C. H., Macindoe, D. M. (1949) *Cricket dialogue*, foreword by R. V. Robins, London.

Thackeray, W. M. (1895) *The book of Snobs and other contributions to Punch*, ed. 'L. M.', London.

— (1906) *Contributions to "Punch" etc.*, vol. 6 of *The works of William Makepeace Thackeray*, biographical introductions by Anne Ritchie (née Thackeray), 13 vols., London.

Theophrastus of Eresus (1992–3) *Sources for his life, writings, thought and influence*, ed. W. W. Fortenbaugh, P. M. Huby, R. W. Sharples, D. Gutas, 2 vols., Leiden.

— (1998) *Sources on physics* (texts 137–223), commentary volume 3.1, ed. R. W. Sharples, Leiden.

— (1999) *Sources on psychology* (texts 265–327), commentary volume 4, ed. P. Huby, Leiden.

— (1995) *Sources for his life, writings, thought and influence*, commentary volume 5, Sources on biology (human physiology, living creatures, botany): (texts 328–435), ed. R. W. Sharples, Philosophia Antiqua, vol. 64, Leiden.

— (2005) *Sources for his life, writings, thought and influence*, commentary volume 8, Sources on rhetoric and poetics (texts 666–713), ed. W. W. Fortenbaugh, Philosophia Antiqua, vol. 97, Leiden.

Tilman, R. (1992) *Thorstein Veblen and his critics, 1891–1963*, Princeton, NJ.

Todd, S. C. (1993) *The shape of Athenian law*, Oxford.

Tracy, S. V. (2000) 'Demetrius of Phalerum: who was he and who was he not?', in Fortenbaugh and Schütrumpf (2000), 331–45.

Trenkner, S. (1958) *The Greek novella in the classical period*, Cambridge.

Trevett, J. (2001) 'Coinage and democracy at Athens', in Meadows and Shipton (2001), 23–34

Tsakirgis, B. (2005) 'Living and working around the Athenian Agora: a preliminary case study of three houses', in B. A. Ault, C. L. Nevett (eds.) *Ancient Greek houses and households: chronological, regional and social diversity*, Philadelphia, PN, 67–82.

Tucker, T. G. (1911) *Life in ancient Athens: the social and public life of a classical Athenian from day to day*, London.

Ussher, R. G. (1966) 'Some characters of Athens, Rome and England', *G&R* 13, 64–78.

(1977) 'Old Comedy and "Character": some comments', *G&R* 24, 71–9.

(1993) (ed.) *The Characters of Theophrastus*, 2nd edn., London.

van de Woestijne, P. (1933) 'Théophraste et La Bruyère', *Revue Belge de Philologie et d'Histoire* 12, 5–28.

(1934a) 'Théophraste la cour et la ville', *l'Antiquité Classique* 3, 231–51.

(1934b) 'Notes sur six Caractères de Théophraste traduits par La Bruyère (XXIII–XXVIII)', *Revue Belge de Philologie et d'Histoire* 13, 24–44.

van Ophuijsen, J. M, van Raalte, M. (1998) (eds.) *Theophrastus: reappraising the sources*, Rutgers Studies in Classical Humanities, vol. 8, New Brunswick, NJ.

van Raalte, M. (ed.) (1993) Theophrastus, *Metaphysics, with an introduction, translation and commentary*, Leiden.

van Wees, H. (2000a) 'The development of the hoplite phalanx', in (id.) (2000b), 125–66.

(2000b) (ed.) *War and violence in ancient Greece*, London.

(2004) *Greek warfare: myths and realities*, London.

Veblen, T. (1899) *The theory of the leisure class: an economic study of institutions*, New York, 1899 (reprinted in, and cited from, 'Great Minds Series', Amherst, NY, 1998).

(2005) *Conspicuous consumption: unproductive consumption of goods is honourable*; excerpted from Veblen (1899), Penguin Books: Great Ideas, London.

Vellacott, P. (1973) (ed.) Theophrastus, *The Characters*. Menander, *Plays and fragments*, 2nd edn., Penguin Classics, Harmondsworth.

Vickers. M., Gill, D. (1994) *Artful crafts: ancient Greek silverware and property*, Oxford.

von Reden, S. (2003) *Exchange in ancient Greece*, 2nd edn., London.

Webster, T. B. L. (1950) *Studies in Menander*, Manchester.

(1956) *Art and literature in fourth-century Athens*, London.

Weil, H. (1890) 'Deux allusions à des faits historiques dans les *Caractères* de Théophraste', *Revue de Philologie* 14, 106–7.

West, M. L. (1969) 'Near Eastern material in Hellenistic and Roman Literature', *HSCP* 73, 113–34.

Whitehead, D. (1975) 'Aristotle the metic', *PCPS* 21, 94–9.

(1977) *The ideology of the Athenian metic*, PCPS supplementary vol. 4, Cambridge.

(1981) 'Xenocrates the metic', *RhM* 124, 223–44.

Whittaker, C. R. (1994) *Frontiers of the Roman Empire: a social and economic study*, Baltimore, MD.

Williams, B. (1993) *Shame and necessity*, Berkeley, CA.

Williams, J. M. (1987) 'The Peripatetic school and Demetrius of Phalerum's reforms in Athens', *Ancient World* 15, 87–98.

Wilson, J. R. (1980) 'Kairos as "due measure"', *Glotta* 58, 177–204.

Wilson, P. (2000) *The Athenian institution of the Khoregia: the chorus, the city and the stage*, Cambridge.

Woods, M. (1992) (ed.) Aristotle, *Eudemian ethics*, Books 1, 2, and 8, 2nd edn., Oxford.

Worthington, I. (1992) (ed.) *A historical commentary on Dinarchus* , Ann Arbor, MI.

Wright Mills, C. (1925) 'Introduction' to T. Veblen, *The theory of the leisure class: an economic study of institutions*, London.

Wrigley, E. A. (1967) 'A simple model of London's importance in changing English society and economy 1650–1750', *Past & Present* 37, 44–70.

Wycherley, R. E. (1961) 'Peripatos: the Athenian philosophical scene – 1', *G&R* 8, 152–63.

(1962) 'Peripatos: the Athenian philosophical scene – 2', *G&R* 9, 2–21.

(1978) *The stones of Athens*, Princeton, NJ.

Zimmern, A. (1961) *The Greek commonwealth: politics and economics in fifth-century Athens*, 5th edn., Oxford.

Zoepffel, R. (2006) *Aristotelis Oikonomika: Schriften zu Hauswirtschaft und Finanzwesen*, Berlin.

INDEX OF REFERENCES TO TEXTS BY AND ABOUT THEOPHRASTUS

The Characters
  1. The Dissembler
     43, 48, 103, n. 289, n. 292;
     §2: 66; §§2–3: 96;
     §4: 81, n.164;
     §5: 87, 97, n.267; §§5–6: 87;
     §6: 66, n. 133;
     §7: n. 11.
  2. The Toady
     43, 47, 48, 62, 76, 96, 117, n. 141, n. 289;
     §2: 66, 83, 93, n. 180;
     §§3–4: 83, 87;
     §6: 78, n. 262;
     §7: 84, 93;
     §9: 94;
     §10: 82, 103, n. 164;
     §11: 89;
     §12: 55, 80, n. 129, n. 133, n. 216;
     §13: n. 11.
  3. The Chatterbox
     38, 39, 42, 54–5, 56, 85, n. 239;
     §2: 39, 77;
     §3: 44, 49, 87, 117, n. 162, n. 164, n. 256;
     §4: n. 11.
  4. The Country Bumpkin
     43, 44, 48–50, 71, 74, 76, 81, 102, 103, n. 59,
        n. 121, n. 162;
     §2: 84, 117; §§2–3: 90;
     §3: 35, 73, n. 121;
     §4: 80, 84, 85–6;
     §5: 36, 55;
     §6: 80;
     §7: 5, 74, 78, n. 21;
     §8: 73;
     §9: 81;
     §10: 71;
     §11: 97;
     §12: 88, n. 139;
     §13: 84, 87, 94.
  5a. The Obsequious Man (§§1–5)
     43, 103, n.216;
     §2: 84;
     §3: 93;
     §4: 56, n. 91;
     §5: 78, 83, n. 133.
  5b. The Conspicuous Consumer (§§6–10)
     3, 64, 99, 103, n. 4, n. 12, n. 27, n. 66, n. 292;
     §6: 42, 101, n. 139;
     §7: 88, 102;
     §8: 93, 99, n. 139, n. 180; §§8–9: 56;
     §9: n.121; §§9–10: 80;
     §10: 23, n. 67, n. 246.
  6. The Morally Degraded Man
     3, 4, 43, 47, 97, 102, n. 4, n. 15, n. 59;
     §2: 3, n. 189, n. 59;
     §3: 3, 89;
     §4: 88;
     §5: 35, 79, n. 21, n.270; §§5–6: 62;
     §6: 77, 88, n. 135;
     §7: 3, 30;
     §8: 91;
     §9: 39; 93;
     §10: n. 11.
  7. The Talker
     42, 48, 64, 86, 117, n. 27, n. 239;
     §5: 7;
     §6: 85;
     §7: 45, 90, 94;
     §8: 82, 89, 92;
     §9: 30;
     §10: 39–40, 79, n. 133.
  8. The Rumour-Monger
     43, n. 144;
     §§2–10: 86;
     §4: 56, 73;
     §§6–10: n. 87;
     §7: n. 180;
     §8: 56;
     §10: n. 133;
     §11: 92, 93, n. 11, n. 233, n. 244.
  9. The Shameless Man
     43, 62;
     §2: 97, 108;
     §3: 74, 82, 90;
     §4: 55, 75, 94;
     §5: 56, 89;

§6: 85, 92;
§7: 92;
§8: 88.
10. The Penny–Pincher
43, 64;
§2: 97;
§3: 81, 89;
§5: 36, 75;
§6: 34, 78, n. 255;
§7: 97;
§8: 80; §§8–9: 55;
§10: n. 139;
§11: 69; 81; n. 162;
§12: 94;
§13: 78, 97, n. 133, n. 162;
§14: 97, n. 233.
11. The Repulsive Man
4, 41, 43, 64, 117, n. 12;
§2: 5, 40, 59, 83, n. 21;
§3: 5, 89;
§4: 94;
§5: 85;
§7: 92;
§8: 79, 82, 85; §§8–9: 93–4;
§9: n. 133.
12. The Tactless Man
43, 64;
§2: 81;
§3: 79, 81, n. 24, n. 164;
§4: 92;
§5: 92;
§6: 64;
§7: 57;
§8: 96;
§9: 31;
§10: 96;
§11: 90, n. 268;
§12: 75;
§13: 92;
§14: 42, 82.
13. The Overzealous Man
43;
§2: 90;
§3: 74, 92;
§4: 81;
§5: 63;
§6: 63;
§7: 55, 57;
§8: 5, 80, n. 21;
§9: 81, n. 164;

§10: 77;
§11: 92.
14. The Obtuse Man
4;
§2: n. 272;
§3: 55, 92;
§4: 89;
§5: 5; §§5–6: 80;
§7: 87;
§8: n. 132;
§9: 74;
§10: 79;
§11: 55;
§13: 50, 87, n. 133.
15. The Self–Centred Man
4, 43, 85, 86, 107, 117, n. 145, n. 289;
§2: 87;
§3: 85;
§4: 2, 97–8;
§5: n. 21;
§6: 85;
§7: 96, n. 27;
§8: 85;
§9: 81, 82;
§10: 33, 39;
§11: 89, n. 133.
16. The Superstitious Man
4, 39, 42, 47, 80, 90, n. 176;
§2: 79, n. 176;
§4: 80;
§6: 80;
§7: 80;
§9: 77;
§10: 80;
§11: 39;
§12: 77–8;
§13: n. 176;
§15: 87.
17. The Ungrateful Grumbler
n. 265, n.289;
§2: 66, 82, 96, 198, n. 213;
§4: n. 176;
§6: 75, 97, 117, n. 164;
§7: 78, 79;
§8: 92;
§9: 96; n. 133, n. 267.
18. The Distrustful Man
4, 39, n. 141;
§2: 74;
§3: 76–7;

§4: 80;
§6: 83;
§7: 97;
§8: 74, 76–7, 84;
§9: 97, n. 133.
19a. The Offensive Man (§§1–6)
5, 48, 64, 84, n. 164;
§§1–6: 84;
§2: 177, n. 126;
§§3–5: n. 21;
§5: 77, 88, 114;
§6: 93.
19b. From another, unnamed Character
(§§7–10)
3, n. 234;
§7: 77; §§7–8: 90;
§9: n. 24; §§9–10: 82;
§10: 75, 114, n. 110.
20. The Disagreeable Man
4, 117;
§2: 81;
§3: 57;
§4: 81, 83;
§5: 73, 78, n. 164;
§6: 82, n. 21, n. 110;
§7: 77;
§9: 66, 80;
§10: 79, 81, n. 133.
21. The Man of Petty Ambition
37, 43, 62, 69–71, 89, 101, 103, 106, 107,
117;
§2: 82;
§3: 57, 79, 89;
§4: 55, 84, 103;
§7: 89, n. 139;
§8: 70, 83, 84, 93;
§9: 56, 89;
§10: n. 164; §§10–11: 89;
§11: 39, 70, 84.
22. The Illiberal Man
41, 43, 77;
§2: 70, 89, 108; §§2–5: 70;
§3: 90
§4: 77, 81, 90, 95;
§5: 57;
§6: 79, 90, n. 164;
§7: 40, 84, 93, 103;
§8: 73, 83;
§9: 85, 96;
§10: 77, n. 255;

§11: 84, 117;
§12: n. 225;
§13: 84.
23. The Boastful Man
37, 43, 48, 64, 85, 101, 106;
§2: 56, 74, 88, n. 135;
§3: 56; §§3–4: 39, n. 87;
§4: n. 139, n. 180;
§§5–6: 69–70;
§6: 96;
§§7–8: 94;
§8: 74;
§9: 80, n. 121, n. 133.
24. The Arrogant Man
4, 43, 81, 86, 107, 141, n. 236;
§2: 83;
§3: 96, 108;
§4: 45, 92;
§5: 107;
§6: 96, n. 264;
§7: 98;
§8: 85;
§9: 81, 117;
§10: 57, 57, 81;
§12: 42, 115; §§12–12: 98;
§13: n. 133.
25. The Coward
29, 38, 39, 106, 108, n. 289;
§1: 39, 74; §§2–8: 57;
§§3–8: 47–8, 63;
§4: 74;
§5: n. 164;
§8: 106, n. 133.
26. The Oligarchic Man
33, 44, 47, 91, 107;
§2: 90;
§3: 22, 66, 91, n. 104; §§3–4: 86;
§4: 83, 91, n. 27;
§5: 69, n. 27;
§6: n. 11, n. 179.
27. The Late Learner
64, n. 59;
§2: 41, 57, 82;
§3: 79;
§4: 89;
§5: 83, 89;
§6: 79;
§7: 88;
§8: 89;
§9: 5, 63, 79, 92, n. 21, n. 104, n. 229;

§10: 55; n. 164;
§12: 74, n. 247;
§13: 79;
§14: 88;
§15: n. 24, n. 224;
§16: 11.
28. The Slanderer
43, 62, 66, 85, n. 194, n. 289;
§2: 55, n. 48; §§2–3: n. 181;
§3: 80; §§3–4: 77; §§3–6: 58–9;
§4: n. 119, n. 121;
§5: 90, n. 164;
§6: n. 11, n. 27.
29. The Friend of Villains
4, 38, 44;
§2: 38, 91;
§§3–4: 66–7;
§5: 38, 91, n.27;
§6: 38, 91, n. 252;
§7: n. 11.
30. The Shabby Profiteer
43, 47, 62, 82, 95, 103;
§2: 82;
§3: 56;
§4: 82;
§6: 79, 89;
§7: 57, 75;
§8: 74; 88;
§9: 74, n. 139;
§11: 39, 77, 78;
§14: 79, 88, n. 164;
§15: n. 139;
§16: 74;
§17: 57, 75, 82;
§18: 82;
§19: 55;
§20: 57.
Concerning weather signs
53–4, n. 171.
Inquiry into plants
16, 54, n. 62, n. 172, n. 174.
Metaphysics
17, n. 64, n. 99.
On the causes of plants
16, n. 173
Citations from *Theophrastus of Eresus: sources for his life, writings, thought and influence* (FHS&G)
FHS&G 1 (= Diogenes Laertius, *Life of Theophrastus*, 5.36–57)

1.1–2 = Diog. Laert. 5.56: n. 68
1.7–9 = Diog. Laert. 5.36: n. 73
1.10–12 = Diog. Laert. 5.36–7: 18
1.11–12 = Diog. Laert. 5.36–7: 45
1.13–14 = Diog. Laert. 5.37: 24
1.16 = Diog. Laert. 5.37: 33
1.16–21 = Diog. Laert. 5.37: 33
1.21 = Diog. Laert. 5.37: 105
1.22–9 = Diog. Laert. 5.38: 25
1.30–1 = Diog. Laert. 5.38: 26
1.31–2 = Diog. Laert. 5.39: n. 68
1.38–40 = Diog. Laert. 5.39: 23
1.40–2 = Diog. Laert. 5.40: 34
1.41–2 = Diog. Laert. 5.50: 39
1.44–5 = Diog. Laert. 5.40: 18, 104
1.52–60 = Diog. Laert. 5.40–1: n. 282
1.60–2 = Diog. Laert. 5.41: 25
1.61–4 = Diog. Laert. 5.41: 88
1.68–291 = Diog. Laert. 5.42–50: 2
1.160 = Diog. Laert. 5.45: n. 215, n. 258
1.165 = Diog. Laert. 5.45: n. 258
1.166 = Diog. Laert. 5.46: n.258
1.185 = Diog. Laert. 5.47: n. 112
1.206 = Diog. Laert. 5.47: n. 258
1.219 = Diog. Laert. 5.47: n. 258
1.236 = Diog. Laert. 5.48: n. 107
1.240 = Diog. Laert. 5.58: n. 258
1.311–20 = Diog. Laert. 5.52–3: 21
1.320–56 = Diog. Laert. 5.54–6: 21, n. 71
1.324–30 = Diog. Laert. 5.53–4: 20, n. 71
1.336 = Diog. Laert. 5.54: 76
1.337 = Diog. Laert. 5.55: 75
1.354–5 = Diog. Laert. 5.56: n. 73
1.361–2 = Diog. Laert. 5.57: n. 88
FHS&G 2.1 = *Suda s.v.* 'Theophrastus' no. 199: n. 95
FHS&G 7A = Cicero, *Brutus* §§169–72: 1, n. 1
FHS&G 7B = Quintilian 8.1.2: 1
FHS&G 12 = Athenaeus 1.21b: 28
FHS&G 15 = Plutarch, *Moralia* 545F: 28, n. 112
FHS&G 18 = list of Theophrastus' pupils: 27, 45
FHS&G 19 = Diogenes Laertius 5.12–13: 20
FHS&G 22 = *Codex Vaticanus Graecus* 742 f. 66v 1.9–12: n. 305
FHS&G 23 = Diogenes Laertius 6.90: 18, 88
FHS&G 24 = Cicero, *Tusculan disputations* 5.107: n. 170
FHS&G 25 = Plutarch, *On exile* 605A–B: n.170

FHS&G 27 = Philodemus, *P. Herc* 240 fr.
16.3–10: n. 283
FHS&G 28 = Aelian 4.19: 63
FHS&G 29 = Themistius, *Orations* 21 252B: 24
FHS&G 30 = Dionysius of Halicarnassus,
Dinarchus 2: 25
FHS&G 21 = Plutarch, *Quaestiones Convivales*
633B: 32, n. 100, n. 126
FHS&G 32A = Aelian 8.12: 25
FHS&G 32B = Proclus, *On Plato's First
Alcibiades* 114B–D: n. 92
FHS&G 36A = Cicero, *Tusculan disputations*
3.69: 104
FHS&G 36B = Athenaeus 5.1186a: 34
FHS&G 53 = Plutarch, *Cicero* 2.4.5–6: n. 296
FHS&G 55 = *Suda* no.1141: 18
FHS&G 61A = Cicero, *On the nature of the
gods* 1.93: 26
FHS&G 61B = Pliny, *Natural History* 1 Preface
19: 26
FHS&G 72A = Boethius: n. 64
FHS&G 133A = Plutarch, *Moralia* 1097B: n.
311
FHS&G 133B = Plutarch, *Moralia* 1126F: n.311
FHS&G 335 = Athenaeus 9.43: 54
FHS&G 365C = Plutarch, *Natural explanations*
19 9–6B: n. 100
FHS&G 436.4a–c: n. 10
FHS&G 443 = Stobaeus, *Anthology* 3.38.43: n.
265
FHS&G 444 = Stobaeus, *Anthology* 3.38.30: 30
FHS&G 446 = Seneca, *On Anger* 1.12.3: 30
FHS&G 449A = Stobaeus, *Anthology* 2.7.20: 29
FHS&G 449B = Hesychius no. 100: n. 12
FGS&G 451 = *Florilegium: best and first
lessons* no. 64: n. 239
FHS&G 452 = *Gnomologium Vaticanum* no.
331: 87
FHS&G 453 = *Gnomologium Vaticanum* no.
327: 126
FHS&G 454 = Mubassir, *Choicest maxims and
best sayings*, 'Sayings by a number of
philosophers': 30
FHS&G 461 = scholion to *Nicomachaean
Ethics* 1145a10: 35
FHS&G 465 = Stobaeus, *Anthology* 2.31.124:
35
FHS&G 467 = Plutarch, *Agis and Cleomenes*
2.1–3: 32
FHS&G 468 = Fulgentius, *Mythologies* 2.1: 113

FHS&G 469 = Stobaeus, *Anthology* 3.31.10: 69
FHS&G 470 = Antonius Melissa, *Loci
Communes* 2.71: 33, n. 100
FHS&G 471 = *Gnomologium Vaticanum* no.
323: 18
FHS&G 472 = *Gnomologium Vaticanum* no.
336: 472
FHS&G 473 = *Gnomologium Vaticanum* no.
329: 31
FHS&G 479 = ps.Plutarch, *On the opinions of
the philosophers* 847F–75A: 116
FHS&G 486.20–2 = Jerome, *Against Jovian*
1.47–8: 53, n. 65
FHS&G 491 = Vitruvius 6 Intr. 2: 26, n. 232
FHS&G 494 = Cicero, *Tusculan disputations*
5.24–5: n. 89
FHS&G 506 = *Light of the soul B*, *Anthology*
ch. 7, *De alacritate*: 71, n. 206
FHS&G 507 = scholion to Plato, *Laws* 1.631C:
107
FHS&G 510 = *Florilegium Monacense* 202: n.
232
FHS&G 513 = Aelian 4.20: n. 170
FHS&G 514 = Cicero, *De oficiis* 2.55–6: 70
FHS&G 515 = Cicero, *De officiis* 2.64: 81
FHS&G 517 = Stobaeus, *Anthology* 4.1.72:
94–5
FHS&G 518 = ps.Aristotle, *Letter to Philip*
4.1–5: 258
FHS&G 519 = Maximus Confessor, *Loci
communes* 46: 15, n. 56
FHS&G 521 = Stobaeus, *Anthology* 2.15.31: 85
FHS&G 522 = *Gnomologium Vaticanum* no.
325: 31
FHS&G 523 = Stobaeus, *Anthology* 3.3. 42: 77,
95–6
FHS&G 524 = *Gnomologium Vaticanum* no.
324: 91
FHS&G 526 = Stobaeus, *Anthology* 3.19.12:
76
FHS&G 527A–B: n.215
FHS&G 534 = Aulus Gellius, *Attic Nights* 1.3,
8–14, 21–9: n. 263
FHS&G 535 = Plutarch, *On brotherly love*
490E: 95
FHS&G 538A–F: 96
FHS&G 539 = Stobaeus, *Anthology* 4.11.16: 32
FHS&G 545 = Mubassir, *Choicest maxims and
best sayings*, 'Sayings by a number of
philosophers' no. 120: 111, n. 298

FHS&G 546 = Walter Burley, *On the life and character of philosophers* 68.7–8: 85, 97, n. 267

FHS&G 547 = Athenaeus 6.254d–e: 88–9

FHS&G 564 = Athenaeus 13.610a–b: 78

FHS&G 577 = Plutarch, *Quaestiones Convivales* 679A, 716A: 88

FHS&G 584A = Porphyry, *On abstinence from eating animals* 2.15.3: 90, n. 68, n. 258

FHS&G 636 = Eustathius, *Commentary on Odyssey* 1.357: 78

FHS&G 644 = Eustathius, *Commentary on Odyssey* 15.93–4: 80

FHS&G 651 = Harpocration, *s.v. kata ten agoran apseudein*: n. 257

FHS&G 654 = Harpocration, *s.v. sustomoteron skaphes*: 24, 85

FHS&G 659 = Philodemus, *P. Herc* 1424 col. vii: n. 153

FHS&G 661 = Stobaeus, *Anthology* 4.28.7: 78

FHS&G 662 = Stobaeus, *Anthology* 2.31.31: 78

FHS&G 689A = Philodemus, *On rhetoric, P. Herc.* 1007/1673 col. 13: 81

FHS&G 694 = Quintilian: n. 64

FHS&G 696 = Demetrius, *On Style* 222: 16

FHS&G 708 = Diomedes, *The art of grammar* 3: n. 26

FHS&G 709 = Athenaeus 6.261d–e: n. 126

FHS&G 710 = Athenaeus 8.347f–348a: n. 126, n. 271

FHS&G 711 = Plutarch, *Quaestiones Convivales* 631D–E: 32, n. 126

FHS&G 712= Athanasius, *Rhetores Graeci* 14 177.3–8: 31

FHS&G 713 = Cicero, *De oratore* 3.221: 31